A Treasure Trove
of Word Origins

Is That What It Means?

by

Max Oppenheimer, Jr.

1531 Yuma • P.O. Box 1009 • Manhattan, Kansas 66505-1009 USA

© 2004 Max Oppenheimer, Jr.

Printed in the United States of America on acid-free paper.

ISBN 0-89745-269-0

Sunflower University Press is a wholly-owned subsidiary
of the non-profit 501(c)3 Journal of the West, Inc.

To Christine, Ed, Lyn,
All those
Who love and respect language,
And a new triad in my life:
Christine, Emily, and Logan Ross

Contents

Introduction	xi
The "Miracle" of Origins	1
Folk Etymology	3
Food for Thought	5
Hostility in Language	8
Cut Out of the Whole Cloth?	11
The Loom of Language	13
Well! I'll Be Darned!	15
No Man Is an Island	17
Beware of Misusing Language	19
Using Language Skillfully	21
All About Humor	23
The Mystery of Language	25
A Primeval Language?	27
Words Born in a Bar	28
Let's Have a Consensus!	30
No Puny Flames These	34

This May Make Your Head Spin	35
Word Origins Clarify Perceptions	37
Associations and Connotations	39
Borrowing from Other Languages	40
Dare We Broach the Subject?	42
Entropy in Language	44
Don't Let This Get Your Goat!	46
Latin, a Key to Many Languages	47
Star-spun Words	49
Linguistic Contamination	51
Subjectivism Has a Place in Language	52
Language Can Be Consistently Inconsistent	54
Travel Broadens Linguistic Knowledge	56
Languages Must Be Learned	57
Language May Be the Basis for Humor	59
Debates Are Rooted in Violence	61
Ache Can Be a Pain to Pronounce	62
Of Shades and Windows	64
Altered Meanings	66
Use Restraint When Tracing Word Origins	67
Critic Climbs Out on Wrong Branch	69
Putting My Best Foot Forward	72
Left Up a Pole	74
Silence Can Be the Cornerstone of Character	76
Indian Words in English	78
Research Can Be Overrated	79
Columnists Affect Each Other	81
Common Sense Is Always Useful	83
Even Geniuses Need Rules	84
Historical and Unusual Word Sources	86
Modern Terms for Ancient Roots	88
Math and Poetry — a Good Mix	90
Don't Ever Lose *Hoffen*	91

A Treasure Trove of Word Origins ix

Language Games	93
The Meaning of Meaning	95
Chad Anyone?	97
Different Languages, Different Rules	99
Testing the Boundaries of Language	100
Gloom, Doom, and Fear	102
For *What* Do the Bells Toll?	103
Cash and the Almighty Dollar	105
How Meanings Evolve	107
The Line Between Man and Machine	109
Like Games, Language Has Rules	111
Migration and Language	113
A New Look at Old Words	114
No Rigmarole Here!	116
They Stole My Thunder!	117
Slang	119
Accuracy in "Signature" Phrases	121
We Don't Have to Learn Anglo-Saxon!	122
Bible-spawned Bird Names	124
Different Views of Reality	126
No Matter the Origin, Buxom Is Good	127
What's in a Name Indeed?	129
The French Academy, Guardian of Language	131
Roots Anchor Meanings in Language	133
Attack and Violence in Language	134
Astronomy Terms Not Always Extra-terrestrial	136
Language Can Be Tantalizing	137
Terror Derivatives from Latin and French	139
Rats! Dreaded Scoundrels Came from the East	140
Chemistry and Language	142
Learning a Foreign Language: Bilingual Method vs. Total Immersion	144
Fractured English	145

China's Name a Misunderstanding	147
The Chinese Language	149
Sign Language	150
Linguistic Origins of Evil	153
Radio and TV Language	155
Language Is Fun and Games	157
Rhetoric Often Spells Deceit	158
Words with Dark Roots	160
The Images Behind the Words	162
Relationship Between Thought and Language	163
This Information Is *Sub Rosa*	165
Multiple Meanings in Different Languages	166
Grammar Rules Must Make Sense	168
Easy with These Neologisms	170
Tricky Problems of Correct English	171
Oxford English Dictionary's Insane Contributor	173
Caveat Lector!	175
Acronyms — Not Always the Last Word on Word Origins	176
Those Pesky Pronouns	178
Language and the Dissecting of Reality	180
Language May Bewitch Our Intelligence	181
The Origins of "Juke" Are No Joke	183
Style Defines the Man	184
Language and Consciousness	185
The Power of Words	187
Colorful Word Origins	188
More About the *Oxford English Dictionary*	190
Complexities of Language, a Wonder of Nature	191
The Politically and Historically Accurate *Squaw*	193
Epilogue	196
Selected Reading	200
Index	202
Word Origins Index	215

~ Introduction ~

WE ALL HAVE heard the expression "born with a silver spoon in his mouth." It is how we might refer to someone who is part of a wealthy family. The phrase originated with the custom of Godparents presenting a child with a silver spoon at the christening. Of course, a child born of wealthy parents did not have to wait until its christening to sup from silver — the child was practically *born* "with a silver spoon in its mouth" and could expect a golden future.

What is crucial to note here is that languages tend to convey meaning through images, also known as metaphors. Why? Most probably because since the very beginning, man, to communicate, relied on pictures of one kind or another, be they figures scratched on the ground, drawings on cave walls, hand signals, or signs and gestures. The habit never ceased, and pictures — whether clearly spelled out in words or fossilized and no longer recognizable over time — are still embedded in language. It is a well-established fact that, as the popular saying goes, "a picture is worth a thousand words." Think about it! We could just say "the child has wealthy parents" . . . or "was born to a rich family," but a terse verbal definition, flat, cold, and colorless, does not grab you the same way, does it?

Isn't a metaphor, describing the colorful scene of a baby, with an elegant silver spoon in its mouth, much more striking and effective? Doesn't it fill the mind with a host of associations linked to all kinds of memorable experiences? Even most single words, *sans* additional modifiers, were once metaphors to begin with, as each one realistically evoked the actual scene or scenario our ancestors associated with its semantic content — the very image that came to their minds when they heard it. The trick is to really appreciate and *respect* each word, to look at it with the know-how to recognize the often-hidden picture therein and with the curiosity to marvel at its fascinating and enlightening origin. Yes . . . I used "respect" intentionally, for the word also conceals an image; its root meaning is "to take a good second look," from the Latin *re* (again) and *spectare* (to look at).

You have heard of fossils? Why not imagine yourself a passionate paleolinguist researching linguistic fossils and word genealogy? Knowing how to dig beneath the surface and expose the original image behind a word fills us with the thrill of discovery and helps us understand it better. From it we learn how our ancestors perceived their universe. Not unlike a skilled geologist looking at rocks to tell us how the landscape evolved over millennia, we have the means of opening up a treasure trove of meanings.

As humankind evolved, became more sophisticated, the simple original word images also had to keep up the pace to express ever more complex shades of meaning that continued to emerge after the original words were first coined. Language had to be fluid. Even a word like *metaphor* widened its semantic scope to meet changing needs. Originally from the Greek, *meta* (after) and *pherein* (to bear), it merely described moving something to another destination and thereby making a change. In the end, language being a tool and tools having to be adjusted to cope with new tasks, a new word, *metapherein*, was formed, signifying more specifically to transfer, to change. Soon, metaphor referred — in the abstract sense — to replacing a meaningful utterance with another, one more descriptive.

This process, by triggering mental associations and connotations, expressed the original meaning with greater appeal to some of the five senses, here the visual one. In a way, we witness a linguistic *metamorphosis* of an expression, and the Greeks never fail to have a word for it — *meta* (change) and *morphe* (form) — while still preserving the essence of the original meaning, yet improving on it by means of a felicitous change of scene.

Another good example is *delirium*. When patients suffer from delirium, they have slightly crazy ideas. We might express it more picturesquely by saying, "They are off their track." Don't look now, but that is exactly what the word meant in the first place in a primitive rural setting. From the Latin *de*, meaning off, and *lira*, meaning furrow, it originally designated some farmer staggering all over his field, unable to plow a straight line. The word gradually gained a more general application to denote mental problems.

I have no doubt that all languages are based on pictures familiar to their users. I would even go as far as saying every word is a poem, every language fossilized poetry. Look at the very complex Chinese writing, which started with pictographs. Now, more stylized, the characters still regale us with appealing images. The Chinese written character for "male" evokes an earlier — at that time more familiar — background, combining the characters for "effort," "strength," and "field." "Look" shows a hand shading the eyes. The sun rising behind trees represents the character for "east." "Happiness" combines a woman and a child, to reflect the enduring Chinese attachment to family values.

View language from this new pictorial perspective and it will make a lot more sense than ever before! It is, after all, merely one of the multiple means of *access to* or (to use a chemical term) one of the *precipitants of* meaning. Beyond speech and writing, these means of access or precipitants may range from interpretation of body movements and grimaces to sign language and, yes, even a blind man's groping, fumbling white cane represents his link to the outside world.

We construct meaning from mental habits, memory, imagination, feeling, and sensations. Such conversion of sensation into perception and eventually meaning has been called *figuration*. Latent cerebral thought, after arising from sense perception, is subsequently abstracted into verbalized thought, always thereby at risk of possible limitations and distortions, and is clearly affected at each stage by past thought. Beyond this, perhaps, a collective force of consciousness in which we all participate, some kind of vast sentient two-way semantic energy field into which we tap and with which we maintain a connected awareness, *enables* both our reality and our meanings. It is what Carl Jung, enlarging Freud's notion of "personal unconscious," called the "collective unconscious," which was made up of universal, cross-cultural, and timeless elements of human experience, the so-called archetypes.

But back to the silver spoon . . . I should be so lucky! I am, however, tempted to say, judging by how my own life evolved, that I should have been "born with a dictionary in my crib." As destiny dictated, language and languages have played a crucial role throughout some eighty years now. In 1922, when I was five years old, my father accepted a position abroad and, within days, I was an expatriate child, transplanted from New York to Hamburg, Germany. At that age, learning the language was not problematical. Because my parents were gone all day at the office, a motherly German housekeeper, who spoke only German and knew not a word of English, raised me. (I beg your pardon! Purists may wish me to use "reared" and reserve "raise" for cattle, although raise is now quite acceptable.) Highly motivated to forget English and blend in with the background (I can still sense the hostile looks around me on my first ride in a Hamburg streetcar, as I was conversing in English with my mother and World War I not forgotten), I learned German quite quickly and naturally. Within months I was just another North German kid, and I cannot even remember how it happened.

The next personal "cataclysm" in my life proved to be more of what might today be called culture shock. At Easter 1930, because of my father's transfer, we moved to Paris. I knew only German and some very elementary Latin. The new situation demanded my acquisition, all at once, of French, Latin, and English, so that I could fit in with my coevals in a French *lycée*. Such French schools offer a demanding program, which, if successfully completed, qualifies one to enter a university or other institution of higher learning. The kids my age were reading Caesar and Vergil in the original. How well I remember this pivotal experience in my life. There was nothing gradual or painless about it! It required total dedication, personal sacrifice, and a great deal of work. Very quickly, at thirteen years of age, meaning became all important, a boogeyman — no vague abstraction, but a formidable challenge to be conquered.

The constant struggle through the semantic darkness surrounding me was a matter of survival, to grope for light, to understand the reality around me, and, even more critical with regard to my classes, to decipher the works of countless French, English, and Latin authors, who were the subject of our studies. Imagine spending hours with huge dictionaries trying, but at first failing, to decipher one single sentence, one rhymed couplet! Yes, to coin another metaphor, I was fighting my own war in the linguistic trenches! This is where I first truly learned to hone the patience and discipline needed to focus on extracting every particle of meaning from a conversation, a lecture, a text, any form of communication. I only wish that I had not been so overwhelmingly absorbed by and fearful of the immediacy of meeting the linguistic challenge. I caught up with the rest of the class soon enough, but the constant pressure of competing for rank and grades did not allow for the relaxed enjoyment and appreciation of the miraculous mysteries and beauties of language. That came much later.

My involvement with languages has been constant ever since. I even used them extensively in the Military Intelligence Service during World War II. After the war, I completed my studies and began a career of university teaching and research in languages and literature, dealing mostly with French, English, German, and Spanish. In the fifties, I was recalled into the U.S. Army and spent the next eight years first in that service, then with the CIA, acquiring Russian and using it in every conceivable manner, ranging from studying, speaking, writing, and translating, to years of Soviet-defector interrogation. In 1958, returning to teaching and research, I started sorting out my by then extensive linguistic baggage. My attitude toward language matured, acquiring new dimensions as I focused, with considerably more empathy, on each as an individual living system, with its own characteristics and idiosyncrasies. I distinguished new patterns, new relationships, new linguistic wonders, previously ignored and now suddenly noticed. Albeit committed to the same task, each language handles it somewhat differently.

I use *empathy* deliberately, as it is a good example of the tricks language plays. The word entered English heavily disguised, denoting "the capacity for participating in or a vicarious experiencing of another's feelings, volitions, or ideas." Would you ever guess it comes from the German *Einfühlung* and literally means "feeling one's self into another person's feelings and emotions." It sounds like what a "walk-in" would do — the label Science Fiction now gives to an alien from another planet who takes over the body of an earthling! Before naturalizing *Einfühlung*, however, English sent it to Greece to clothe it in Hellenic attire and give it a more scholarly, professional look. It did not even bother to give it an English appearance, because, as we shall see in a moment, English does not do that.

Reflecting on the evolution of English, in layman's terms, three significant facts explain most of it. First, there is an Anglo-Saxon or Germanic foundation. Second, after the Battle of Hastings and the Norman conquest of England (1066), French, the language of the court and nobility, was *superimposed* upon Anglo-Saxon, the language of the lower class, in effect doubling the vocabulary of English into perhaps the largest of any language. English words reflect to this day their social provenance and rank. Third, when English takes in a foreign term, it admits it as is. For example, *depend*, from Latin through French, literally means "to hang from" (*de*, from; *pendere*, hang); *circumstance*, from Latin, means "to stand around" (*circum*, around; *stare*, stand). Other languages, like German and Russian, insist on loan translation by translating every part of the imported word into Germanic and Slavic roots respectively. For *depend* and *circumstance* we have the German *abhängen* and *Umstand*, and the Russian *zavicyet* and *obstoyatelstvo*, respectively — genuine native terms in which the Germans and Russians catch the meaning and the picture.

After years of trying to capture language in its richness and complexity with cold formulas, principles, and diagrams, I have long given up the quest for what (echoing quantum physicists) might be called a linguistic unified field theory for all languages. It would be forever frustrated by unpredictable exceptions and deviations from the norm. I prefer to observe and surprise language in action and wend my way through the extraordinary intricacy of its semantic maze or symphony, delighting in new discoveries at every step. After all, which would you prefer when walking through beautiful nature's meadows and woods, a richly illustrated flora and fauna guide or a dry botany and biology text? Rome's Horace in his *Ars Poetica* answers for us: "*Omne tulit punctum qui miscuit utile dulci, lectorem delectando pariterque monendo.*" ("He wins on all points who mixes the useful and the sweet, both delighting and instructing the reader.")

One more warning, before I let you read in peace! The evoking of false metaphors by language can, besides delighting, also distract us from the correct meaning of words. Here is a graphic example. I once heard a talk-show host define in error *vituperative* as *hostile*. I explain in one of my essays that *vituperative* might be associated with hostility, perhaps even in most cases does imply it. Still, an accurate dictionary entry has to define it merely as "given to censure, characterized by wordy abuse." From the Latin *vitium* (vice, fault, blemish) and *perare* (prepare), it in no way includes the meaning of hostility. A verb simply denotes an action, never the feelings of the actor, which here could range from paternal, to concerned, and, yes, hostile. One of my readers, a trained professional and scientist, just could not accept this explanation, insisting it meant hostile. I don't recommend him as a lexicographer.

An important lesson with respect to language is to be learned from this incident, affecting all communication and reflecting the potential misuse of language by each of us, especially the media. The message is always at the mercy of the humanness of the sender and receiver. If you will forgive the pun and mixed metaphor, the ironclad train of logical thought we dispatch is always at risk of being derailed by the bewitching hazards of the picturesque landscape through which it travels. The great Austrian philosopher Ludwig Wittgenstein (1889-1951) said, "Philosophy is a battle against the bewitchment of our intelligence by means of language." Although he does not mention emotional hazards in his statement, they can never be disregarded, embedded as they are in the metaphors, associations, and connotations generated by language.

Isn't it ironic that on October 25, 1946, at England's Cambridge University, the same Wittgenstein, cool logician that he was, when facing the equally famous Karl Hopper in their dramatic (albeit only ten-minute-long) debate, "lost it, went ballistic." Bewitched by something in the language, I suppose, and definitely hostile, he started wielding an iron poker at his "Austrian landsman," until Bertrand Russell ordered him to put it down. Therefore, when using language, remember Ulysses, who tied himself to the mast of his ship to escape the songs of the sirens, and cling fast to hard logic against the lure of images. The metaphors woven into the loom of language might distract and confuse you.

The first 103 essays herein (pp. 1-183) represent columns originally written for the Sun City, Arizona, *Daily News-Sun* from March 15, 1999, to the present; the final seven essays (pp. 184-193) were written for the *Arizona Senior World* during 2002. They have been titled and edited for publication here as *Is **That** What It Means?*

Language lovers interested in exploring the subject further may find the Selected Reading section useful.

The "Miracle" of Origins

Have you ever wondered by what miracle the countless expressions and words we use every day are woven on the loom of language? How were they coined? Whence do they come?

Isn't your curiosity piqued just a bit? By the way, *pique* comes to us directly from the French where it means to prick or sting. Perhaps you think it is just so much trivia. Well now, *trivia* and trivial come from the Latin *tri* (three) + *via* (road), and crossroads, where three roads cross, is the place people might meet and exchange unimportant news and gossip.

When a knowledgeable geologist looks at a rock, it might tell him a fascinating tale about its origins — what awesome floods or glaciers shaped it, what cataclysms framed its odd symmetry, to paraphrase William Blake. Fossils embedded in the rock might even yield clues as to the animal and vegetal world that dominated the area and affected the lifestyle of our forefathers who inhabited it. The same holds true with words. In many cases they can tell us a great deal about how past generations thought, perceived their universe, reasoned about natural phenomena, and even viewed the social order that ruled their everyday life. In that sense, language is "fossilized poetry" bequeathed to us from the past with all the imagery that an evolving human mind was capable of, as it assimilated and transmitted experience with its new time-binding tool: language. Knowledge of word origins can shed much light on how language came about, why we use certain words to designate certain objects or express certain feelings. Suddenly the veil that clouds their origin is torn, the mystery of their meaning vanishes, and it all seems clear and logical! We see with x-ray eyes the images behind the words, their bare identity, and their true nature. It gives us, as Paul Harvey would say, the *rest* of the word's story.

Consider, for example, the phenomenon of folk etymology (the origin and historical transformation of words). Have you ever wondered how the *Florida Keys*, the elongated islets shaped like bones — Key Largo or Key West — ever got their name? They don't open locks! Elementary! In 1527, no doubt in search of profitable real estate, the Spanish conquistador Álvar Nuiñez Cabeza de Vaca (his last name means "cow head," because one of his ancestors during the 13th-century Crusades marked an unguarded mountain pass with the skull of a cow), together with his luckless companions, was washed up on the coast of what was to become Florida. Perhaps, haunted by dreams of his bones drying on the beach, he named the new landscape *cayo hueso*, or islet shaped like a bone. Later on, Americans, unfamiliar with the meaning of the Spanish words, by a process known as folk etymology distorted the foreign terms into more familiar English sounds and came up with Key West.

Hoosegow, a jail or lockup, was also formed by folk etymology when Americans transposed into something meaningless, but sounding more like English, the Spanish *juzgado*, *i.e.*, judged or sentenced. In fact, *Arizona* most probably owes its origin to folk etymology. Derived from the Pima Indian words *ali shonak* (place of the little spring), I have no doubt that the Spaniards practiced folk etymology by replacing the incomprehensible Pima lingo with *árida zona* (arid zone), later shortened to its present name. (William A. Douglass of the University of Nevada at Reno, a scholar of Basque, in 1979 suggested as origin *aritz ona*, a Basque word meaning "good oak." Although Basques were involved in a silver strike at a site of that name [1736] and there is an Aztec word *arizuma* signifying "silver bearing," I do not accept that derivation.)

If you draw a family tree upside down, the lines tracing ancestry are three-pronged, resembling the foot of a bird. The French monks that drew these genealogical trees named them *pied de grue*, meaning foot of a crane. Again by folk etymology, in 15th-century England, this was named and spelled *pee-de-grew*, *pedegru*, finally *pedigree*. We now have pedigreed horses and pets.

> **Arizona** From Spanish, *árida zona*; originally from Piman Indian *ali shonak*, meaning "place of the little spring."
>
> **Attic** Derives from Attica, the Greek state, where Athens stood. The Attic style featured elegance and simplicity, a small row of columns atop another larger one — and eventually any top story of a building.

In future essays I shall share with you a *treasure trove*, from French *trésor* (treasure) + *trouvé* (found), of word origins. Many are even socially significant, casting a light on how our ancestors viewed each other. Thus *lady* and *lord* reveal how in the past their servants and helpers thought of them. The main task of a lady, when she was the farmer's wife, was to bake bread. *Lady* is a contraction of an earlier Old English contraction of *hlaf* (bread) + *dig* (to knead). *Dig* (German *Teig*) gave us dough. The *lord*, by equal right, was the *hlafweard*, or loaf-ward or warden, guardian of the bread. A *steward*, or *sty* + *ward*, was once a keeper of the pigs. The *servant*, *hlaf-aeta*, was the loaf-eater. A *knight* (from Anglo-Saxon *cnicht*, *cneoht*, meaning boy, youth, military follower) came to mean successively a youth, a servant, finally the servant of a noble. A *knave*, from German *Knabe* (boy), is now a pejorative term. And, interestingly, the usual American term *ladybug*, as well as the preferred British version *ladybird*, are not so named out of childish fancy, but in honor of "Our Lady," the Virgin Mary, especially since they are beneficial insects and considered a kind of blessing.

Folk Etymology

Just to remind you, we call folk etymology or popular etymology the transformation of words — usually those foreign to our ears — in order to make them more compatible with, sound more like, other better known or better understood words in our own language. *Asparagus* becomes sparrowgrass, *chaise longue* chaise lounge. New word creations, albeit often akin to gobbledygook, can be quite amusing. Occasionally they may be the involuntary gibberish of individuals deprived of a somewhat broader education or vocabulary. Thus, a *thug* (from Hindi *thag*, thief, and Sanskrit *sthaga*, rogue, *sthagati*, to conceal), who had spent his life kowtowing to his Mafia bosses and who was now ready to offer evidence against them in exchange for a reduced sentence, was asked by reporters how he spent his free time in the hotel where he was lodged. "I eat crackers with caramel bear" (his version for Camembert) was his reply. A perfect instance of the folk etymology process! Incidentally, *kowtow* is a similar case from the Chinese: *ko* (strike, bump) + *tou* (head), to kneel and touch the forehead to the ground in deep respect. *Chink*, an offensive term for the Chinese, is also formed by folk etymology from the Chinese *Junguo ren*, pronounced *junkwo zhen*, and meaning a Chinese person.

What about *gibberish* used in the paragraph above? This word and the verb to gibber are partly imitative of the sound of nonsense, besides being related to the 11th-century Arabian alchemist Geber. To avoid death on charges of having consorted with the devil, he wrote his treatises in seemingly nonsensical language. Other imitative or onomatopoeic words are jabber, giggle, gabble, buzz, hiss, bobwhite, cuckoo. As long as we are on the subject of Arabs, the Rock of *Gibraltar*, Prudential Insurance Company's trademark, was named after its Arabic conqueror, Tarik: *Jabalu't Tarik*, Tarik's Mountain, later *Jibal Tarik*, produced *Gibraltar*. In Italian it became *Gibilterra* by assimilating the last part of the name with *terra*, meaning land.

When Spanish explorers were trespassing on territory that is now in Colorado, no doubt reminded by their priests of their sinful ways, they named one of the rivers *Río de las Ánimas Perdidas* (River of Lost Souls). But that did not sound right to the French who followed them there. The French just do not use such an expression as "lost souls." They preferred something more Gallic (from Gaul), such as *Rivière du Purgatoire* (Purgatory River). That, however, was just too *highfalutin* (probably from high + fluting or blowing) for our plain Yanks, who quickly changed it, by folk etymology, to (would you believe?) Picketwire River, its name to this very day.

The irreverent French trappers and hunters in the Wyoming territory — sex and women constantly on their minds since otherwise not available — called the gorgeous peaks rising before their eyes Tetons, because they reminded them of *tétons*, (teats, breasts), or, I shudder to think, the underbelly of a sow lying on her back. I suppose we got even by calling these intruders *frogs*! This derisive and pejorative epithet for the French was not, as is often erroneously assumed, inspired by the French justifiable appetite for consuming tasty frog legs. The epithet, believe it or not, originated with the coat of arms of the French kings, the so-called lilies of France or *fleur-de-lis*, which is a stylized iris. In the Middle Ages, the predecessor of the royal shield was decorated with frogs rampant, perhaps tracing back to some feudal lord with estates located in a marshy region. According to John Ciardi, E. Cobham Brewer's *The Dictionary of Phrase and Fable* (1870, Rev. 1894) describes the heraldic device as "three toads erect saltant" (from Latin *saltare*, jump). Brewer claims that Nostradamus (1503-1556) called Frenchmen *crapauds* (toads) because of this.

As you noticed, I have a passion for language. Originally, *passion* (from the Latin *patere*, to suffer) meant suffering. Later Christians used the word to refer to the passion, or suffering, of Christ. During Chaucer's time, in the late 14th century, passion began to signify such powerful emotions as anger, rage, and even love. Now it expresses a more violent emotion of sexual love.

Food for Thought

What can be more French than a *bistro* (*bistrot*, if you prefer the alternate spelling used in French), one of the charming pubs, or bar-restaurants, that dispense beverages often with food? Don't look now, but this word has traveled all the way from Russia and back without earning frequent-flyer miles. The origin of *bistro* has two versions, but their combination is the most logical and likely, going back to the Russian occupation of Paris after the fall of Napoleon I in 1814. The Cossacks frequented Parisian restaurants and, often in a hurry, tried to speed up the relaxed style of the owners or waiters by impatiently shouting, "*Buystro! Buystro!*" — the Russian word for "quick." Try doing that today in Paris and you'll never get served. You might get a lecture on good manners to boot.

But wait! Now a year after first publishing the paragraph above, I discovered the *real* story — and here it is, a lesson in scholarship!

> Dear Reader,
> I must hang my head in shame,
> and yet I only have myself to blame.
> Any excuse I make is just plain lame!
> Since Berlitz's granddad knew language fame,
> I trusted Charles Berlitz just for his name,
> when he came up with this outrageous claim,
> that the word "bistro" from the Russian came.

> Of course, I should have wondered just the same,
> whether Charles wished my naiveté to frame.
> And so he did, indeed, and now my aim
> is to correct the error and reclaim
> your trust, which Charles Berlitz caused me to maim.
> So here below the truth we shall declaim
> on "bistro" and conclude this language game.

Actually the origin of *bistro* or *bistrot* (the French Academy never expressed any preference for either spelling), a word designating a small European wineshop or restaurant, first appeared in the late 1800s in a book authored by Father Basil Antoine-Marie Moreau (1799-1873). A certain Louis Piéchaud came up with the ingenious and amusing hypothesis about the word's etymology. Allegedly, during a Russian philology course at the Sorbonne, it was suggested that, in 1815, after the Congress of Vienna and Napoleon's defeat, the thirsty soldiers of Tsar Alexander I, then occupying Paris, had demanded to be served their food and beverages "*buystro, buystro.*" A clever anecdote, but, if true, why did three quarters of a century lapse before *bistro* appeared in a book or any slang dictionary?

It is not surprising that Charles Berlitz, whose family is famous for having charged more than anyone else for language courses without better results and who himself wrote controversial books on *The Bermuda Triangle* and *The Mystery of Atlantis*, fell for it. It is always fun to come up with unusual word origins, like those of *testimony* and *testify*. The Latin word *testis* means witness and its diminutive, *testiculus*, testicle. This verbal association originated with the early practice of placing the hand on the seat of manliness when swearing an oath to some statement. The *King James Bible* calls it euphemistically "swearing hand on the thigh." Derivatives with Latin *ad*, meaning to, *con* against, and *pro* forth, gave us attest, contest, and protest respectively.

A more scholarly search for *bistro* yields more likely possibilities. *Bistre* in French means swarthy, tanned, and a Western French regional *bistreau* (pronounced like *bistro*) means a cowherd. It eventually came to mean a strong lad or plain "*macho*," maybe referring to the bar owner. This is not very convincing either. Not all *macho*s are tanned and swarthy and not all bar owners are macho. Much more likely is to relate *bistro* to *bistrouille*, now more correctly spelled *bistouille*, designating a cheap bad alcohol and even coffee mixed with alcohol. The word *bistrouiller* means to make up bad beverage mixtures, and is still used in the wine business. The French poet Jean Richepin, who knew both his slang and his liquor, used *bistringot* for gambling den. Truthfully speaking, we cannot state with certainty that this is the definitive origin of *bistro*. *Bistringue*, dating to 1906, introduced in Canada in 1909, is a cabaret and was added to the French Academy dictionary in 1954. Nevertheless, you can have a great inexpensive meal in many French bistros. *Bon appetit!*

Let us continue, however. If you have breakfast in a Parisian bistro, you might be served a delicious French *croissant*. Well, not just French. The word, referring both to an ascending crescent moon and the tasty flaky bakery product shaped like one, is originally the translation of the German *Hörnchen*, little crescent or horn. It came from Vienna where after Poland's King Jan III Sobieski in 1689 defeated the Turks, laying siege to the city, the bakers to celebrate the victory made rolls in the shape of the crescents that adorned the Islamic banners. So, when in Paris eating croissants, think of Jan Sobieski and not Saddam Hussein!

But getting back to the expression "to boot," *boot* is from the Anglo-Saxon *bōt-profit*; related to English "better," it once was even used as the positive instead of good. We used to say *bōt*, better, best, from the Aryan *bhud-good*. In an old English game, players exchanged articles and an umpire would tell them what each should get "to *boot,*" or in addition. The extra amount was placed in advance in a cap, into which the umpire's hand was constantly dipping. Hence the game's name, "Hand in Cap," and, you guessed it, the *handicap* of golfers, defining both the allowance a golfer gets and his weakness. From the old *bōt*, meaning also advantage, came bootless errands and the pirate's booty. A child's bootie comes from the French *botte*, the boot as footwear. Now, of course, "to boot" means in addition or besides, and also refers to compensation, usually in cash, for the difference in value between things or real estate bartered: "He traded something and gave $10 to boot."

With regard to the pronunciation of "boot," I am reminded that many New Yorkers rather carelessly pronounced duty or New York as "dooty" and "Noo York." This may have been partially influenced by the German and Yiddish "*Nu?*" meaning "What of it? . . . What next? . . . So?" Unlike what your foreign-language teachers told you, there's always a reason.

And here is another interesting illustration of "the story behind the word." *Panic* comes from *Pan*, the Greek god of flocks and shepherds. Travelers, whom he often startled, dreaded him. His name surfaced in the Greek phrase *panikon deima*, the panic fear.

Hostility in Language

Hostile feelings between two nations are often reflected in the words or expressions of their language. Once firmly embedded in daily speech, they may persist long after all reasons for their initial use have vanished and are lost in oblivion. Let us for a moment again become paleolinguists (from Greek *palai*, long ago; *linguists*, dealing with ancient or fossil forms) and unearth some of these xenophobic language patterns. By the way, in Greek, *xeno* is stranger and *phobos* fear, and, by implication, hatred. Perhaps you remember when the British referred to syphilis as the "French Disease," and France quickly got even with its neighbor across the Channel by calling it the "English Disease" (*mal anglais*). What about *pardon my French*, meaning excuse my profanity, or *to take French leave* — i.e., abruptly, without permission? The French retaliated (from the Latin *re*, again, + *tal*, of such kind) or gave *tit for tat* (earlier, *tip for tap*, from the French *tant pour tant*, meaning so much for so much, which also gave us to taunt in the sense of paying back) by saying *to take English leave* (*filer à l'anglaise*). A *French postcard* is pornographic and a *French walk* is a bum's rush. To execute the latter, you grab a person by the seat of the pants and his collar, then, in a manner of speaking euphemistically, "escort" him forcibly to the door.

For many years, England and Holland were bitter rivals on the sea. Dutch figures prominently in English xenophobic expressions. Dutch *duitsch* and German *deutsch* once designated all of Germany instead of just the Netherlands. From the Old High German, *diutisc* meant popular, national. However, later on it became debased just as *Slav*, originally from the Russian word *slava* meaning glory, gave us *slave*. The Dutch, popular at home, were less liked across the Channel. In the 16th and 17th centuries, they tied brooms on their mastheads, boasting that their vessels swept the seas. The British expressed their contempt for their colonial rivals by means of expressions that still survive: a *Dutch auction* is one where the auctioneer starts with a high figure; a *Dutch anchor* is something valuable that has been left behind, from a story of a Dutch captain forgetting his anchor and losing his ship; *Dutchman's breeches* is a small patch of blue in a stormy sky, sufficient to make a pair of pants for a Dutchman.

Dutch treat is where you pay your own share and "treat yourself," and a *Dutch bargain* is one agreed upon over liquor. *Dutch comfort*: I am grateful it is not worse! *Dutch concert* is a cacophony (Greek *caco*, bad, and *phonos*, sound), where every musician does his or her own thing. *Dutch courage* is induced by liquor. *Dutch defense* means an outright surrender; *Dutch feast*, where the host gets drunk before his guests; *Dutch gold*, a cheap alloy of copper and zinc; *Dutch luck*, undeserved good fortune; *Dutch nightingale*, a frog. The list continues. *Dutch praise* ultimately criticizes. *Dutch reckoning* is an invoice that is higher than it would be were it itemized. If you talk like a *Dutch uncle* it means you don't mince words, but scold. A *Dutch wife* is a pillow, used especially in the tropic colonies to refer to a man who did not take a native woman. We also hear occasionally, "If that's the truth, I'm a Dutchman," for "I'll be damned!" *Double Dutch* is double talk or gibberish, and to be *in Dutch* is to be in trouble.

Expressions reflecting dislike of foreigners or strangers are found in many languages. In Montana, Cornish miners call an assessment, where you pay instead of receiving, an *Irish dividend*. The Romans did not trust the people of Carthage, a region they called Punica. *Punica fides*, *Punic faith*, meant treachery. *Vandalism* comes from the sacking of Rome in 445 A.D. by Genseric, king of the Vandals. In Old English, *wealh*, referring to a non-Saxon or foreigner, was what the earlier inhabitants, Waelisc or Welsh were called, whence to *welsh* on a deal. *Walnut* from *wealh knutu* is the foreign or Welsh nut, and to the people from Manhattan the sound of derision, *ppfht*, is a Bronx cheer. In ancient Spain, the inhabitants of Cordova, where Cordovan leather comes from, were reputed cheats, as concisely stated in the proverb "*Cordobés, mala res; de una aguja hace tres*" — "A Cordovan is a bad animal; out of one needle he fashions three." According to the proverb, Cordovans, when trading, may well shortchange you.

Pagan is another socially discriminatory term. Christianity spread more rapidly in the cities than in the outlying districts of the Roman Empire.

According to English historian Edward Gibbon (*Decline and Fall of the Roman Empire*), any countryman (Latin *paganus*, villager, rustic — hence ignorant) living on the other side of the tracks, if you'll excuse the anachronism, was likely to be an unbeliever. However, Gibbon may be in error. Under the Caesars, *paganus* also meant "civilian," as opposed to *miles,* soldier. The Christians called themselves the "soldiers of the Lord." All others were pagans. A *heathen*, on the other hand, was first a dweller on the heath or open country, from the German *Heide*. Joseph T. Shipley, who also writes penetratingly about word origins, summarizes this xenophobic attitude by citing a brief conversation between two cockney kids: "Who's that?" . . . "Dunno." . . . "'Eave (heave) 'arf (half) a brick at 'im (him)!"

Not all word derivations are hostile, even if they contain names of people. *Neighbor* is a *nigh boor*, or nearby farmer, from the Dutch *Boer* (the Boer War in South Africa) and German *Bauer*. Where does *nigh* come from? In Old English, instead of near, nearer, nearest, people used *nigh* (positive), *near* (comparative), *neth* (superlative). Thus, the infrequently used word *nethermost* is actually a superlative, plus a comparative, plus a superlative. Talk about overkill and redundancy! *Savage*, through the French *sauvage*, comes from the Latin *silva*, the forest or the wilds, hence *sylvan*. *Pennsylvania* means Penn's forest! However, *California* is the name of a princess in a very popular Spanish medieval romance of chivalry, *Las Ergas de Esplandián* (*The Heroic Feats of Esplandián*), a sequel to *Amadis of Gaul,* two among the many novels the Knight of La Mancha (Don Quixote) read from "dawn to dawn" until he blew his brain from reading so much fiction about knights and damsels in distress. Folk etymology also played a part in shaping the name *California*, because the Golden State, especially in the summer, reminded the Spanish of *calor* (heat) and *forno* (in Modern Spanish, *horno*, furnace). Still, a novelist's fictitious princess of the same name, living in an earthly paradise, gave the state its name.

Now you may think all this is *hocus-pocus filiocus*, designating both the tomfoolery a magician engages in and the kitchen Latin he utters while doing so when making things disappear before your very eyes. Actually, these words are a distortion of the Catholic sacrament, changing bread into the body of the Lord's Son: *Hoc est corpus filii* (This is the body of the Son). After the trick is completed, the magician may add, "Presto! Change-o!" Is it surprising that magicians are also known as *prestidigitators*, from *preste* (agile, nimble, quick) and *digitus* (finger, or sleight of hand)? *Prestige*, originally, referred to delusion, a conjurer's trick, the power to dazzle, to charm, and then the status obtained due to the ensuing public admiration. The Latin *praestigium*, delusion, is linked to *praestringere* (to bind, compare string) and *prae* (before) — in other words, to blindfold or hoodwink. In the next essay I shall tell you more about how words are combined like Tinker Toys to produce new meanings. Remember also that whenever a word is needed to express something new in our lives, presto, as though by magic, it appears in our language.

Let us dwell a while longer on xenophobic expressions. Speaking of *dwell*, it is now a stylish word, not normally used if you live in a hovel, but once had a rather unpleasant meaning. Originally it meant to stun, to make giddy, and then to mislead, from the Sanskrit *dhwr*, to mislead. In Old High German, to dwell (*twellan*) had shifted its meaning to express the result of stunning, namely to delay, to retard. Used intransitively, that is without a direct object, it meant to delay, to linger, hence to dwell in a place. As to *hovel*, a small hut, it is a diminutive of the Anglo-Saxon *hof* or *hofa*, house. *Hof* (now mostly yard, court), is still used in Germany to name fancy palaces, even castles, estates, or luxury hotels such as Frankfurter Hof, equivalent to the Frankfurt Palace Hotel.

Cut Out of the Whole Cloth?

In the 15th century, *whole cloth* was synonymous with *broadcloth* — cloth that reached across the full length of the loom. In early use, the phrase "cut out of the whole cloth" retained its literal meaning: something that is made out of the full amount of everything that composes it. Later, however, tailors were pulling the wool over the eyes of their clients, cheating them, and, in the United States, the expression came to mean the exact opposite. Tailors were using patched or pieced goods, or even artificially stretched cloth instead of the whole material. Thus, the phrase now means a lie, something without foundation. Rest assured, however, that what I write about is the whole truth without any holes in it, and not an out-and-out lie "made out of whole cloth."

Speaking of cloth, the *Moirae*, called *Parcae* by the Romans (the Fates as we know them), were three in number: *Clotho* (her name rings a bell and may have influenced the old Teutonic word *clathe*, cloth), the one who spins with her spindle; *Lachesis* (the Greek root means to give by lot), with a staff who assigns us our fate; and *Atropos* (from *a*, not, + *tropos*, turn), who never yields, cannot be avoided, and is often pictured with a pair of scales, a sundial, or a cutting instrument. The names for different types of cloth, however, were often coined from their place of origin followed by the word cloth, which was later dropped.

Calicut cloth, whence *calico* comes, is from the city of the same name in India. *Cambric linen* and *chambray cotton* are named from Cambrai in Flanders, now in France. *Cheviot* is from the Cheviot Hills sheep. Kashmir gave us *cashmere*. *Cretonne*, a cotton similar to chintz, often with floral designs, comes from Creton in Normandy. *Damask* and *damascene*, the latter inlaid iron or steel like that on Kurdish flintlocks or swords, originated in Damascus. Those *denim* jeans you wear, at least the material, came "*de* (from) *Nîmes*," the Roman city in southern France. *Duffel* bag comes from the place of the same name near Antwerp. *Frieze*, the coarse wool material, originated in Friesland, the coastal region between Holland and Germany. However, *frieze*, denoting the fine embroidery and the architectural decorations reminiscent thereof, comes through the French *frise* from Phrygia, a 13th-century country of west-central Asia.

Would you believe that the delicate *gauze* could possibly survive all the bullets exchanged on the war-torn Gaza strip in Palestine? *Jersey* material is not from Newark, "NuChoysy," but from Jersey in England. *Lawn*, not the stuff you have to mow, but rather the plain woven cotton or linen fabric, is from Laon in France. *Lisle* thread is from Lille, which you can reach via toll road A, straight north of the Charles de Gaulle Airport in Paris. You will need cash or credit card, no *tokens*, from Old English *tacn*, German *zeigen*, to show. To show was the first meaning of "to teach" from the Sanskrit *dic*, whence Latin *dicere* (to say), whence also *valedictorian*, the one who says good-bye to his alma mater and his classmates. The heavy woolen felted finish *melton* is from Melton Mobray, a hunting ground in Leicestershire, England. And *muslin* cotton is from the Italian *mussolina*, diminutive of Mosul in northern Iraq.

The yellowish cotton *nankeen* is from Nankin in China. Maybe the Chinese did offer "bribes" to Bill Clinton. He will tell you that he uses the original meaning from Old French *bribe*, once merely a charitable offering, just like the one Al Gore received in the Buddhist temple. It meant crumb, piece, what you give to a beggar. *Briber, brimber*, meant to beg. The meaning grew, with the help of politicians, President Clinton excluded, of course, from a gift begged to one demanded in exchange for a favor. Speaking of China: south, north, west, and east (to the Chinese a compass is the south-pointing needle) are in Chinese *nan, bei, shi,* and *dung,* respectively. So *Nankin* is the south city, *Beijing* the north city, and *Shanghai*, from *shang* (above) and *hai* (sea), means exactly that. *Shan* is mountain, so *Shi Shan* means western mountain. *Silk*, from Greek *Seres* (the eastern race, maybe referring to the Chinese) through Latin *sericus*, French *soie*, more likely from Old English *sioloc*, German *Seide*, Russian *sholk*, is related to Old French *sarge* that gave us *serge*. We could go on and on with *sleazy* from Silesia, *poplin* from Italian *papalino,* first made in Avignon, the seat of a second papacy and pope, and *tulle*, used for veils or evening dresses, from Tulle in France.

Tornado	From Spanish *tornar*, to turn, influenced also by Spanish *tronada*, thunderstorm, and *tronar*, to thunder; Latin *tonare* led to French *tonnerre* — thunder.
Treasure Trove	From French *trésor* (treasure) *trouvé* (found).
Trivia	From Latin *tri* (three) + *via* (road); thus, *crossroads,* where three roads cross, is the place where people might meet and exchange unimportant news.

The Loom of Language

Although we do not with certainty know how human language originated, by analyzing words, focusing on their creation, when needed, to express and communicate human thought, we can directly observe how, from one root word, additional nuances of meaning evolve by additions and adjustments to such root words. The latter and their meanings are like living cells, which combine with other elements (prefixes and suffixes) to produce, in a way, offsprings, in fact an entire generation of them, each with its distinctive meaning. The result is a quilt, a structure, a fabric displaying an entire network or family of meanings. That is how language is, in a sense, woven.

Regarding cloths and fabrics, *fabric* is from the Latin *faber* (someone who can make, fabricate); hence, with the addition of the proper qualifier, *faber ferrarius* (iron) or *faber tignarius* (log, beam), we have either a blacksmith or a carpenter. *Fabric* is also related to the Latin *facere*, to make. Now that's a *"fact,"* past participle of the same verb (*facere, factus*), meaning "something done, made, real." *Feat* has the same root, and *defeat* is something undone. For those of you that know Spanish, *hacer* (to make) is the same verb, since *h* and *f* were to a degree interchangeable. But I am *digressing* — from the Latin *di* (aside) + *gradire* (past participle, *gress*), to step. Now here is another *fertile* (from Latin *ferre*, to carry, to bear) cell. It mushrooms into *grade* (a kind of step), *gradual* (step by step), *degree* (also a step in itself), *graduated* (marked off by steps), *degrade* (lower one step), *egress* (to step out), the same as *exit*, from *ex* (out) + *ire* (walk), *progress* (step forward), *transgress* (step across), *aggression* (step toward or against), *congress* (step or come together). The basic root of this word (through Sanskrit *griddhra*, greedy, and Aryan *gardh*) meant "to desire" and implied stepping toward what one wants. You can really see how our forefathers put two and two together logically.

Not all cloths are named after places. The stiff cotton fabric *buckram*, though originally from Bukhara in Central Asia, now Uzbekistan, more probably comes from the French *bougran* and may be influenced by *bouche*, French for mouth, because of the holes in it. *Satin*, from the Arab *zaytuni* (Marco Polo called it *Zaitun*), came from the medieval Chinese seaport of Tzu-Ting, now Chuanchow. But satin also comes from the Italian *setino panno*, bristly cloth, and from Latin *saeta*, bristle. *Gingham* is not from Guincamp, France, as some have claimed, but from Malay *gingan*, striped. *Dimity*, a type of cotton where two threads are woven as one, is not from Damietta, Egypt, but from Italian, Latin, and Greek words combining *di* (two) + *mitos* (thread). Similarly, *twill* reveals its Anglo-Saxon root *twi* (two). *Tweed* is a mistake, as the Scots pronounce twill "tweel." Then, to obscure matters further, it was influenced by the river Tweed. *Drill*, from German *drillich*, translates the Latin *trilix*, or triple thread. Numbers are found in *biscuit* from French *bis* (twice) + *cuit* (cooked) and Dutch *Zwieback* (two-baked); and don't forget the trade name *Triscuit*, thrice baked. This may attract *centipedes*, each with one hundred feet (see *century, centennial, centenarian*, all having one hundred in common), and the dream come true of every podiatrist or foot doctor.

Sometimes this propagation of word cells is overwhelming. The richly embroidered silk and gold fabric *baldachin* or *baldaquin* comes from *baldacco*, Italian for *Baghdad*, but is also related to bawdry, once meaning finery, now unchastity, loose behavior. *Alpaca* is the animal from *al* (the) + *paco* (probably American Indian for red). *Brocade* contains the Spanish *brocare*, to pick. *Chenille* designates the wool cotton. It is French for little caterpillar, from Latin *caniculum*, little dog (*canis,* dog; remember *cave canem,* "beware of the dog," also a caveat or warning) — truly opening a can of worms. The Old English called *caterpillar* "*this wyrm among frute.*" It is folk etymology from the French *chatte poilue*, or hairy female cat. However, other words added to its meaning: a robber was also called a *piller*, hence pillage, and a glutton was a *cater*, making caterpillar a "greedy plunderer," which I suppose it is. You can see how the metaphors multiply as a result of mental associations. *Pillage* is straight from the French, related to Latin *pilar*, to strip the hide from, as well as *pilus*, hair. So *ex* + *pilar*, French *épiler*, yields epilation, the removal of hair.

But let's quit while we're ahead! *Head*, ultimately derived from Latin *caput,* is related to countless words such as capital, chief, achieve (*ad* + *caput,* or come to a head), cape, . . . and on and on.

ℭ Well! I'll Be Darned! ℭ

Let us return once more to cloth and material, if you'll forgive the bad pun on "darn," actually a euphemism for "damn." *Chintz*, formerly chints, plural of chint, is from the Sanskrit *chitra* (pied), of more than one color. Because chintz is often gaudy, the adjective chintzy may have evolved into meaning cheap, even stingy. *Cotton*, related to Spanish *algodón*, comes from the Arabic *quin*. The Arabs or Moors occupied Spain until 1492, when they were expelled. *Crepe*, from French *crêpe*, from Latin *crispus* (curled, undulating), designates both the cloth and the pancake. *Georgette*, a crepe with a pebbly surface, woven from hard twisted yarns, is from Madame Georgette de La Plante, a 19th-century French dressmaker, often called a *modiste* (from Latin *modus*, measure), and related to *mete* (to mete or measure out punishment). Elegant clothes are made to measure. *Pile*, from Latin *pilus* (hair), is related to *peluché* (wool and silk velvet-like cloth), whence *plush*. This is not to be confused with *posh*, about which I shall write on another occasion.

Velvet is from French *veluet* and *velu* (shaggy), as is *velours*. *Crinoline*, from Latin *crinus* (mane) and *linum* (line, flax), contains the French word *crin* (horse hair from mane or tail) and linen. Both the cloth and color *khaki* are from the same Hindi word meaning dusty. It may serve as *camouflage*, which reminds me that many years ago a guide I had met in Srinigar, in northern India, asked me in a letter to send him a "camelflesh" outfit for hunting. It took me a while to grasp his meaning: in a way he practiced some homemade folk etymology, distorting camouflage into camelflesh. The second syllable of *mohair* is again folk etymology from Arabic *mukhayyar*, the chosen, past participle of *khayyara*, to prefer. It refers to a cloth of goat's hair. The same word, through the French, produced *moire*. The thin soft clothing and curtain fabric *pongee* is pure Chinese: *pun-chi* means own loom and implies fine quality.

The words *taffeta*, French *taffetas*, Persian *taftah* (woven), from *taftan*, to twist or spin, are all related, as are *voile* (pronounced *wahl*), veil, and Latin *velum*, which means sail, curtain, or covering. Thus, *reveal* is to pull back the veil. The prefix *re-* always means back or again, since both meanings are closely related. A word like *gabardine* has a much fancier story. French *gaverdine*, *galvardine*, once referred to a pilgrim's cloak and originated, by this ever-fertile folk etymology, from the old word for modern German *Wallfahrt*, pilgrimage. Incidentally, when you travel in Germany, you will see countless signs such as *Einfahrt* and *Ausfahrt* — on ramp and off ramp — from *fahren* (to journey). It has nothing to do with flatulence or scatology! On the other hand, *gabardine* might also have been influenced by the Spanish *gabán* (great cloak), or vice versa. The soft lightweight cotton *Nainsook* is from two Hindi words, *eye* and *delight*, delight of the eye. *Seersucker* is from Persian *shir u sukkar*, milk and honey. Come and get it!

We may never know where *corduroy* comes from. It might be from French *corde du roi*, cord/cloth of the king, or *coeur du roi*, king's heart, or even *couleur du roi*, king's color. *Coeur* (heart), from Latin *cor*, is almost daily on everyone's lips in the form of "cardiac." You all know where leathers like *Moroccan* and *Cordovan* come from, the first from the country in North Africa, the second from the city in southern Spain, where until 1492 the Moors flourished, as they did in Granada. What about *tabby*, a plain silk taffeta? It owes its origin to the great Umayyad prince Attab, after whom a quarter in Baghdad was named. From that quarter came *attabi*, whence *tabi*, a striped cloth, and, of course, the tabby cat with its gray and tawny coat striped or mottled with black.

By now, I don't have to tell you that *meow* is formed by onomatopoeia. Still, nothing with language is always simple! *Tibbie* was also a pet name from Tibalt, Tybalt, Theobald (*Theo God*, hence meaning "bold in God"), in the medieval beast epics so popular in Europe. Chapter 10 of William Caxton's 15th-century translation of the tales of *Reynard the Fox* (*renard* is fox in French; in Germany the epic was called *Reineke Fuchs*) is entitled "How the kynge sent Tybert the catte for the foxe." In Shakespeare's *Romeo and Juliet*, Tybald asks, "What wouldst thou have of me?" and is taunted by Mercutio, "Good king of the cats: nothing but one of your nine lives."

I'll stop here before I exhaust yours.

No Man Is an Island

The often said "No man is an island" means that no individual is sufficient to him- or herself. The word *isle*, from Old French *isle*, from Latin *insula* (island), has influenced many words. It even changed the spelling of the etymologically unrelated word island, which was once spelled *iland* and came from the Anglo-Saxon *iegland*, from *ieg,* or watery land. Thus island is redundant, as people forgot the original meaning of *ieg*, which already included "land." By the process of spelling assimilation, isle has even affected the spelling of unrelated words like *aisle*; adding an *s*, although its French source, *aile*, from Latin *ala* (wing of a bird; side of a church separated from the nave by pillars; wing of a building) had no such letter. *Ala* also shows up in a plane's aileron or little wing. The original Latin *insula* survives in peninsula, which literally means almost an island (Latin *paene*, almost). Island and isolationist are both insulated and isolated from the outside. The drug *insulin*, first isolated in 1922 by Dr. F. G. Banting of the University of Toronto, was thus named because it comes from so-called anatomical islands (from Greek *ana*, up, again, + *tome*, cutting; one volume of a set of an author's works printed apart or cut off from the others is a "tome"), namely the glands of the pancreas called, after their discoverer, the islands of Langerhans.

In the body, islands are cells or tissues surrounded by materials of a different structure. Thus, the *Island of Reil* is the central lobe of the cerebrum (pretty cerebral, eh what?), from Latin *cerebrum*, French *cerveau* (brain). This, of course, assumes you don't have a vacuum between your ears. In Late Latin, *vacuum* was popularly replaced by vocitum, *voitum*, which through Old French *vuide*, *voide* (Modern French *vide*), gave us our *void*. Vacuum and void are so-called doublets. From all this we get *avoid*, which first meant to make empty or void, but later, by confusion with French *éviter* (avoid), shifted its meaning. The same root is found in the adjective *devoid*, but not in the verb *divide*. The French *dévider* means to unwind into a skein and *diviser* means to divide.

Returning to Reil, it suggests, merely by sound, *rile*, another form of *roil*, to make a liquid turbid by stirring it and, figuratively, a person angry. Although the origin is unknown, these words may be related to French *rouille* (rust), or even *brouiller* (to mix, confuse, jumble). The human mind is amazing, yet ultimately logical. *Brouillon* in French means rough draft. I know mine can be jumbled, confusing, and even illegible (from *ill*, not, and *legere*, to collect, and when you collect written words "to read"). See also English *embroil* in a dispute. Broiling fish is from French *brûler*, to burn, but don't take if literally, for "burnt" it might not taste good. Now, if you let nothing rile you, you may lead the life of Reilly (also spelled Riley). This gentleman was not from Ireland. He was a Gypsy lord, from the Gypsy word *rye*, gentleman, changed by folk etymology to a name more common to English speakers. In 1857, George Borrow wrote *The Romany Rye* (*The Gypsy Gentleman*). *Gypsies* (Egyptians) came from India to Europe and spoke Romani. *Rye* (not the grain) is from Sanskrit *raj*, *raya* (lord), whence *rajah*. The *maharajah* is Hindu *maha* (great) + *raj*. The feminine is *maharanee*.

Speaking of Reilly, the expression "living the life of Reilly" originated in a comic song of the 1880s about a saloonkeeper in a small town in the

Middle West, who made so much money he converted his saloon into a hotel. The song, "Is that Mr. Reilly?," was sung by the original Pat Rooney vaudevillian:

> Is that Mr. Reilly, can anyone tell?
> Is that Mr. Reilly who owns the hotel?
> Well, if that's Mr. Reilly, they speak of so highly,
> Upon my soul, Reilly, you're doing quite well.

I also read that H. L. Mencken, a great source for English expressions, claims that "the life of Reilly," more an American than an English expression, grew popular after 1898, when James W. Blake and Charles E. Lawlor (who wrote the lyrics and music to "The Sidewalks of New York") wrote "The Best in the House is None Too Good for Reilly." Edward B. Marks claims that in 1899 his firm published a song, "Everything at Reilly's Must Be Done in Irish Style." The expression was also much used in the Ned Harrigan and Tony Hart plays of the day, which showed the Irish getting ahead as cops and politicians.

Beware of Misusing Language

We know that language is a precious, almost miraculous tool, giving us time-binding, the characteristically human ability of transmitting experience from one generation to another, especially through the use of symbols and, of course, words. But how efficient is it? Any time we pose this question about a tool, there are two sides to consider. How good is the tool, and how good is the one using it? The first to make a serious original contribution to this subject was Alfred Korzybski (1879-1950), a Polish-born American mathematician, engineer, and finally semanticist (from Greek *sema*, sign, and *semainein*, to signify, show by a sign, mean). In *Science and Sanity: An Introduction to Non-Aristotelian Systems and General Semantics* (1933) he propounded an approach to language that rejects the Aristotelian language structure, with its "is" of identity, as tending to confuse words with the things for which they stand, and to see everything as either right or wrong, black or white, a dangerous overuse of dichotomy (remember Greek *bi* or *di*, two, and *tome*, to cut, thus meaning to cut in half or in two).

Now don't rush to the library to read *Science and Sanity*! You might be tempted to cut me in half after you open this formidable 800-page monster. User-friendly writers, such as Stuart Chase (*The Tyranny of Words*, 1938), as well as two of my former colleagues, S. I. Hayakawa (*Language in Thought and Action*, 1949) and Wendell Johnson, have written more readable popularizations of Korzybski's work, thus rendering a great service to careful, accurate thinking and communication. I propose to be even more user-friendly by giving you in simpler, more concise terms the nuts and bolts of their thesis and recommendations to avoid misusing both spoken and written language.

First, in observance of the principle of "non-allness," we must be constantly aware that we only know a narrow band of reality. Nobody knows everything about anything. Using an attitude of humility every time we make a statement about almost anything, we should add to it "etc. . . . etc." Hayakawa launched a journal called *ETC* to reinforce this message: when pontificating about someone or something, first, above all, exercise humility, and think "etc. . . ." because we can never give a complete picture of the subject in question.

Second, everything in the universe is in a perpetual flux. Our world is a dynamic process, a dance of electrons and atoms (*atom*, originally thought to be no further divisible, hence from Greek *a*, not, + *tome*, cut). So, when talking about your fellow humans, use dating. What I now say applies to John 1998, or John 1999, or, more accurately yet, John at 1:03:22 p.m., 1:03:23 p.m., the Catholic Church in 1640, in 1650, today, etc. . . . Before you know it, you'll be perfection personified, quite careful about judging anyone or saying much of anything, lest you not be 100 percent accurate. The world will enjoy some welcome silence and less rhetoric from politicians and talk-show hosts. Our senses deceive us so easily. For example, think of a fan spinning and you'll call it a disk. When it stops spinning, you see only blades where earlier there was a disk. Even our eyes deceive us!

And third is the principle of uniqueness: no two things in our universe are identically alike, not even a row of printed dots. So, speaking about persons and things, use indexing and, above all, never label. Almost all words can become generalizing, erroneous labels. You talk about "fathers," "sailors," "Republicans," "Communists." Are they really all alike? A student writes a bad theme and the teacher, unthinkingly, calls him a "bad student." What a serious misuse of language! Watch your language! You might tell him that he wrote a sloppy paper, but not label him as a bad student. The teacher may have done lasting harm by mislabeling. You call someone a Communist. Are you qualified to do so? How much do you really know about Marx, Engels, Hegel, Feuerbach, and dialectical materialism, the essence of Communist theory? Are Russian and Chinese Communists quite alike? Are all Democrats the same? But read on for "the rest of the story."

Using Language Skillfully

The fourth principle of language usage is more *abstruse* (from Latin *ab*, away, + *trudere*, to push, that is to conceal). It is called *abstracting* (from Latin *ab*, away, + *trahere*, to tract, pull, draw). When you abstract you draw, isolate, separate from a person, object, or situation some particular characteristics, and never, by any means, all of them. Ultimately, abstracting constitutes a quick, impressionistic, usually incomplete "from off the top of your head" evaluation. In fact, my personal opinion is that we would find it difficult to even think in abstractions. What do such abstract concepts like Poverty, Good, Evil, really mean? To get a handle on them you just about have to imagine, evoke the image of a beggar, a saint, or a serial killer, respectively. No two individuals will define such abstract labels the same way. At least, when using abstractions, be aware they may not, in every mind, evoke identical images. When traveling down the ladder of abstraction, think of the increasing degree of specificity attained, as you move from cattle (least specific, most abstract), to cow, to Holstein, to Betsy, the favorite cow you just milked (and the most specific, least abstract).

With the fifth principle, the structural differential, we find semanticist Alfred Korzybski at his best — or worst, and most obscure. He points out, quite correctly, that, at the highest level, most of the "Great Reality," the totality of the energies, life processes, and principles of the universe, are beyond our senses and our ken, outside the human visible, audible, perceptible levels. At the next level, a small portion of the universe is at least perceptible to us in varying degrees, although to no two individuals exactly alike. At least each one of us abstracts it as well as his or her senses permit. At the final level, when we attempt to communicate parts of the perceptible and perceived portion, language hardly allows every one of us to do it exactly the same way. Each of us shall describe it differently, in greater or lesser detail, as he or she perceives it. When communicating our perceptions, we are further limited by our respective abilities, mental and physical, our previous experience, and our command of the art of language. The variations are infinite. I may notice more on a printed page, whereas you may be more observant of nature. We all enjoy different degrees and areas of abilities. Korzybski illustrated the above three stages (entire universe, perceptible portion, limited labels communicated with the aid of symbols — here language, to describe the latter) by drawing three circles, each one comprising a decreased number of dots, some with threads hanging from them and going nowhere as they escaped human understanding, perception, labeling, and communication, respectively.

The sixth and final principle pertains to degrees. That is where old Aristotle really dropped the ball, or whatever else he was playing with in Ancient Athens. He said that at any one time a thing must be either A or not A. Nothing can be further from the truth, and believing his statement muddled much of the thinking of Western Civilization. Reality is far more complex and multidimensional than Aristotle postulated. Two-valued logic or dichotomy (from the Greek word meaning to cut in two or half) may apply in some rare instances, but most of the time we must think in terms of degrees, because many things in nature exist on a scale or in varying shades and nuances. Very little in life is either black or white.

By now all of you are certified General Semanticists, aware of the limitations of the tool of language and of the principles governing its correct usage. As such you will see right through the fallacies or sleight of tongue of students of symbolic logic, especially when they use, or rather misuse, language instead of sticking to algebraic symbols in their sophistry. Consider, for instance, the false premises and conclusion of the Liar Paradox of 6th century B.C. poet, prophet, and "miracle worker" Epimenides: All Cretans are liars; I am a Cretan, therefore I am a liar. The statement violates at least two principles of general semantics, the one of non-allness (how can one be sure all Cretans are liars?) and the one of degree (does a liar necessarily tell only lies?). It cannot be true! If the impossible were true, the first premise correct, and all Cretans liars, then, because the statement is made by a Cretan, that is a liar, it would translate as: no Cretans are liars and I am not a Cretan. It is gobbledygook! Language, used correctly, does not permit it. It does not work like mathematical equations. In language, "a Delicious equals an apple" does not guarantee the reverse to be true. It does not work like x = y, and thus y = x in algebra.

Biscuit From French *bis* (twice) *cuit* (cooked), a process of baking, then drying in low heat to keep longer.

Croissant French translation of the German *Hörnchen*, little crescent or horn. Originally, from Vienna: after Poland's King Jan III Sobieski, in 1689, defeated the Turks, bakers celebrated with rolls made in the shape of the crescents that had adorned Islamic banners.

All About Humor

There is good humor, bad or ill humor, and black humor — but then there are the four humors, and thereby hangs a *tale* (from Anglo-Saxon *talu*, designating both speech and number, as well as Anglo-Saxon *tellan*, to list in order, hence English *tell*, to count like a bank *teller*, and to recount with the meaning of relating a story). The four *humors*, spelled *humours* in Britain, owe their origin to the Latin *humidus*, moist, humid, and *humiditas*, humidity, and refer to the four principal bodily fluids: blood or *sanguine* (French *sang*, blood; Latin *sanguinis*, bloody), *phlegm*, *choler* (yellow bile), and *black bile*. Back in earlier times, when psychiatry was a great deal simpler, a person's disposition might range anywhere on a scale extending from enraged to laid back and the difference attributed to the predominance of one humor or another. Eat too much rare meat, turn beet red, and you'll be labeled sanguine. Too much phlegm, which is cold and moist, would classify you as phlegmatic, even sluggish. A sorehead might be deemed choleric with a surplus of yellow bile. A melancholic sad sack had too much black bile. Either way, choleric or melancholic, you qualify as bilious. Humor eventually designated good humor at the happy end of the scale.

Melancholy is from Greek *melan* (black) and *chole* (bile). Thus, Philipp Melanchthon (1497-1560) translated into Greek his German surname Schwarzerd as, literally, "black earth" (notice how you can spot in the German our English words "swarthy" and "earth"). Professor of Greek and follower of Luther, he was the first to extensively formulate the Protestant doctrine. However, after he wanted to reconcile Roman Catholicism and Protestantism, his name was mud, black mud no less, to Luther, who "blackballed" him, if you'll pardon the pun. It proves that if you fight over religion, you are right back where you started from, but with bruises. Name changes into other languages are frequent. Mozart changed his middle name from Greek *Theophilus* (*theophile*, or God-loving) to Latin *Amadeus*, synonymous with the German name *Gottlieb* or "God love."

A person's disposition may also be revealed by his *complexion*. Ruddy may signify a person is choleric. *Complexion* (from Latin *cum*, together, + *plectere*, past participle *plexus*, to braid, plait, interweave), just as complex, refers to a bundle of interwoven fibers — in other words not a simple fabric. This verb root together with the Latin *plicare* (French *plier*), to fold, generate many English words: *complicate* (fold together), *implicate* (fold into like a spider a prey in his web), also *imply*, even *employ*, with the idea of folding in and involving all, derive from the same source. *Duplicate*, folded twice, yields twofold, as well as *duplicity* or "doubleness" (a little used word) of heart and thought. *Simplicity* is Latin *sine* (without) and *plica* (fold). Then the idea arose of weaving together the characteristics of persons to reflect their personality, and, all the way through to the Middle Ages, the four human qualities were hot, cold, dry, and moist. Combining these and the Latin word *temperare* (to mix, apportion, moderate, regulate) gave us the idea of *temper* for individuals and *temperature* for things. Latin *temperare* is also related to *tempus* (time), *tempestas* (season), even *tempest*, or a manifestation of the stormy season. You can see the loom of language working full blast.

From the same Latin word for fold come *explicit* (folded out so you can see it all) and *implicit* (folded in so it is there but not obvious). *Obvious* comes from another root, *ob* (against) and *viare* (travel). Thus something obvious comes right up against you so that you cannot miss it. The French *plier*, to fold, gave us *pliant* and *pliable*, that which can be folded. Even *replica*, to fold again, and *reply*, to fold back, have the same origin. *Simplicity* may also have been influenced by the Latin *simplus* (one), *simul* (like), and the same corresponding words in French, *simple* meaning simple or one, and *semblable*, *simuler*, meaning respectively similar, alike, and simulate, act like. Actually, once you know, it is quite simple!

The Mystery of Language

Have you ever wondered where all our approximately 4,000 languages and more than 6,000 dialects come from? After the flood, if you believe the Bible, Noah's descendants, having arrived in Babylonia, attempted to build a tower that would reach to heaven. Jehovah, evidently a believer in high-rise zoning restrictions, was displeased by such presumption and "confounded the speech of the builders" so that they could no longer understand one another. This presumably created the diversity of human languages, but we do not know whether before this biblical event took place we had more than one language. There was a time in the early 1900s, at least in Europe, when no linguistic research subject pertaining to an original primeval language (in German *Ursprache*) was acceptable, either as a doctoral dissertation or a scholarly publication. It was frowned on, just as the subject of cold fusion might be suspicious to a physics department in our days. Such restrictions no longer apply, but the idea of one primeval tongue is still met with a measure of skepticism, and, I respectfully submit, rightly so.

Experts in historical linguistics, some with further impressive language backgrounds, such as Merritt Ruhlen, have tried to elucidate the mystery of the origin of language and trace the evolution of a possible single mother tongue. The goal is to demonstrate that all extant languages share a common origin. For this purpose one must classify all existing languages and discover whether they have common elements and thus may be assigned, together with others, to language families. In a sense one must create a family tree of languages with one original mother tongue at the summit. The difficulty lies in that some such exotic tongues as Basque, Caucasian, Burushaski, Sino-Tibetan, Yeniseian, Na-Dene, and Ebonics (just kidding with this last one!) are not easily linked to any others. Therefore, Ruhlen does not provide us with solid evidence or conclusive proof of a single primeval tongue.

There have been other attempts to prove the existence of such a primeval language or even to hazard a guess as to the first words uttered by mankind. The famous Wilhelm von Humboldt (1787-1835) assumed from the very first the existence of such a prehistoric language. Adolphe Pictet (1799-1875), Swiss linguist and historian of primitive Aryan civilizations, was the first to mention the concept of linguistic paleontology. Pictet studied Indo-European origins of the early Aryans and examined in great detail the words related to terrain, flora, and fauna, to establish the chronology of contacts between Uralic (Finno-Ugric and Samoyedic) and other language families. The Russian Nikolai Marr (1865-1934), albeit one of the world's greatest authorities on Caucasian languages and Basque, exhibited dubious scholarship, perhaps bordering on madness, when he founded the New Theory of Language, claiming that ultimately all languages derived from the Japhetic language family, named after Japheth, third son of biblical Noah (and this before the TV special on the Ark). Marr is also famous for indirectly triggering, after his death and waged by his disciples, the only linguistic controversy in which a powerful dictator such as Joseph Stalin thought it fit to personally intervene. To his credit, old Joe solved it without chopping off any heads or sending anyone to Siberia. He had his gentle moments.

Another important authentic paleolinguist, with whom I corresponded in the early 1980s, was Richard Fester, a gifted German amateur, not an academic. He wrote many books among which are *Tongue of the Ice Age: The First Six Words of Humanity* (1962), *Primeval Words of Mankind: An Archeology of Language*, and *The Stone Age Is at Our Door*, combining linguistics, archeology, anthropology, biology, and behavioral sciences. Fester amassed a huge impressive collection of thousands of terms from over one hundred languages, many quite exotic, to show intriguing similarities among them. He dared propose a primeval vocabulary, the first six archetypes of human language: *BA*, *KALL*, *TAL*, *OS*, *ACQ*, and *TAG*. These syllables or sounds, according to Fester, could have undergone an infinity of variations by permutation of letters or addition of other vowels and consonants. I shall give you some further details on this controversial, but tantalizing, theory as well as my own thoughts on this topic in another essay, "Migration and Language."

A Primeval Language?

In "The Mystery of Language" we focused on whether one single primeval language (*Ursprache*) might have been the ancestor of the approximately 4,000 or more tongues scattered on the surface of our planet. I wrote about the gifted German paleolinguist Richard Fester, who, after studying over one hundred languages, including some quite esoteric, had advanced the very controversial theory that he had discovered the first six words, the principal archetypes of human utterance: *BA*, *KALL*, *TAL*, *OS*, *ACQ*, and *TAG*. Lack of space forbids going into greater detail, but Fester proposed that these syllables through permutation of their letters, substitution of consonants and vowels, addition of others, had been at the origin of all languages. *BA* might have generated *BAU*, *BE*, *WA*, *AWA*, *BIS*, and so on. Thus, the six archetypes could well have generated all words of all existing languages.

After studying similar sounds as they occurred in many languages, Fester thought that each sound and its permutations covered a wide range of related meanings. Thus *BA* sounds in many languages are linked to the meanings of body parts (paw, belly, paunch), women (wife, widow), human habitation (build, *bauen* in German). In many African Negro tongues, *BA*, *PA*, and *WA* refer to man, father, son. The sound *TAL* appears in many languages to be linked to the concept of valley, dale, and dell, something flat or slightly hollow. Noteworthy is that Wisconsin Dells owes its name to the French *dalle* meaning tile, because of the flat rock formations in the locality. Sounds like *AC*, *CAC*, and especially *ACQ* occur in thousands of geographical names worldwide for places where there was water and ice, and often fail to occur where there is none. Check a map of southern France and note the many localities ending in *AC*, such as Padirac, Figeac, Nérac, Bergerac, Aurillac. Even viewed with skepticism, Fester's elaborate lists of words grouped by core meanings cannot be ignored.

Is it mere coincidence that in places as distant from each other as Carnac in Brittany (France) and the Carnac in Egypt there are heaps of stones? In the French Carnac they are called *menhirs* and *dolmens*, somewhat similar to Stonehenge; in Egypt they are old temples; and

Scottish Gaelic, Old Irish, and Welsh *carn*, English *cairn*, all designate rounded or pyramidal heaps of stones made as a monument, memorial, or marker. Some linguists have speculated about the existence of primeval words "*carn*" and "*ac*" meaning "stone" and "big," respectively. Along similar lines, why could not the names of rivers like Elbe and Labe on the one hand, and Seine, Saône, Oise on the other, be a primeval generic term for a stream of flowing water?

One thing is certain. Many erudite scholars and linguists, with their heads in the clouds or in the dust of libraries, fail to see the forest for the trees and do not allow the awesome beauty, the exquisite artistry, and the esthetic qualities of language to emerge occasionally through the dense mass of factual details. An awesome linguist like Merritt Ruhlen, mentioned in the previous essay, may even in the dedication of his book, *The Origin of Language: Tracing the Evolution of the Mother Tongue* (1994), surprise us with ambiguities like "For my twins, Marian, Ricky & Johnny" [*sic*]. A careful reader wonders whether the author miscounted his progeny, forgot their names, could not tell them apart, or mistook "twin" for "triplets."

What do I personally make of all this? My considerate guess is that humans had from the beginning the potential for verbal communication. Languages then originated simultaneously in many parts of the world. Later, when human groups explored the planet, traveling much more than we realize, their primitive tongues enriched themselves by mutual contact and borrowings. Thus, the same Latin spoken by the Roman legions in contact with various local tribes produced no fewer than fourteen Romance languages: Aromunian, Catalan, Corsican, French, Galician, Italian, Ladino, Moldavian, Provençal, Portuguese, Rhaeto-Romance, Romanian, Sardinian, and Spanish.

Words Born in a Bar

I just glimpsed some of our New Age teens trying to make a statement on TV with their fancy hairdos and graphic tattoos. It was all I needed to launch me on today's word quest! The word *tattoo* has two meanings. When it is a call or signal on a bugle or drum to inform soldiers they must return to quarters before taps, the word comes from the Middle Dutch *taptoe*, like the *tap* of a keg, and *toe*, to shut (German *zu* means shut). Literally it is an order: "Close the tap on the keg!" or "Time for the tavern to close." When it means injecting pigments beneath the skin of individuals to scar them permanently, it is of East Island origin, as Maori *ta* means to scar and Tahitian *tatu* means pricking. Now, a variation of *tap* is *tamp*, to plug, which means to tap or strike the charge and fill the hole for blasting. *Temper*, from the Latin *temperare* means to moderate, regulate, also to mix clay and water and is related to Latin *tempus*, time, with a wide range of meanings. You temper steel to soften it after it was previously hardened. Distemper implies unregulated or immoderate temper.

If you do not suffer from a bad temper, you may be inclined to "caper," that is to cavort and leap about in a gay and frolicsome way. With *caper* we again have a word with different origins and multiple meanings. From the Dutch *kaper*, the latter from *kapen* (to take, plunder) it means privateer and the pirate Captain of such a vessel. It might even be related to the Latin *capere* (to seize, take) and the German *kaufen* (to buy, trade). From the Latin *capparis* (first thought to be a plural because of the *s*, later dropped to make it a singular) it means a prickly shrub, the berries of which are a favorite condiment to spice up certain dishes. The French love their codfish in a rich sauce with capers. Then, corresponding to the verb "to caper," we have the meaning of a gay, unrestrained leap. Hence, by semantic extrapolation, springs the meaning of a capricious madcap escapade, even illegal, ranging from a mere prank to a serious crime. Finally, from Scottish Gaelic *ceap*, a shoemaker's last or clog on an animal's foot (Latin *cippus*, post), the Scottish, because of its appearance, even apply the term to a piece of buttered bread, usually with cheese on it.

From here, believe it or not, I lead you to *taxi*. The word is a shortened form of *taximetercabriole*, much too much of a mouthful for the foreign drivers that drive them in New York City. (I am reminded of one of the longest words in German, *Panzerkraftwagenaufselbstfahrlafetten*, a full-track armored car with mounted gun turret). *Cabriolet* from the French is a two-wheeled carriage, named from its often bouncing or leaping motion (compare the Latin *caper*, goat, a cavorting beast; in French, *chèvre*; in Spanish, *cabra*). Hence spring many words: *capricious*, jumping all over the place in mood and whims; the musical term *capriccio*, lively in tempo; *caprice*, a sudden impulsive change in action; the island of *Capri*, noted earlier, thus named because of the many goats on it. You can easily reach the island from Naples. Its blue grotto may be entered from the sea with the help of skilled oarsmen taking advantage of a dipping wave uncovering its opening.

Taxi, on the other hand, comes from the Latin *taxare*, to charge. Tax always refers to something levied on persons or property for the support of a government either in the form of labor (*task* comes from the same Latin *taxare* or French *tâche*, meaning work, task) or money. *Meter* means to measure, and every taxi (much easier to say than the above eight syllable word) has an instrument with "capering" numbers rising upward to your final fare. Now, *sedan* is a horse of a different color, if you'll pardon the mixed metaphor. In the 17th century it was a popular means of transportation, a closed seat on two poles carried by two bearers, one in front and one behind, something like a litter. In 1634, Sir Sanders Duncombe secured a monopoly for this conveyance in London. He called these new means of transportation "sedan chairs," from Latin *sedere*, to sit. Compare *sedentary* — you know, what a couch potato does — and *sedation*, which causes you to want to sit. Car manufacturers later borrowed the term sedan for automobiles. However, *limousine* comes from the woolen coats worn by the shepherds in the French province of Limousin. Happy touring!

Let's Have a Consensus!

It was quite gratifying to receive a letter from a reader who enjoys my ramblings on language and wrote to me about his interest in collecting lawyerly and other redundancies such as: last will and testament, cease and desist, metes and bounds, part and parcel, nook and cranny, hue and cry, aid and abet, leaps and bounds. I trust my scholarly fan will not object to a few comments regarding such alleged redundancies. May I suggest that true redundancies, where the repetition of words adds nothing to the intended meaning, are such expressions as "irregardless" and "general consensus." The first one probably springs from a blend of irrespective and regardless and contains two negatives, one of them obviously superfluous: the Latin prefix *irr-* signifying "not" and the suffix *-less* with the same effect. Consensus literally means that all together are in full consent regarding a matter. Originally consensus meant the harmonious working together of all parts of the body from Latin *cum* (together) + *sentire* (to feel), later the agreeing of all involved. The word "general" is here entirely superfluous, repeating the idea contained in *cum*.

Before I take up my reader's examples one by one, allow me to point out that in a perfect language there should be no synonyms. Why, indeed, should we need two tools to perform the same task? Therefore, when synonyms appear in a language, usage usually attaches to each word distinctive shades of meaning that prevent them from being identical twins. Now, I should like to take the above-alleged redundancies one by one and see whether some of them may be logically explained.

Is *will and testament* truly a redundancy? Old English *willan*, past *wolde*, German *wollen*, means — at least etymologically — to wish or will what is well (same root) for you. The Sanskrit *varati* means wishes. Attest, contest, protest, however, are related to Latin *ficare, facere*, Spanish *hacer*, French *faire* (to make), and *testis* (a witness); in other words, testify. Testicle, as earlier noted, is a little witness from the time when instead of swearing on a Bible, one's hand was placed on the seat of manliness. Detest is to call down the gods from heaven to witness against someone. When a man dies without a witness to what he desires to be done after his *demise* (Latin *demittere*, literally send down from) he dies *intestatus* (intestate), or without a will or testament, a witnessing document. It could be argued that will is the wish and testament the legal document to execute it.

Cease and desist: Latin *cedere*, first meant to go, proceed, move, hence later to yield. The Latin frequentative (to do something frequently or repeatedly) of the same verb was *cessare*, French *cesser*, English *cease*. If one yields often enough, one stops: cessation. Desist, from Latin *desistere*, *de* (from) + *sistere* or *stare* (stand, stop), means to stand away or down from. The legal expression, far from redundant, is precise: you not only stop, but you stand away and don't move close again. Stop and continue stopping.

Metes and bounds: Old English *metan* meant "to measure." *Bounds*, from Old French *bodne*, now *borne* (road marker), is the limiting line of an area. Anglo-French *metes et bounds* designated the boundaries of land established by reference to natural or artificial monuments along it (stream, ditch, fence), as distinguished from those established by beginning from a starting point and proceeding by stated compass courses and specified distances. Butts and bounds, by contrast, are abuttals (land contiguous, from Latin *cum*, with, and *tangere,* touch, in contact with other landmarks) and boundaries in relation to other properties The remaining alleged tautologies (duplication, in Greek from *tautos*, identical, and *logos*, speech) will be considered forthwith.

Part and parcel: *Parcel*, from the French *parcelle*, is a particle, a smaller portion of a part and, in precise legal terms, justifiable, like the subdivision of a division.

Nook and cranny: *nook*, probably from the Norwegian *nok*, means a hook, hence an interior angle. *Nick*, as in the nick of time, German *Knick*, means a bend, crack, crease, dent, notch. In the good old medieval days, when Sun City, Arizona, was but a dream and vision of a Shangri-La, a tally was used to register attendance in colleges and churches. The tally was a stick of wood and attendance was indicated by a nick or notch on it. Students or worshipers arriving in time had their attendance nicked and thus arrived in the nick of time. *Tally*, from French *tailler*, to cut or carve, refers to the old system of record keeping, where each of two persons kept a double-notched stick cut in half so that both had a record as a check of

Duodenum	Meaning twelve in Latin, the part of the intestine is so named for its length of twelve times the breadth of a finger.
Cent	From Latin *centum*, one hundredth of a dollar. **Dime**: From Latin *decima pars*, tenth part. **Nickel**: From German *Kupfernickel*, or copper nickel, and St. Nicholas (the goblin Nicholas), who was blamed by miners when they found metal without copper content.

transactions. *Tailler* comes from Latin *talis*, like, although a cut does not always result in two like parts. *Cranny*, from French *cran*, notch, crevice, cog, catch, has almost the same meaning. The popular usage of reduplication or paired phrases in such expressions reflects the notion of a thorough search in every possible hiding place and a natural predilection for balanced near synonyms for emphasis.

Hue and cry: *Hue* has two distinct meanings. As color, it comes from Anglo-Saxon *hiw*, which first meant form, then appearance, then color. Today we use hue as a finer division of the primary colors. Our hue and cry is echoic or onomatopoeic. It comes from French *huer* and means to scream, hoot, actually shout *"Uh, Uhu!"* to apprise others of danger. Times of crisis and urgency, when danger is present or the pursuit of felons is in progress, should justify repeated vociferous outbursts and constitute mitigating circumstances for repetition.

Aid and abet: Here we have a definite shift in meaning. Originally from the same Old Norse, the verb *beita*, to bite, and the feminine noun *beita*, food. English "to bait" means both to incite (animals or persons) and food given as a bait or lure in fishing. Old French *abeter* (not *abêtir*, which means to stultify, make like an animal) also means to incite. Hence our abet, which over the years acquired a positive meaning, namely to incite in the sense of encouraging. The reduplicated paired phrase, evidently for emphasis, again represents a crescendo, not merely to aid, but to further encourage. Another well-known paired phrase, which is definitely redundant, is *without let or hindrance*. Old English *lettan* means to delay or hinder.

Finally we have *leaps and bounds*: *Lobster* is really a "leapster" from Anglo-Saxon *hleapan*, to leap. Old English *loppe*, is a flea. Even the German *lox*, or salmon, a fish that "leaps upstream" to spawn, is related. New Yorkers like their bagels with cream cheese and lox or smoked salmon, from a German-Yiddish term. However, leap is from a common Teutonic root that also means to run, German *laufen*, Old French *aloper*, whence English to lope. Interloper, an unlawful intruder, means literally to run in between, and elope signifies to run out or away. To bound, bounce, caper, frisk, comes from the French *bondir*. Arguably the expression *leaps and bounds* means both to run and jump alternately, a more accurate, not entirely redundant picture. All these examples reinforce the fact that in most languages graphic pictures or metaphors exist behind the words. Even in Chinese, the written sign (once a pictograph) for *look* is a hand shading the eye, for *east* the sun rising behind a tree, and for *perfect* a large ram, a symbol for ideal perfection.

No Puny Flames These

While on a cruise to Alaska I heard the emcee of a culinary show come up with what appeared to be a spurious explanation of the origin of the name of *Crêpes Suzette*. According to him, Napoleon, eager to please his mistress of the moment, asked the chef to give the crêpes her name. Not so! It would have been out of character for Bonaparte to act thus. Besides, the dish does not date that far back. A more likely version, although possibly also apocryphal, cites a restaurant owner named Marie as the creator of this famous delicacy. But wait! The story is not over.

The French chef Henri Charpentier, who died in California at the end of 1961 after a long and brilliant career during which he successively served Queen Victoria, Edward VII, John D. Rockefeller, and other luminaries (today he would be cooking for the likes of Michael Jordan, Tiger Woods, or Barbara Walters), also claimed to be the originator of this sought-after dessert. He recounted that once, while sprinkling cognac over crêpes ordered by the Prince of Wales, the future architect of the "cordial understanding" between England and France, the combination caught fire because of the hot chafing dish. The resulting "flaming" delicacy so pleased the future Edward VII that Charpentier, wishing to claim for himself the invention of the new recipe, thought of dedicating it to his illustrious client. The Prince, gallant as always, opted instead for naming it after his current lady companion. Thus Suzette made gastronomic history. The Italian proverb "*Se non è vero, è bene trovato*" ("If not true, the story is nevertheless well invented or imagined") comes to mind. When eating crêpes, just enjoy their flavor and that of their name, and don't sweat the small stuff — in this case, equivocal history.

You may reproach me for adverting your attention to or advertising fancy food, when dieting may be a concern. *Advert*, literally turn or direct to (Latin *ad*, to, + *vertere,* past participle *versus*), to turn, also forms adverse and adversary where *ad* signifies a warning and circumstances or persons turn against you. Through the French *avertir* (warn) and *avertissement* (notification, advice, warning), the English *advertise* (the *d* restored because of the awareness of its Latin derivation where a *d* is present) originally meant to warn, a good thing to remember if you are prone to be taken in by excessive advertising. In the meantime, the French have come to use other words for advertisement, namely *annonce* and *réclame*, something Americans must remember if they wish to be understood in a country many of them falsely think hates them. I always point out that the French are too busy hating one another to have time for us. English-French textbooks list numerous words that are identical in both languages, but carry different meanings, referring to them as false friends (*faux amis*).

The word *hate* illustrates a phenomenon I shall *revert* to (*re*, again, back, + *vert*, turn) in another essay, namely the presence in the English language, after the 1066 French Norman invasion, of both the Germanic Anglo-Saxon word and that of Latin or French. In this case, *hate* comes from the German *hassen*, but odious or hateful from the Latin *odium* through the French *odieux*. The *odium teologicum*, certainly present in the Kosovo affair, is the bitterness and hatred developed by unyielding views when dealing with religion. The following are all derivatives: *avert* and *averse*, implying to turn away; *versus*, usually abbreviated "vs.," meaning in contrast to or as an alternative of (a turning is implied); *version*, which is something turned into something else like the corrected or translated version of a text; even *vertigo*, where everything is turning around in your head. All are related and represent derivatives (from Latin *derivare*, French *deriver*, to lead water away from a river, by extension to take anything from something else) of the same original Latin root meaning "turn."

This May Make Your Head Spin

Let us continue with the prolific number of words deriving from the Latin *vertere* (versus), to turn (*prolific,* from Latin *pro*, forth, + *alescere*, grow; Latin *proles* means offspring, hence *proletariat*, the lowest social class whose main task in Rome was to produce offsprings). *Conversion*, both in a religious and chemical sense, as well as convert, literally mean together (*con*) + turn. A *pervert* from *per* (through, through and through, thoroughly) + *vertere* (turn) is someone who turned completely into something bad. The prefix *per-* in perish, perdition, perplexity, perforate, perfidy, performance, and countless other words, reflects the same idea of through or thoroughly to the bitter end.

Conversation originally meant associating with others — physical intimacy — hence the saying that "one may know people by the conversation they keep." In law, criminal conversation still means sexual intercourse. Only in the 17th century did *converse* begin to mean to talk together with others. Verse, as in poetry, was text that turned at the end of a line, when it was still customary to write prose continuously, without spaces in between. Today we have convertible automobiles, which can be turned from sedans into open cars at the push of a button. (I remember when on my TR-3 and TR-4 it took me thirty minutes to turn the roof up or down.) The right side of an open book is the *recto*; turn the page and you have a *verso*. *Vertex*, from the same Latin word meaning whirl, summit, the pole of the heavens, and *vortex* or whirlpool all have embedded in them the idea of turning. Now vertex may mean the point opposite and farthest from the base, the intersection of lines as in an angle, or the highest point of zenith. Hence a line drawn up to it is *vertical*. A vertiginous height is one that gives you vertigo and makes your head spin.

In Lower Latin the verb *vergere*, to bend, a variation of *vertere*, still containing the notion of turning, gave us *diverge*, to bend away or apart, and *converge*, to bend or come together. A diversion allows us to turn away from what we are doing and is milder than a distraction, which literally pulls us away (Latin *trahere*, to pull, note traction). *Verge* (Latin *virga*, rod) and *virgin* (Latin *virgo*) may be related in that virga may also have referred to a green branch or twig and a genuine virgin should still be green. The rod, perhaps once a phallic symbol, was carried in processions as an emblem of authority. That is where verge also acquired its meaning of edge or border. Once "within the verge" was used to mean within the turning or boundary of the power of the Lord High Steward, *i.e.,* twelve miles around the King's court. Then it became the limit or edge of that territory. Gradually the use of verge as limit and brink was expanded to include not only territory, and came to mean, more generally, on the brink of a place or an action: on the verge of suicide or, on a more positive note, of hitting the jackpot.

Some languages like Latin and Russian have a frequentative, which signifies repeated action. *Versare* was the Latin frequentative of *vertere* and meant to turn many times. Hence *versatile*, meaning capable of turning, changing, adapting — not merely once, but often — to different skills as circumstances demand. Versed and conversant, able to turn to or master different skills are also related. But let us quit, while we are still ahead, with *animadversion*, meaning a critical attitude prompted by hostility (made up from *anima*, mind, + *ad*, against, + *vertere*, turn), lest I generate it among you my faithful readers.

If the action in Kosovo can be called a war, although none of our military was killed and the enemy had no weapons to match ours, I might end this piece with the origin of the word. *War* is Teutonic, Middle English *werre*, Old High German *werra*, strife, and *weren*, to protect. The root of such words is still found in the German *Wehrmacht*, armed forces, literally protective might. The *w* did not exist in Latin or early Romance languages and even now only occurs in foreign terms. It became *g* in French and resulted in *guerre*, Italian and Spanish *guerra*. This interchangeability of *g* and *w* gave us doublets like guard and ward, guardian and warden, guile and wile, guarantee and warranty.

In light of contemporary events, I would like to end by quoting the words of Talleyrand, Napoleon's foreign minister, in 1815 at the Congress of Vienna: "One can do anything with bayonets except sit on them." No truer words were ever spoken! When a nation has weapons, it feels compelled to keep using them.

Word Origins Clarify Perceptions

Gossip — malicious — is a truly terrible thing, but the word itself has a fascinating story and shifting meanings. Originally *godsip*, a combination of *god* + *sibb* (kinsman, related), it referred to a person spiritually related to another by being its sponsor at baptism, as a Godmother or Godfather. *Sib* + the diminutive suffix *-ling* gives us the modern English social science term for children of the same parents: *siblings*. Then gossip also started meaning a companion or crony. Now, both Godparents and cronies are apt to talk and reveal intimate details about the persons they are related to, hence the meaning of *telltale*, and eventually the term was applied to the talk itself and often to false rumors spread about someone. The same shift occurred in Scotch, where gossip is *cummer*, from the French *commère*, literally *cum* (together) and *mère* (mother) — that is, fellow-mother or Godmother. Today, the French word refers to an inquisitive and talkative, rather unladylike woman, a gossip. The Old French counterpart *compère*, once Godfather, then crony, formed our rarely used English *compeer*, from Latin *cum* (together) and *par* (equal), meaning an equal in rank, age, and prowess, a peer.

Recently, an educated long-time journalist scoffed at my suggestion that word origins and the images they contain, when explained, might enlighten us on the way our ancestors perceived their reality. Let us once again prove our contention by illustrating it with the word *villain*. We shall show how our forefathers perceived the word and how its meaning changed under the influence of evolving social attitudes. Latin *villa* is a diminutive of *vicus*, hamlet. It once meant a farm with all its buildings. Under Italian influence it began to mean a mansion. A group of villas became a village. An unsophisticated Italian song about country life similar to the later madrigal is an Italian *villanella,* and the French poem composed of five tercets and a quatrain with a rustic theme is a *villanelle*. A dweller on a farm was a *villein* or *villain*. Check in a good dictionary and you shall find the first spelling meaning a peasant farmer under the feudal system, the second reflecting the city dwellers' contempt for country bumpkins, gradually evolving in meaning from baseborn to criminal. Hence come villainous and villainy.

The French *ville* grew in meaning and now refers to a city, just as the Anglo-Saxon *tun*, enclosure or fence (German *Zaun*), progressed in meaning to homestead and finally to the larger town. The French *ville* is found in countless English and American city names: Nashville; Gloversville, where gauntlets and mittens are made; Pottsville, where, I believe Casey swung his bat; and Louisville. The Latin *vicus*, hamlet, Greek *oikos*, house, gave us Anglo-Saxon *vic*, settlement. *Bailiwick* is, therefore, the settlement or territory controlled by a bailiff. Makes good sense, doesn't it? Lower Latin *baiulivus* was the man in charge of a fort. The Latin *ballium*, probably once interchangeable with *vallum*, wall or rampart (in Spanish *b* is pronounced to this day like a *v*), meant castle wall, which gives us London's Old Bailey. The Latin verb *baiulare*, to carry, to take care of, exercise friendly custody with a guarantee of producing an individual when needed, gave us *bail*. *Interval*, now any space, once was the space between ramparts, just as *interlude* was the play between courses or acts, from Latin *inter* (between) + *ludus* (game).

This is probably enough of a language dose for the moment. *Dose*, Greek *dosis*, derives from *didonai*, to give. The pharmacist gives, you take. *Posology*, from Greek *posos* (how much?) is the medical science of *dosage*.

Associations and Connotations

You have just been ushered to your theater seat. Looking forward to an entertaining performance, you open the program. After leafing through the ads, you finally reach the part pertaining to the play you have come to watch. Following the play's title and author, the program usually lists the cast or *dramatis personae*, literally people of the drama, in other words the characters or actors that are to appear in the play. The term may also be used for the characters in a novel or poem. It comes to us from the Latin *persona*, French *personne*. Originally it really meant a mask, especially one worn by an actor in Greece and Rome. Thus the word, possibly from the Etruscan *phersu* (mask), gradually came to designate the actor, role, or character, and by extension any person. This is hardly surprising, since, as Shakespeare puts it so well, "All the world's a stage, and all the men and women merely players."

In 1909, Ezra Pound wrote a volume of poems entitled *Personae*. He had in mind the masks of the actor, recalling Yeats's demand that the poet objectify his experience through an imagined personality, a mask. Joseph T. Shipley in his *Dictionary of Word Origins* points out that *persona* is a combination of the Latin *per* (through) + *sonare* (to sound). At first, buying his proposed etymology requires a certain leap of faith on our part. We must, however, remember that in ancient times the audience could not see the actors' faces. They wore masks corresponding to the characters they portrayed: the mask of Apollo, the mask of Pan, for instance. Thus the spectators did not need a program to know who played and impersonated whom. Some masks may have been equipped with megaphonic mouthpieces, which validates Shipley's idea that persona was thus named because the sound came through the mask. Although I do not disagree with Shipley in essence, I find it hard to believe that the transition from *personare* (resound, sound forth, shout) to mask and finally to person evolved that abruptly. It must have taken several intermediate expanded uses of the word to gradually include more and more associated meanings.

I have always claimed that the human mind, aided by its five senses, can distinguish semantic nuances long before language provides us with the terms to express them. Even then, language relies on associations, connotations, and even context to communicate meaning as closely as possible, often by using existing words for a new purpose. Perhaps nature has endowed us with this ability to communicate by means of a relatively limited number of words. Our brain, then, already aware of the general contents of the communication, anticipates and fills in a portion of the background and details. Thus the average, not highly educated, individual need not retain too formidable a vocabulary to function adequately. For instance, the simple English noun or verb *run* can acquire countless derivative meanings, such as a run in your stockings to name just one.

I submit that the use of *personare*, to sound forth, gradually grew to include to "perform upon a musical instrument," then to "act or speak through a mask." The past participle *personatus* meant disguised and counterfeit, which supports this theory of shifting meanings. Eventually the word referred to the actor and later to any person. We might add that parson is a doublet of person. However, in the 11th century it became limited to the person in charge of parish affairs. Remember that at one time parson and person were pronounced alike, just as other similar pairs like clark and clerk.

Borrowing from Other Languages

As I have frequently pointed out and as you may have noticed on your own, our words and phrases are highly metaphorical and abound in graphic images that seem to communicate meaning to our brain much more compellingly and vividly than, say, an equation $x + y = z$. There is a reason why, when teaching children the alphabet, we use books with many pictures. Everyone knows a picture is worth a thousand words. And hereby hangs a theory I formulated forty-one years ago entitled, "The Bane of Our Linguistic Insensitivity."

Besides the innumerable metaphors that enliven our speech and drive home the message more forcefully, such as "no ax to grind," "play with fire," "leap of faith," "wash one's dirty linen in public," "jump to conclusions," other less obvious images are concealed within many of our words to which most of us are totally insensitive, if not blind. This is due to a little-known fact of how English (unlike German or Russian) adopts foreign words. When English pirates words from the Latin or French, it does so directly, without essentially changing their foreign garb. Consider such words as *depend, circumstance, progress, result, perplexed*, all from the Latin or their corresponding French synonyms *dependere, circumstare, progredi (progressus), resaltare, perplexus,* respectively. As you can see, the original Latin word is still pretty much preserved in the English loan-word.

On the contrary, when German and Russian adopt the same words, they proceed by a process known as loan translation. Instead of introducing them into their language without change, they translate each element of the adopted word into a German or Russian root, which faithfully reproduces the image or metaphor concealed in the original. Thus, for anyone knowing Latin, *dependere* (our *depend*) literally means to hang from; *circumstance* is that which stands around; *progress* is to go forward; *result* is to jump back; and *perplexed* is thoroughly woven through. I shall not encumber this essay with the German and Russian equivalents, but be assured that they all faithfully translate into German and Russian words the images contained in the original. Thus, whereas English speakers ignorant of Latin most probably miss the graphic images reflected in the words, their German and Russian counterparts cannot help but be aware of them. The original image is evident in their own language. For example, in the case of *dependere*, German translates *de* as *ab* and *pendere* as *hängen*, resulting in *abhängen*, a literal translation.

The big question is: does it make any difference as to perfect understanding and communication? The answer would have to be determined by subjecting many people to carefully devised tests that would require them to give accurate definitions of such words. I submit that it might be easier for someone conversant with Latin to come up with concise definitions by relying on the knowledge of the concrete image illustrating the word's literal meaning. Thus, *circumstance* is whatever is (stands) around (surrounds) a particular event. With regard to a word like *result*, most of us have a linear picture of something coming after something else. I suggest that if you knew that the Latin *resaltare* literally means "to jump

Cake	From Old Norse *kaka*, German *Kuchen*, Dutch *koek* — *koekje* (a little cake) has come to be our cookie.
Calico	From *calicut* cloth, from the city of the same name in India.
Dandelion	From French *dent de lion*, lion's tooth — the flower of the unwanted "weed" is spiked like the teeth of a lion.

back," you would more readily comprehend the legal meaning of *result* as signifying "revert" in "the estate will result to John after Peter's death."

I am not prepared to issue a final verdict in this matter. Still, I suggest that the more we are aware of the makeup of words, the more professionally, efficiently, even artistically, we shall use, enjoy, and respect them, as would a mechanic tools, a musician notes, and a painter colors, according to the mastery of each. One last piece of evidence! The Latin *cedere*, to go, also came to mean *cede* — because if you go away, withdraw, you yield to someone. It gave us a whole slew of words where only the prefixes alter the meaning: *recede*, go back; *secede*, go apart from; *intercede*, go in between; *succeed*, go under, hence come after, replace; *antecede(nt)*, come before; *accede*, go toward; *deceased*, gone from or off. Although there is no "abcede" (go away?) in English, abscess is the hollow filled with pus where the flesh receded.

Maybe, you all had better learn Latin!

Dare We Broach the Subject?

Today, we shall once again broach the subject of the adequacy of language as a tool for communication. But first, the word *broach* comes from Latin *brocca*, spike. The diminutive is *broccola*, stalk, Italian plural *broccoli*, the vegetable. After making a deal, the "broker," a name later applied to the middleman in any transaction, would broach or prick open a cask of wine to celebrate the occasion. Now back to our subject. It is safe to say that there is at least some analogy between language and mathematics. They are both symbolic means of representing the world. In some respects, if one considers the various attributes of language, such as wealth of metaphors, musicality, emotional impact, it might be described as more varied and richer. However, mathematics is indisputably more precise and, although I dislike the term, more objective. (After all, we cannot completely detach ourselves from our subjective self.) In any event, I cannot imagine anyone reacting emotionally to $x + y = z$.

Now, the quantum physicist and mathematician Werner Heisenberg once said that contemporary science, today more than at any previous time, has been forced by nature herself to pose again the old question regarding the possibility of comprehending reality by mental processes, and to answer it in a slightly different way. We too are entitled to pose the question as to the accuracy of language in reflecting reality. Without going into galactic mathematical complexities, it is possible for a layman to understand what, in the world of particles, the Heisenberg uncertainty principle means. Very simply stated, it means that if we try to measure both the position and the momentum of a particle, we cannot simultaneously measure both these properties with arbitrarily high precision.

With your indulgence, I herewith propose a parallel linguistic uncertainty principle. Relying on the two basic tenets of general semantics ("the word is not *the thing*" and "the map is not *the territory*") and insisting on absolute 100 percent precision, we can safely assert the following: for anything out there in the universe that we can perceive with our five senses and wish to communicate, no words or linguistic symbols are capable of completely and precisely conveying the totality of the meaning contained in the object of our perception. Conversely, no word, as a mere linguistic symbol, with its limited meaning varying from user to user, can possibly have an exact counterpart that corresponds to it 100 percent out there in the universe. Language, a mere symbolic representation, can never express the infinite variety and complexity of life. It can only suggest and sketchily evoke it.

I can hear all of you objecting and clamoring: "If this is so, how is it we do manage to communicate?" The key word is "manage." I am merely saying that we may not always be communicating as well as we believe. Of course, in many simple situations, by meeting each other half way, anticipating the tenor of the intended communication, since we share a large quantity of knowledge and experiences, we manage to achieve at least a reasonably acceptable overlapping of our respective meanings. However, in countless other imaginable scenarios, where opinions, beliefs, or highly abstract notions come into play, we might not have the meeting of the minds we count on language to ensure. There is bound to be some loss of meaning (the technical term is entropy) in the mutual transmission of information. We cannot always express all we mean.

Entropy in Language

Entropy is a term borrowed from thermodynamics, designating the measure of the amount of energy lost in a system and thus not available for doing work. In communication theory the term designates the measure of the efficiency of a system (here a code or a language) in transmitting information. Experience has shown that a number of different messages can be sent by selection from the same set of symbols. Simply stated, there always is a degree of uncertainty that may result from any one message, and the latter may fail to communicate in various ways.

History tells us that the misinterpretation or mistranslation of a single Japanese word, *mokusatsu*, may have doomed the fate of Hiroshima and Nagasaki. Social usage and taboos, face-saving considerations, and other complexities have exerted a strong influence on the Japanese language. Thus *mokusatsu* can mean either "ignore," "withhold comment," or "have no comment." Some authors, including Charles Berlitz, claim that before dropping the atom bomb, the United States warned Japan of a new weapon of hitherto unknown destructive force and gave our enemy an opportunity to surrender to avoid disaster. The Imperial government announced that, pending cabinet discussion of the matter, it was following a policy of *mokusatsu*. Evidently that was the wrong answer. It was allegedly translated as *ignore*, and we all know the rest of the story.

Other such cases exist, especially in foreign relations. I have always maintained that, had I been the interpreter, I would not have translated Krushchev's famous phrase *"Vas poxoronim!"* as "We shall bury you!" I might have opted for a lighter, less confrontational, "We'll have the last laugh!" or "Who laughs last, laughs best!" Slavic people just seem to have a morbid sense of humor that prompts a Russian to tell you that "the praise of his mother's pig's knuckles will be sung on her very deathbed." We would choose other expressions to rave about someone's culinary skills. Krushchev did not literally mean what he said. It was an unfortunate metaphor inherent in the Russian language.

French, for many years, was the principal diplomatic language. Now the French verb *contrôler*, which appears on the surface to be the same as our "to control" (one of these "false friends" I once wrote about), means primarily to verify. On a train the *contrôleur* is the ticket collector. When the word was used in the 1905 treaty between Russia and Japan and falsely translated by "dominate," you can imagine the negative reaction.

Without becoming paranoid about your use of language, do take a moment to ponder the thousands of words we use routinely without considering every possible ramification of their meaning. Does *wealth* mean the same to Bill Gates and to some poor fellow working for peanuts? Do the rapist and his victim define *justice* from the same perspective? Does the teenager on his first date really feel love or should he use *infatuation* (from Latin *in* + *fatuus*, foolish)? Does *compassion* mean the same thing to everyone? Asked to define the latter, knowing the origin of the word can be of help. *Compassion* comes from the Latin *cum* (with, together) + *patere* (to suffer). At least we can now visualize that true compassion entails vicariously participating in someone else's suffering.

To hit the bull's eye with a pistol takes skill and practice. We take language for granted, but to be verbally on target requires the same. A talented musician will detect subtle differences in a composition. A gifted user of language will do so with shades of meaning. Take a phrase like *to shock*, a kind of verbal catchall. Associate it with different scenarios and you will see the meaning range from horrify to outrage, fill with indignation, disgust, or even electricity (electric shock). Recently I was asked to distinguish between faith, belief, and surrender to the unknown. Faith has many meanings. In the context of the question it implied foregoing positive knowledge. Surrender always suggests original resistance. Belief ranges from conviction to supposition or suspicion.

Nowadays, we hear the very forceful *impact* used everywhere, in most cases wasted, instead of *to affect*, which means to drive or transmit with a forceful impact. Puns can *impact* the scabrous with the sublime in a word . . . nuggets of wisdom being *impacted* in tons of verbosity . . . *impact* the area with military . . . images *impacting* the human retina. For a TV host to say "Reserves called to serve in a war will impact their families" is poor style. Language can be a miracle or, at times, a shimmering mirage!

Don't Let This Get Your Goat!

John F. Kennedy, Jr., is no more, and the word *tragedy* is repeated over and over again by the media. What do tragedy and a goat have in common? Tragedy is from the Greek *tragoidia* or goat song, from *tragos* (he-goat) and *aeidein* (to sing), because drama probably originated with the sacrifice of a scapegoat. The typical Greek tragic hero was usually a person of significance, who was undone either by some personal flaw such as hubris or by the will of the gods. *Hubris*, from the Greek *hybris* (pride or insolence), ranges from pride and ambition to overconfidence and may well apply to this unfortunate young man, since he took chances beyond his level of skill and experience as a pilot. I remember being warned, when I had my pilot's license for visual flying only (not being certified for instrument flying), that merely flying through clouds could cost me my license.

According to the Bible, the sins of the people were laid upon the *scapegoat* or escape goat, which was then dismissed into the wilderness. The Latin term was *caper emissarius,* or emissary goat, which is what the French call it: *bouc émissaire*. The German *Sündenbock* literally means sin goat. Christ, of course, is the Divine scapegoat who takes upon him all the sins of the world. The word *buck*, originally a male animal, comes from Old English *buc*, *bucca* (he-goat). *Buckwheat* comes from another Anglo-Saxon word, *boc,* meaning beech tree. The verb buck is to behave like a goat and jump vertically, hence the exhortation "buck up"! From Anglo-Saxon *buc*, a wooden jug, comes the meaning to wash, also encountered in the old, no-longer-used French word *buer,* to wash. In modern French the noun *buée* still means steam. The wooden frame used for *sawing* or *sawbuck* (there is also a sawhorse) comes straight from the Dutch *zaagbok* (*sägen* in German is to saw). It is not unusual for a machine or contraption to derive its name from an animal. Examples include *crane*, which takes its name from the bird and *easel* from the Dutch *ezel*, German *Esel* or donkey. In French, *easel* is *chevalet* or little horse.

Named after *monkeys* are monkey board (footboard at the back of a vehicle), monkey boat (small boat used in docks and on the Thames River), monkey bridge (in the engine or boiler room), monkey cap (like those worn by bellboys), monkey foresail (on a sloop or schooner), monkey gaff (for the better display of signals), monkey-rope (for safety), monkey suit (naval uniform, also a tuxedo), and many others, all the way to monkey wrench. *Butcher*, from French *boucher*, was once a killer of goats, since *bouc* is a male goat in French. But where does the expression "get one's goat" come from? From horse racing! Stable hands have learned, through many years, to place a goat in the stall with a nervous race horse. The horse becomes accustomed to having the goat next to him and calms down. If the owner of a rival horse, however, can steal or "get this goat," the deprived horse becomes even more nervous and is apt to lose the race.

Book is from the Anglo-Saxon *boc*, *boece*, a beech tree, boards of which were used for writing. The Greek *papyros* gave the French *papier* and our *paper*. Along the same lines, Latin *codex* (or *caudex*) is the trunk of a tree or a split block of wood. From these, wooden tablets were made on which *codices* and *codes*, or systems of laws, were written.

Latin, a Key to Many Languages

"*Alea jacta est!*" This famous Latin phrase meaning "The die is cast!" is attributed to Julius Caesar as he prepared to cross the Rubicon River. A Roman law required any General entering Italy from the north to dismiss his troops before crossing this river. A wise precaution, because Generals approaching capitals with troops have been known to employ them to topple governments! The same words are often used to show that one has made a daring and important decision, but not without having carefully weighed and pondered the pros and cons and realized the seriousness thereof.

The word *iacta* (sometimes spelled *jacta*, although Latin had no *j*), past participle of the Latin *iacere* (*jacere*), has two closely related meanings: to cast, throw (French *jeter*) or to lie (French *gésir*), which logically enough is the position one occupies after having been thrown with sufficient vigor. *Iacta* has been extremely fertile in the production of English words, either directly from the Latin or indirectly through the French. *Fertile* also comes from the Latin *ferre*, to carry or bear, here in the sense of producing, like to bear children. In a word like *jettison*, which means to throw cargo overboard, the root *jeter* is clearly evident. The result of jettison is jetsam, equipment or cargo thrown overboard to lighten the ship in time of distress and which has sunk to the bottom. *Flotsam* from French *flotter*, Latin *fluctuare* (to float), is the same thing, but floats. A Captain who jettisons too much may no longer be *affluent* (Latin *ad*, toward, + *fluere*, flow): wealth no longer flows toward him.

Jetty, from the French *jetée* (the action of throwing or thrusting), refers to a structure thrown or thrusting out into the sea. Other less obvious derivations abound. At first sight, in a phrase like "the subject or object of one's attention," there appears to be little difference between the words "subject" and "object," both more or less meaning motive, cause, reason. However, in both logic and grammar, the two are almost opposites. In the above phrase, *subject*, from the Latin *sub* (under) + *iacere* (to throw or, here, lie), is the basis or initiator of our attention. *Object*, from Latin *ob* (in the way of) + *iacere* (throw or lie), is what offers itself to our senses, the recipient rather than the initiator of our attention. The subject performs the action, while the object is acted upon. The subject of our attention means something initiates or triggers our attention. The object of our attention means it receives our attention.

Subjective means concerned with the subject, usually oneself. Objective, as in "to be objective," means, in theory, that the "I" detaches itself and is unemotionally focused on the object under consideration. Philosophically, one might argue that one cannot really ever detach oneself from oneself. Every new prefix changes the meaning of the word it is attached to. *Ab-*, from or off, in *abject* is literally cast off in spirit or pride. The prefix *ad-*, to or toward, in *adjective* is a word thrown at or attached to a noun. *De-* (from) in *dejected* gives the meaning of being cast from and down, usually in spirit. The Latin frequentative (denoting repeated action) of *iacere* is *jactare*, whence jactation or boastful display. From the double frequentative *jactitare* we have jactitation (quite a mouthful!) meaning repeated and often physical boastful display or even jerking and twitching of the body.

A Treasure Trove of Word Origins 49

Other prefixes yield: eject, inject, interject, reject, project — meaning to throw out, into, in between, back, and forward, respectively. *Trajectory,* with the prefix *tra-* (short for *trans*, across) means a path through space. A jet throws forth liquid or gas. I shall quit before you object — that is, throw words or (Heaven forbid!) heavy objects in my way (*ob-* denoting against). Knowing the literal Latin meaning gives us a clear picture of and helps us define these words.

Star-spun Words

"When you wish upon a star, makes no difference who you are" goes the song, and reveals the very root, if not of *to wish*, at least of *to desire*. *Desire* is from the Latin *de* (from) + *sidus* (star; the stem changes to *sider* when declined). This relationship between *star* and *desire* is more evident from the less-used verb "to desiderate," a frequentative of "to desire," meaning to seek or long for, literally to be away from one's lucky star. We do not have many frequentatives (verbs indicating repeated action) in English, but in languages that do, like Russian, they are usually formed by adding extra syllables to the word, as here: desi(*de*)r(*at*)e. The French *desirer* and the given name *Désirée* or Beloved come from the same source. Recently, I was told that a linguist on the web claimed desire came from *de* + *sire*. This, I believe, is pure fantasy (my euphemism for hogwash). *Sir*, shortening of *sire*, is via French *sieur*, from Latin *senior* or elder, and French *Monsieur* (Mr.). It means literally my senior.

Astrologers observe the stars to see how their groupings and conjunctures at someone's birth influence the future. *Consider,* from Latin *considerare* (*cum*, together, + *sidera*, stars), meant to examine stars together and take them into account when determining their effect on our fate. The adjective considerate first designated one who has given careful thought to something and then one who has given thought on behalf of others. In scientific lingo, sidereal bodies are stars. If propitious stars or planets are missing at your birth, it may spell *disaster,* from Latin *dis* (away) + *aster* (star). Aster is also the star-shaped flower, and asterisk is the little star in printing (*).

Astronomy is the *nomos* or law of sidereal bodies; *astrology,* from Greek *logos* (speech), is a kind of applied astronomy, science, or superstition, depending on your belief system. The ancient Romans ascribed much importance to the heavens and stars and had a third word for star: *stella*, now often a woman's name. When watching a play, we expect a stellar performance. A *stellionate*, from the Latin *stellio*, a crafty person, literally a lizard (from Latin *lacertus* and French *lézard*) with star-shaped spots, now means in Roman civil and Scots law a fraud, such as the sale of the same property to different persons or the sale of something which belongs to another as one's own. That would not qualify as a stellar performance!

Stellular means shaped like a small star or radiating like one. Several stars together (Latin *cum*) form a constellation. *Star*, an ancient Teutonic word from the same word in Sanskrit, is found in many Germanic languages such as *Stern* in German. *Consternation*, not related to stars, means dumbfounding terror and is from the Latin *cum* (together) + *sternere* (to spread or strike down). *Dumbfound*, from Latin *fundere* and French *fonder*, both meaning melt, fuse, as well as confound and confuse, are less forceful and conjure the image of a *centripetal* (Latin *petere*, seek, hence seeking the center) meltdown. The adjective *stern* meaning serious and stiff has nothing to do with the German *Stern*. It comes from Anglo-Saxon *styrne* and rather evokes German *starr*, rigid, although our *stiff* corresponds to German *steif*. More likely, *stern* comes from the Greek *stereos*, rigid, whence *stereotype*, a rigidly repeated pattern, also influenced by the solid printing plate of type metal. The *stern* of a ship comes from Old Norse *styra*, the act of steering, German *steuern*, and was affected by the old *austern*, now *austere*, from a Greek word meaning dry. Since the dry wind blows from the south, it is also related to Latin *auster*, south. Greek *sternon*, chest, gives us *sternum,* a bone connected

Kowtow	From the Chinese: *ko* (strike, bump) + *tou* (head), to kneel and touch the forehead to the ground in deep respect.
Neighbor	A *nigh boor*, or nearby farmer; from Old English *nigh, near, neth* (the positive, comparative, and superlative), and Dutch *Boer* (peasant or farmer).

to our ribs, and, when cracked, very painful. Again you see how artfully the loom of language weaves the same threads into the fabric of other languages.

Linguistic Contamination

Recently, a local weatherman commented on meteor showers and the dazzling show they can provide. Just as weathermen often miss their forecasts, their knowledge of linguistic terms is not always "up to snuff." These last three words (if I may digress), meaning up to par, were first used to describe primarily a person's physical condition, for people once believed that our quite sensitive sense of smell was the one most easily affected by any health problems. It was held that if you can sniff well, you should be in good health. But back to our weatherman who said meteors meant things flying in the air. Let us be more precise!

The Greek *meteoron*, from *meta* (beyond) + *eoros* (to lift up), designated a thing in the heaven above, an astronomical phenomenon. The word aerial has the same source. Actually, as Joseph T. Shipley in his book on word origins correctly observes, medieval natural history distinguished four types of meteors: aerial, or winds; aqueous (Latin *aqua*, water), or rain, snow, dew; luminous (Latin *lumen*, *lux*, light), or rainbow and halo; and igneous (Latin *ignis*, fire, hence ignite), or lightning and so-called "shooting stars." When the latter land on earth, they are called meteorites.

Speaking of aqua and water, should you ever visit the region of southern France known as Provence and the Rhône Delta, also known as the Camargue, not far from the magnificently preserved Roman city of Arles, where Paul Gauguin and Vincent Van Gogh painted for a while, don't miss Aigues-Mortes (Provençal *aigue* is from Latin *aqua*), a city, whose name means "dead waters." Aigues Mortes, the walls of which you can still walk, was once a seaport. From there, in 1248 and again in 1270, Louis IX, better known as Saint Louis, launched the Seventh Crusade for Egypt and the Eighth or last Crusade for Tunis, respectively. Aigues Mortes lies now far from the Mediterranean, because the river's alluvial deposits have caused the water to recede a great distance — hence the name "dead waters."

Speaking of aerial and air, *debonair*, a word used by Chaucer to describe some of his characters in *The Canterbury Tales* (written between 1387 and 1400), does not come from the French *de bon air*, of good appearance, as an English teacher once wrongly tried to make me believe. Too late to get my money back! The expression rather comes from the French *de bonne aire*, where *aire* can have several meanings, but here designates the nest of a bird of prey. The corresponding English term used in falconry, *aerie*, refers to a nest or brood of birds of prey — eagles and hawks — and hence debonair means of good breeding or race. The word is related to area, *i.e.*, surface or site. In other words, you have a good background.

Strange combinations of meaning have affected these words, almost as though by contamination, here between *area* and Latin *aurum* (gold), as well as *aurea* (golden circle), *aureus* (ancient Roman gold coin). The *u* from *aurum* was inserted into *aureola* or *aureole*, from French *aréole* (reddish circle around an inflamed point or a tit) and French *aureole* (halo, nimbus), from Latin *areola*, diminutive of area. Latin *area* has run through a series of meanings: a plot of ground, a threshing floor somehow connected with arid because it is dry, and a ring around a heavenly body. Paintings and statues of saints often displayed them with "lambent (from Latin *lambere*, to lick) circles of golden areolas about their heads" (as described by English essayist and critic Thomas De Quincey, 1785-1859), originally a disc, not merely a ring, perhaps to both indicate sanctity and protect them from pigeon droppings. Meanings grow by association and connotation. New words are created, old ones acquire new, but related, meanings, spreading like semantic weeds. Thus *aeronaut* is from *aer* (air) + *nauta* (sailor), and, believe it or not, related to *nausea*, which itself was once limited to seasickness.

Subjectivism Has a Place in Language

Today, instead of writing about word origins, I shall endeavor to broach a more elusive subject, one might say a hitherto — at least to my knowledge — totally neglected dimension of language study. It is an area of linguistic research, which linguists have shunned, especially those bound by and fearful of the restrictive (albeit often arbitrary) rules governing the *do's* and *don'ts* of scholarly research and publication, deeming it too difficult to support any potential findings with strictly measurable, factual, concrete data. Anyone developing a thesis in the humanities field, which encompasses languages, is rightly or wrongly held to the same strict standards of logic, cause and effect, and step-by-step reasoning required in the exact sciences. Such standards exclude, of course (and understandably so), anything smacking of dubious divine illumination. Should, however, any cultural and intellectual enlightenment founded on solid, reliable study and experience also be peremptorily declared off limits?

On the other hand, academic discipline perhaps relies at times too stubbornly on the so-called "objective" approach, even when exploring those realms of knowledge where new discoveries may be accessible only to subjective sensory perception and individual intuition. Why, in our constant efforts to fathom our complex universe, should we be content with focusing solely on a reality presumed to be as it is in itself, entirely independent of mind, rather than on one perceived and known through living experience? Why, indeed, ignore the unlimited emotional, intuitional faculties available to us, falsely declaring such cognitive processes the prerogative of only artists and dreamers?

The question I should like to pose is whether different languages express meaning with equal efficiency, and, more specifically, always communicate it with exactly the same intellectual, emotional, pictorial, musical, or, as it were, artistic impact. The immediate obvious answer is "No!" Languages differ in many respects: in musicality, even onomatopoeia, involving the auditory sense to enrich communication; in metaphors, adding graphic imagery often worth a thousand words; in size of vocabulary; and in varying degrees and shades of precision and clarity illuminating conceptual subtleties, as a strategically disposed floodlight might enhance the lines of a marble statue.

Generally, only by mastering two languages to perfection may we be fully aware of such differences, which may vary from the patently obvious to the highly sophisticated. Thus, a title like *The Taming of the Shrew* cannot be adequately expressed in German, the closest translation being "The Taming of the Unmanageable or Rebellious One," a linguistic and stylistic disaster. Perhaps I can illustrate my point about the differences in languages by resorting to an example accessible to those of you not skilled in a second language. Consider two recent movies, like the British *The Ideal Husband* and the French *Autumn Tale*. Can you possibly imagine employing American actors, speaking American English, to portray the characters and duplicate the action of either film? Both works are so typical of their respective cultures and regional locales, so imbued with the essential characteristics of the respective national types, so patently British and French in their respective entirety, that they would ring false and be inconceivable in any other setting. In that sense, languages — like people and objects — possess a soul that touches our soul and makes it resonate. To truly appreciate this you must learn to love them!

Language Can Be Consistently Inconsistent

Fearful lest I do not meet my biweekly deadline, I always prepare my newspaper columns in advance and quite a lag occurs between the time I write them and when they are read. By the way, if biweekly means once every two weeks, how would you express twice a week? The answer is semiweekly. To prove to you how illogical and inconsistent human language can be, take biannual. Through assimilation with biweekly, it should mean every two years, but it means, instead, semiannual or twice a year. To express the thought of every two years, use biennial.

Students of language who seek immutable scientific laws to explain linguistic phenomena may be disappointed. In nature and the universe one might be tempted to search for a unified field theory like the one potentially comprising both the macro world of relativity and the micro world of quantum physics, but in language there is too much human input or even "tampering" to allow for such expectations.

I just returned from a trip abroad where I constantly stumbled across examples to prove this point. The French call the oblong cream puff, usually chocolate- or mocha-covered, with whipped cream or custard filling, *éclair*. It means literally lightning, from the Vulgar Latin *exclariare*, Latin *exclarare*, to light up, illuminate, from the same root as our "clear." The French called it thus, because it can be swallowed in one gulp, at lightning speed. Why do we then illogically call the rich French pastry consisting of several oblong layers of puff paste with a filling of whipped cream, custard, or jelly, created at the end of the 19th century, a napoleon, when the French call it a *mille-feuille*, literally "thousand leaves." Of course they also called a twenty-*franc* gold coin a napoleon, after the diminutive French emperor, as well as a man's high boot, and a card game with five-card hands where the highest bidder has to make the tricks he commits himself to making. I suppose the General's profile appeared on the face of the coin, he wore high boots to look taller, and his enemies would have liked to cream him with the pastry. Just kidding!

Both terms, *paste* and *pastry* (formerly it used to be called pasty), are, of course, in no way related to past or passed. They originate from the Latin *pasta*, from the Greek *paste, pasta*, barley porridge. A more remote origin is the Greek *pastos*, sprinkled. The word paste is still used for the dough (German *Teig*) mixed for making pastry. It is also applied to a mixture of flour and water used as an adhesive, and to similar substances, including diamond paste, that is diamond dust in a jelly or oil, used as an abrasive.

Cake is an old Teutonic word, Old Norse *kaka*, German *Kuchen*, Dutch *koek*, diminutive *koekje*, whence our cookie. From the practice of the large restaurants along Broadway, in New York's theater district, of having a large *cheesecake* as the main window display (I remember Lindy's in the 1930s), the word was transferred in movie, newspaper, and theater slang to the main display in their publicity, *i.e.*, to the pretty legs of actresses. After all, cheesecake, like little girls, is made of "Sugar and spice/And all things nice." English actress Nell Gwyn (1650?-1687), in the epilogue of a tragedy, once protested: "Nay, what's worse, to kill me in the prime/of Easter-term, in Tart and Cheesecake time!" *Tart* comprises three words. The cake comes from the French *tarte*, from the Latin *torquere*, past *tortus* (to twist), as the pastry is twisted. Tart, meaning sour, is from Old English *teart*. *Tart*, the disreputable woman, combines the bitter taste with *sweetheart*: a short and bitter sweetheart is a tart!

Travel Broadens Linguistic Knowledge

When traveling, one can occasionally pick up some interesting data on word or name origins. While in Germany, a friend asked if I knew the origin of the name of the German automobile known as Audi. I was aware there once had been a German car maker called *Horch*, which in German means *"listen!"* Apparently someone working for that firm decided to strike out on his own. Barred from using the same name, he simply substituted the Latin equivalent for "listen!" — *"audi!"* The car's four-ring emblem symbolizes the fact that four firms participated in forming the new company.

However, to return to our own language, we all know that the Latin *quintus* (five) gave us *quintuplets* and *quintessence*. When perfume is distilled to give it its final aroma, the ultimate degree of distillation is five times, hence quintessence. However, the word was first used by the Pythagoreans to designate ether, the fifth and last or highest substance in ancient and medieval philosophy above fire, air, water, and earth, which permeates all nature and is the constituent matter of the celestial bodies. Now it is used to refer to the most perfect or ultimate level of distillation or extract of almost anything, such as, for instance, "the quintessence of music is melody" and "the quintessence of wit is brevity."

The Latin *torquere* (past participle *tort*), to twist, is the source of many English words. Twisted tow (fiber from flax, hemp, or jute), when lit on a stick, gave us *torch*, French *torche*. *Torche* also meant a bunch of twisted straw used to wipe or dust and yielded the French *torchon*, a rag used to *torcher*, or wipe and dust. *Torture* implied twisting the limbs. I guess Tomás de Torquemada of Inquisition fame — one might call him the quintessential torturer — was aptly named. Think also of the torque on a car engine. Hence we also derive tortuous and torsion. However, *turtle* and *tortoise*, having in ancient times been regarded as infernal creatures, probably owe their name to mythological Tartarus, the infernal (of, or relating to, the dead) regions. To extort is to twist something like money or the truth out of someone. To distort, to twist away or apart, and to contort (also note contortionist) to twist together, both refer to misshaping, the first ideas, the second face or body.

A retort is a witty or sharp reply twisted right back to counter someone's remark. It may also be a glass vessel often used in chemistry with its neck bent back. From the Lower Latin *torquementum* we have Latin *tormentum*, English *torment*, a stone-hurling war engine as well as an instrument for torture. Both used torsion. Related verbs and the resulting anguish all have the same origin. *Tornado*, the whirling storm, came to us from the Spanish *tornar*, to turn. It was also probably influenced by Spanish *tronada*, thunderstorm, and the verb *tronar*, to thunder. Latin *tonare* gave us French *tonnerre*, thunder, which is also close to the German *Donner*. The Norse God Thor, son of Odin, with his famed hammer and goat-drawn chariot that produced thunder as it rolled by, gave us *Thursday*, *Donnerstag* (or *Thunder Day* in German). Sanskrit *tan* is to resound.

Our distaste for "hurtful twisting" is also the basis for the legal *tort*, an injury done someone or a wrongful act not including breach of contract. Mentioned in a previous essay are the delicious pastries *torte* and *torta*, German *Torte*, as well as the open-faced tart favored by the French (*tarte*), made of twisted dough. The human *torso*, the body's stem, however, comes from Greek *thyrsos*, the staff surmounted by a pine cone or by a bunch of vine or ivy leaves with grapes or berries, carried by Dionysus (Bacchus) and by satyrs engaging in mad revels and Bacchic rites, often without the benefit of torches.

Languages Must Be Learned

The fundamental feature of human language is that it has to be learned. It is not innate. Animal sounds are inborn and, it appears, remain uniform within a species with only slight variations. Human children have to learn the meanings their parents attach to the human sounds they make. Scattered cases of feral or isolated children, some thirty to forty in all, from Wild Peter of Hanover in 1724 down to Kamala and Amala, the wolf-girls of India in 1920, have shown that a child reared by animals, abandoned to live on its own in the wilds or otherwise cut off from human society, fails to develop speech. Isolation past the age of seven may render the child permanently mute.

A Los Angeles girl locked from babyhood to age thirteen (when neighbors found her and alerted the police) in an attic room, given food, but never spoken to, had by that time lost the power not merely to speak, but even to think. There is not a word we utter, a concept we use, an idea we form, that does not directly or indirectly depend on the larger community for its existence. Meaning, and what else is objective reality if it is not meaning, is the joint property of those who communicate. Part of that meaning may not communicate. Then the delicate question arises: "Is it still meaning and, if it is, to whom?" *Solipsism* (from *solus*, alone, + *ipse*, self), is an epistemological (pertaining to the methods and grounds of knowledge) theory that the self can know nothing but its own modifications and states.

Plato in his *Cratylus* called language a tool to educate one another and to organize and classify being. German philologist (one who studies historical linguistics) and scholar Wilhelm von Humboldt (1767-1835) stated that language was not an action, but an efficient, purposeful operation. He called it the work of the intellect. The constant and similarly formed elements available to the intellect to raise articulate sounds to an expression of thought, as completely as possible expressed in its context and stated systematically, is what shapes language. This interplay between thought and language, catalyzed by the input of associations and connotations and based on real life experiences, may generate surprising semantic variations. Especially interesting is the process whereby a single word (signifier) describing a complex multidimensional event sprouts variations that become semantically independent. The result is that each variation springing from the original root word assumes a meaning that corresponds to only one element of that complex event.

The Latin *petit* means "he goes for something, he seeks, he asks for." Greek *piptei* of the same root is a frequentative present of the same root, but signifies "it falls," and similarly Old Hindu *patati* means "it flies." *Patati* is also the root for *petition* and *appetite*. How can there be a possible connection between these meanings or a logical transition from one to the next? Well, the following example of one action, one event, includes them all and might well explain to what such simultaneous triple meaning is attributable: the swoop of the goshawk down upon his prey. The original content, namely "to go for, to fall, to fly," of the root *pet* may have initially occurred to humans observing the hawk's action and may have been used to describe it, as they lumped the entire process together as one. Later, each successive phase of the event acquired its own independent signifier and meaning. Likewise, "to seek," German *suchen*, Gothic *sokjan*, corresponds to Latin *sagire*, to scent, and Greek *hägeitai*, he leads — all of which describe the action of the hound who scents, seeks, and leads his master in a hunt. (In Greek the same root may mean to opine, to believe.)

Language May Be the Basis for Humor

How gratifying to discover that there was sufficient interest in language and its role in human culture and thought to be asked by Arizona's Rio Salado (Salt River) Sun Cities Lifelong Learning Center to present five two-hour lectures on the subject! We covered many aspects of language, such as the mystery of its origin, animal and body language, general semantics, and the possible misuse of language, the linguistic metaphors we live by, the images embedded in our English words, the adequacy of translation, or, in extreme cases, the virtual impossibility thereof, the merits of bilingual education, the problems of learning foreign languages, and anything else the audience wished to bring up.

Those of us involved with the written word might think of ourselves as experts, because we creatively and intellectually use language throughout life, but my challenge is to make *everyone* look at language more thoughtfully, more analytically, with eyes wide open rather than "wide shut," as a recent film title puts it.

Language also presents many opportunities for laughter, especially when recalling examples of double entendre (ambiguity of meaning, if you prefer) from careless headlines, such as: "Prostitutes Appeal to Pope" and "Teacher Strikes Idle Kids." As a last resort, foreigners provide bottomless gold mines of fractured English as a source of mirth: "If this is your first visit to Moscow, you are welcome to it" . . . and in a Paris hotel, "Please leave your values at the front desk" . . . or better yet, a Paris store sign, "Dresses for Street Walking." In Acapulco, there was the assurance that "The manager has personally passed all the water served in the hotel," and, finally, a Norwegian hotel kindly requested ladies "not to have children at the bar."

It is of interest to note that where English has only two words to

> **Bluestocking** Now a pedantic woman with literary pretensions; may be traced back to Venice in the 1400s to the *Della Calza* society (literally "of the stocking," as they wore *blue* stockings. In Paris (1590) and England (1750), *Bas-bleu* clubs (French for "bluestocking") were formed.
>
> **Bulldozer** 1890s American term for a heavy machine with tank treads and large earth-moving blade, called a "bull dose" or "to bull dose." Originally, the term referred to flogging slaves, administering a *dose* strong enough for a bull.

distinguish semantic shades pertinent to language, namely "language and tongue," French has three: *langage* (language), *langue* (a specific language: French, German, Spanish), *parole* (the spoken tongue). The origin of language will undoubtedly remain a mystery, but not that of the word *story*. A *storey*, later *story*, whether the floor of a house or a tale, comes from Latin *historia*, from a Greek root meaning to know and French *estorie, estoire*, eventually *histoire*, where it means both a story (tale) or history (the discipline). The reason that the same English word means both floors and tales may be that buildings once depicted (by means of pictorial and sculptural art) historical, legendary, and literary subjects and that "storied windows" told a legend for each floor.

Story and history may be related to *histrionical* (connected with the stage) from Latin *histrio*, an actor, probably one who made others laugh, more remotely from Sanskrit *has*, to laugh, and *hastra*, a fool. In the 16th and 17th centuries, *histrio, histrion*, were used for actor from the Etruscan *hister*. *Histrionics* now contemptuously refers to stagy conduct intended to produce some particular effect on others. The top story or attic derives its origin from Attica, the Greek state, where Athens stood. The adjective grew to mean elegant and designated an architectural style marked by simplicity and refinement. The Attic style often featured a small row of columns on top of another larger one, as on the Pantheon of Athens, hence it eventually meant any top story. Sanskrit *attaka* was the highest room of the Indian house, from the root *atta*. *Loft* and *lofty* are both from the Anglo-Saxon *lvft*, German *Luft* (air). The verb "to store" and the noun "store" are from Old French *estorer*, Latin *instaurare*, to begin with, install, repair, replenish. Similarly, from Latin *restaurare* (present participle *restaurans*), French *restorer*, we have to *restore* and *restaurant*, where we can restore ourselves. German *Boden* means both attic and ground. They must have thought of it as the bottom of the roof!

Debates Are Rooted in Violence

Reading about debates between contenders for the office of President, you may think they are engaged in nonviolent friendly discussions. Maybe so! However, the root of the word rather indicates they are beating each other down. *Debate* is from the French, *de* (down) and *battre* (beat). When the contenders *discuss* topics, from *dis* (apart) and *quatere*, past participle *quassus* (shake), they are trying to shake each other apart. Worse! The frequentatives *quassare* and *quassicare* mean to break, shake to pieces, hence our verb "to quash." The latter is a doublet, one meaning to make void, without effect (to quash a sentence), the other to beat down, to crush. Debaters would be wise to wear helmets, casques, or casquets.

Casque, from the same French word, is related to the French *casser* (to break), Italian *caseo*, as it breaks the blows aimed at it. Not unrelated are the Portuguese *caska* (bark), Spanish *cascara* (rind, shell, peel), and finally the English *cascara* used in medicine. *Cascara amarga*, or bitter bark, also known as Honduras bark, was once used in the treatment of syphilis and skin diseases. *Cascara sagrada*, or the sacred bark, the dried bark of cascara buckthorn, is used as a cathartic or mild laxative. A doublet of *cascara* is cask, a tub, but the diminutive *casket*, little tub, comes from cask meaning chest (not a part of the body, but a container). You don't believe me? Open Shakespeare's *Henry VI* (2.3.2) almost at the very end, and read: "A jewel, lock'd into the woefull'st cask/That ever did contain a thing of worth."

This meaning of chest was influenced by the French *cassette*, a small case, from Latin *capsa*, chest, and the verb *capere*, to hold, seize, from which also come captive, capture, captivate, even capsule, capacity, and chassis. You can see how the human mind, as it needs and dreams up new more specific, yet related meanings, creates new words from the same root. Cask has two additional forms, thus yielding triplets: the noun case or receptacle, and the verb to encase. Now *case*, an event, and the expression *"in case"* come from Latin *cadere* (*casu*) to fall. Thus, the compound *escheat* traveled a long journey from Latin *ex* + *cadere*, to fall out, through French *échoir*, and came to have a legal meaning, to revert. When someone's heirs could not inherit the estate, the latter escheated to the lord. Of course, the former claimants felt cheated, which has the same origin, as the estate "fell out of their possession." Old French *cheoir*, to fall (the noun derived from it, "chute," fall, is still used, but the verb is now replaced by *tomber*, as in *tombé*, a ballet movement with accent on the descent), yields our *chute*, which involves falling. *Parachute* literally means stop falling.

Chance depends on the fall of the dice, as does *casual* (of little importance). Casuistry (specious reasoning, originally practiced by Jesuits and justified by precedents found in thick case books, as in common case law, to resolve right or wrong cases of conduct), casualties (fallen ones), on occasion (fall in your path; from Latin *ob*, against), occident (where the sun falls at night), accident (fall against you; from *ad*, against), are all related. *Cash* first meant a case where money is kept, hence cashier. Now to *cashier* someone from the army comes from French *casser*, to break. From the previously mentioned *quatere* we also have *percussion*, with *per* meaning through and through, concussion with *con* meaning together, repercussion with *re* a reduplication of percussion, even quake and the Quakers, who shook and trembled as they spoke in tongues in ecstatic fervor at their religious gatherings. Where *casemate*, a fortified masonry position through which guns may be fired, ultimately comes from is uncertain. From an old Italian word, it comprises *casa*, house, and Latin *mattus*, stupid, drunk. It might also be related to the meaning to kill (Spanish *matar*). Linguistic roots sprout like plant seeds.

Ache Can Be a Pain to Pronounce

Why would any sane person pronounce "ache" as though it were written "ake"? Shouldn't it, instead, be pronounced like the eighth letter of the alphabet *h*? Well, in current English we opt for "ake." Samuel Johnson and his *Dictionary* bear most of the blame. He derived "ake" from Anglo-Saxon *acan* and Old English *aece* and arbitrarily decided the modern spelling of this word. Shakespeare, sparing himself many a headache, not only distinguished between the two forms, but also used them for puns and riddles.

In *Much Ado about Nothing* (3.4) we read:

> Beatrice: . . . By my troth I am exceeding ill. Heigh-ho!
> Margaret: For a hawk, a horse, or a husband?
> Beatrice: For the letter that begins them all — H.

An epigram by John Heywood (1566) shows the former pronunciation of ache and solves the riddle:

> H is worst among letters in the cross-row,
> For if thou find him either in thine elbow,
> In thy arm, or leg, in any degree;
> In thine head, or teeth, or toe, or knee;
> Into what place soever H may pike him,
> Wherever thou find ache, thou shalt not like him.

We also read in *Wits' Recreation* (1640), an anthology whose author is unknown: "*Dolor Intimus.* Nor hawk, nor hound, nor horse, those h h h,/But ach itself, 't is Brutus' bones attaches." In Shakespeare's *Antony and Cleopatra* (4.7) we find a similar pun: "Scarus, wounded: I had a wound here that was like a T,/ But now 'tis made an H."

In Shakespeare's *The Tempest* (1.2), Prospero says: "Fill all thy bones with aches, make thee roar,/That beasts shall tremble at thy din." John Baret in his *Alvearie, or Triple Dictionarie* of 1573 (English, Latin, French) explains: "Ake is the Verbe of the substantive Ach, ch being turned into k." As a substantive (a word functioning as a noun), then, *ach* was written *aches* and pronounced as a dissyllable (a word with two syllables). When a verb, it was written *akes*, and its pronunciation was monosyllabic. This distinction is invariably marked in the old texts. Thus, in *Romeo and Juliet* (2.5) we read: "Lord, how my head akes [*verb*]! What a head have I!" In *Coriolanus* (3.1) another verb: "and my soule akes to know." Finally, in *Othello* (4.2), still a verb: "That the sense akes at thee!" In all cases when it was a noun, it was spelled *aches* and was pronounced as two syllables and like the plural of the letter *h*. Perhaps Johnson should have left well enough alone!

In most English words of this kind and of Teutonic (a fine English term, although my spell checker rebels at it) origin, the verb has taken the *k* spelling and sound, while the corresponding noun prefers the *ch* spelling and sound. Some of you may not until now have thought of them as a pair: bake-batch, break-breach, make-match, speak-speech, stick-stitch, wake-watch, and, yes, most probably, eat-etch. English *to eat*, Greek *edein*, Latin *edere*, Anglo-Saxon *etan*, German *essen*, all with the same meaning, did, indeed, give us *to etch*, which, after all, means to eat with acid. With regard to eat, language wrought some more fine-tuning. In German, when people eat, we must use *essen*; when animals eat use *fressen*. (English only has one word.) *Fressen* is only applied to people when they display bad animal-like eating habits. In Anglo-Saxon, the word also existed: *fretan*. It gave us our *fret*, which literally meant to eat away, then to be gnawed with care and worries.

Latin *obedere*, an intensive form of *edere*, meant to eat away, devour. The past participle *obesus* first designated a person eaten away, actually lean. Soon it reverted to an active meaning, describing persons who eat all they can and become *obese*. Fat people might wish the original meaning resurrected, from Latin *resurgere*, to surge or rise again. In the olden days, Jenny Craig promised to make you obese or lean. You figure!

Of Shades and Windows

Stated as kindly as I can, media personalities are not always the best source for accurate information on questions of language. Recently I heard a TV newscaster talk about "commodification," a word you will not even find in a crossword-puzzle dictionary, because it does not exist. I also heard an alternative medicine expert on a local radio station attribute the origin of the expression "health nut" to the fact that people once believed a diet of nuts and dried fruit guaranteed good health. To this I say, "Nuts! nerts! nertz!" — an exclamation in colloquial usage since about 1925 and capable of expressing a wide range of sentiments: disgust, contempt, defiance, anger, and even impatience with one's self. Please observe that I did not say, "It's the nuts!" which would signify I deemed the statement excellent. General McAuliffe, of the 101st Airborne Division, replied "Nuts!" to the German invitation to surrender at Bastogne during World War II's Battle of the Bulge. Under the circumstances, I consider that a euphemism. The German interpreter must have labored long on it.

The word *nut,* besides meaning a hard-shelled dried fruit, has (since about 1915) designated a person ranging anywhere from insane, foolish, and gullible, to one of unusual habits or beliefs, eccentric, irresponsible, or even humorous. With the increasing popularization of psychology, the word was used less and less in the sense of insane, referring rather to eccentricity and humor. It might even be applied to one performing an unusually generous, funny, or emotionally touching act. Once again you can witness how a single word may resonate over such a wide scale of nuances in our mind. It is as though an endless succession of windows of slightly altered meanings keep opening up in the perceptive and cognitive portions of our brain. Much like the Windows computer operating system, once opened, those in our mind may remain so, if not intentionally closed; they will be superimposed on our mental screen, always semantically distinguishable, depending, of course, on individual linguistic proficiency.

Returning to what inspired this column, the word "nut" could be originally applied to any person fanatically enthusiastic about anything, a true fan, be it of sports like golf, tennis, and, yes, healthy living. No need to resort to almonds and raisins, although they might be good nutrients for the human body, if not for the little gray brain cells in the "nut" of a talk show host, as Agatha Christie's detective Hercule Poirot might opine. To be off one's nut means to be crazy, irrational, in a tantrum. We also use the term to refer to a hard to solve problem or task, when we say that such and such is a hard nut to crack, demonstrating once again the metaphorical nature of language as one image is applied to varying scenarios.

In a non-metaphorical sense, the word "nut" designates perforated, usually hexagonal, metal blocks, a projection on the shank of an anchor, the ridge in a stringed musical instrument, the piece on a violin bow to tighten the hairs, testes (pardon my French!), and a doughnut or spice nut, depending on the occasion and context. In British English, "for nuts" may mean "at all" in "he cannot write or she cannot sew for nuts."

Many expressions use nouns, and mostly adjectives, of nationalities, such as "pardon my French," "French leave," "French illness," "Dutch uncle." As mentioned, they are usually, to a certain degree, derogatory and originally sprang from hostile feelings between nations and a tendency by one to credit unworthy qualities to the other.

Altered Meanings

How about doing some linguistic housecleaning? The origin of a word can cast a great deal of light on its precise meaning; however, as a language evolves, even purists, no matter their frustration and despair, cannot prevent speakers of the language to alter such meaning, just as one might use a tool for a different purpose than originally intended. Thus *aggravate*, from the Latin *aggravare*, to make heavier, from *gravis*, heavy (hence our adjective grave), originally meant to weigh down and even to exaggerate. Then it specifically meant to make worse as in "the weather aggravated his cold." Recently, shuddering as I heard on TV that a beekeeper had "aggravated the bees and been stung," I was reminded that to many people, aggravate means to annoy or irritate. I visualized the poor insects loaded down with heavy burdens, desperately trying to maintain their lift! No wonder they stung him!

Nevertheless, the word is now mostly used informally and loosely to mean "to irritate, annoy," thereby depriving English of an elegant and succinct way of expressing "to make worse" in one word. To annoy is less strong than aggravate and means to "harass, pester, disturb." Irritate is still milder, signifying to "excite to impatience." Hearing aggravate misused, I console myself with the thought that a bee sting would be much worse.

To *tantalize* means to torment and to tease by arousing expectations. *Harass*, correctly accented on the first syllable (few people know this), implies persecution through repeated demands and threats. Tantalize has come into our language from mythology and an age when the gods punished any man challenging them and endeavoring to equal them in power. The giant Sons of Terra (Earth) and Titan once rebelled against the gods. One of them, Tantalus, as punishment, was immersed in a pool up to his chin. Each time he tried to drink, the waters receded. Fruit dangling over his head drew away whenever he reached for it. To tantalize is to arouse, and then kill all expectations, as when a girl acts responsive, but then rejects a boy.

Harass comes from early English *hare*, Old French *harer*, originally to set the dogs on someone. It is related to *harry*, from Anglo-Saxon *herian*, to lay waste, Old English *here,* and Modern German *Heer*, army. Perhaps Spanish *herir*, to wound, has the same origin.

Many English speakers also appear to have a fuzzy idea of the difference between reluctant and reticent. Again, when in doubt, go to the source! *Reluctant*, from Latin *re*, indicating backward motion, and *luctare*, to struggle, wrestle (French *lutter*), is to refrain from doing something by wrestling with one's self. *Reticent*, from Latin *tacere*, to remain silent (French *se taire*), designates someone who exercises restraint in speaking and communication, maintaining a kind of silent reserve.

Another phenomenon in language is impoverishment through linguistic inflation. Particularly disturbing is the overuse of "hero," especially when applied to two confused American soldiers who bungle across the Kosovo border, are rescued, and returned to their country in triumph, rather than being court-martialed as AWOL. From the Greek *heros*, the word once referred to a legendary figure endowed with great courage, favored by the gods, and often believed to be of partly divine descent. The word is related to Sanskrit *vira* (meaning hero), and Latin *vir*, and Anglo-Saxon *wer*, meaning man and modern virile. *Werewolf* is literally *man wolf*. Would you believe it is even related to Latin *servare*, to protect, from the Aryan root *SAR* with the same meaning of protect + *vir* (man)?

Use Restraint When Tracing Word Origins

When searching for word origins, it is wise to refrain from exuberant (from *ex*, here an intensifier, plus *uberare*, to be fruitful) extremes of fancy and to remain within the bounds of sound scholarship and common sense. Some imaginative amateur linguists have derived east, where the sun rises, and Easter, the season when the Lord arises, from yeast, which also makes things like dough rise. Now this is a stretch! From the Greek *eos*, Sanskrit *usas*, related to the Aryan root *us* (to burn) and Sanskrit *vas* (to shine), *east*, like all the names for the cardinal points, is a very old word indeed. In the same vein, *west* does not owe its name to the fact that the sun "wasteth" there. It is rather from the Sanskrit *vasta*, the house where the sun resides at night. The latter is *vasati* in Sanskrit.

South is from Old High German *sunth*, the *n* dropping as it did in tooth, from *tanth*, Sanskrit *danta*, Latin *dens*, possessive case *dentis*, whence *dentist*. *North* may come from the Umbrian *nertru* (left), and the Greek *nerteros* (lower, infernal), but, of course, more directly, from the Germanic *Nord*. The word *tooth*, from Latin *dens*, recalls a linguistic law we owe to Jakob Grimm, of fairytale fame, who was also a distinguished philologist (again, literally from Latin and Greek, a lover of learning and words, like all of you, my readers). Very simply put, the law (later refined by Danish philologist Karl A. Verner) states that certain consonants in Greek and Latin words are predictably converted into other consonants in English and German cognates: *g* to *c* or *k*, *h* to *g*, *d* to *t* or *z*, *p* to *f* or *v*.

Thus Latin *genus* converts to English *kin*, *gelidus* to *cold* or German *kalt*, *hostis* to *guest* or German *Gast*. *Dens* and *duo* yield *tooth*, *two*, and *Zahn*, *zwei* respectively, while *pater* and *penna* give us *father*, *feather*, and *Vater*, *Feder*. This should help you learn German more easily, especially if you arm yourself with Mark Twain's advice to use only diminutives when speaking German. The humorist had observed that all German nouns, whether masculine, feminine, or neuter in gender, become neuter when adding the suffix *-chen*, which gives them a diminutive meaning. Your German style might sound bizarre ("My little son had a little flu and in his little bed played with his little train, while his little mother worried" — or in German, "*Mein kleines Söhnchen hatte ein kleines Grippchen und in seinem kleinen Bettchen spielte mit seinem kleinen Zügchen, während sein kleines Mütterchen sich um ihn sorgte*"), but what an absurd way to economize on memory or RAM, if you prefer computer lingo!

Let us now sink our teeth into the derivatives of tooth, teeth. From Latin *in* and *dens*, literally into and tooth, we have *indent*, with meanings ranging from cutting into to forcing inward. During colonial times, indentured servants, who exchanged a few years' work for their sea passage, were given a document outlining their contract with their master. Both copies were either indented or, if written on one sheet, torn, so that, if need be, they could be matched and their authenticity verified. *Dandelion* is from the French *dent de lion*, lion's tooth. Sanskrit *danta*, Greek *odon* (tooth), yield odontology and odontologist, who can charge you

> **Éclair** In French, means "lightning," from the Vulgar Latin *exclariare*, Latin *exclarare* (to light up, illuminate). The French so named it because it can be swallowed at *lightning* speed — in one gulp!
>
> **Gibberish** Related to 11th-century Arabian alchemist Geber, charged with consorting with the devil. To avoid death, Geber wrote his treatises in seemingly nonsensical language.

more than a dentist because of his fancy title. *Mastodons* were different from elephants and mammoths in that they could have two sets of tusks, but mainly because they sported a nipple-like (*mast* is Greek for breast) projection on their molars. A trident is a three-pronged scepter or spear carried by such VIPs as Poseidon, son of Cronos, brother of Zeus (Jupiter), chief mythological sea god. It may also prove a handy weapon against muggers. Sanskrit *adana* (food), as well as Greek *edein*, Latin *edere*, German *essen*, and our *eat* all spring from the same root.

Critic Climbs Out on Wrong Branch

Well, I finally received sonic flak from a reader about my definition of biannual, occurring twice a year, and biennial, occurring once every two years. I value any reader's comments, even those of a critic who, perhaps scanning my column too rapidly, failed to realize that I was explaining the meaning of these two words as they apply in general to events, journals, etc. . . . not merely plants. Applied to plants, biennial may, indeed, mean continuing for two years. For example, a biennial like the parsnip requires two growing seasons to grow from seed to seed. As to *flak*, it comes from the German *Fliegerabwehrkanone*, or antiaircraft gun, and is now used in slang to mean criticism.

Do any of you who watch *Jeopardy* on TV ever wonder where this word comes from? Do its brilliant contestants know? Originally, it evolved from Lower Latin *jocus partitus*, a divided game. In ancient Rome, when a game was a draw, the players divided the wager. Hence originate the Anglo-French *juparti* or *jeu parti*, again, literally, a divided game, but now meaning an "alternative" or poem treating amorous problems in dialogue form. From there the phrase was applied to evenly matched opponents, where the result of the game or match was uncertain and the stakes, sometimes even their lives, were in danger, the present meaning of jeopardy. As to jeopardize, the verbal ending *-ize*, from Lower Latin *-izare*, is often used in the sense of to make, to do, hence the meaning of placing someone or something in danger or harm's way.

Many of you know the story of the Gordian knot. A Phrygian oracle informed the people that a wagon would bring them a king who would put an end to their troubles. Soon Gordius, a mere peasant, appeared in his wagon and became king of Phrygia. In gratitude he dedicated the wagon to Zeus, and the pole of the wagon was fastened to the yoke by a knot of bark. Another oracle prophesied that whoever managed to untie the knot should reign over Asia. Alexander the Great took a shortcut (no pun intended), severing the knot with his sword, and thereby fulfilled the oracle, adeptly solving a knotty problem. *Knot* itself is a common Teutonic word, Anglo-Saxon *cnotta*, Old Norse *knutr* (knot), and *knötir*, also meaning ball. It became German *Knoten*. A cognate of the word produced our verb *knit*. The knots (one knot = one nautical mile = 1.15 statute miles per hour) a ship travels in an hour are measured by a log line. The length of a knot marked off on a log line is 47 feet, 3 inches and has the same ratio to one nautical mile as twenty-eight seconds has to one hour. Thus the number of such knots or divisions running out from the log reel within a twenty-eight-second interval indicates that the identical number of nautical miles will be covered within one hour by the ship if it (or should I in true naval fashion say "she") maintains the same speed and does not hit an iceberg.

A *knout*, Russian *knut*, of Scandinavian origin and related to knot, is a lash of knotted thongs. The word *log*, like clog, which once was a synonym, is onomatopoeic (imitative of sounds) suggesting something bulky and clumsy. Back in the 15th century and later, the speed of a ship was calculated by dropping a piece of wood, a log, with a measuring device into the water alongside the vessel. The record of speed and of other ship data was kept in a logbook, and the term log later applied to the recording of any journey or travel data and facts. I'll tell you about loggerheads some other time, lest I weary you and we end up being at loggerheads!

A colleague of mine recently enlightened us on the scientific aspects of a cruise he took, and I just returned from a 4,893-nautical-mile (5,627 statute miles) cruise around South America from Valparaiso, Chile, to Rio de Janeiro, Brazil. Allow me to dwell on a few linguistic data that attracted my attention during the trip. The word *mile*, Anglo-Saxon *mil*, comes directly from the Latin *mille*, plural *milia*. The Roman mile was *mille passuum*, a thousand paces or 1,618 yards (our mile is 1,760 yards). The Romans counted the pace from where the foot touches the ground to where it touches again.

During the cruise I foolishly entered a poetry contest, although I usually only translate poetry and don't write it. We were instructed to write about the journey. I pretended to have found in the ship's library a lost sonnet from Shakespeare, which he wrote while taking the same cruise some 500 years earlier to gain inspiration for *The Tempest*. I carefully observed all the rules of the Shakespearean sonnet (rhyme sequence, abab cdcd efef gg), with each quatrain self-contained and the last two verses the conclusion. My only deviation was to use Alexandrine (twelve-syllable) lines, instead of Shakespeare's decasyllabic (ten-syllable) ones. The sonnet was as follows:

> Land where the pyramids in the jungle rise high,
> As Mayan priests, to stem some dreaded final day,
> To the counting of time their awesome skill apply,
> And in their bloody rites their hapless victims slay.
> Land of fabled Incas, of El Dorado fame.
> Victims of Spain's grim lust for the coveted ore,
> As the conquistadors in waves to their shores came
> Ravaging their empire and plunging it in gore!
> Argentina, whose name rings like a silver bell
> Praised as the purple land, pampas, where gauchos ride,
> And rhyming payadors (traveling country singers with guitars)
>   of Martin Fierro tell,
> While dancing the tango defines the nation's pride.
> No wonder your beauty remains a constant lure
> Your magic to enjoy, your hardships to endure.

Unfortunately, I aimed too high. The three judges on the panel rolled their eyes and declared the winner to be a gentleman who cared neither about rhyme nor syllabic order and who wrote about Magellan, of Magellan Straits fame. My comment?

> The three judges were not amused
> This sonnet thing had them confused.
> No way they would give an award
> To one who tried to ape the Bard.
> Instead they gave it to some man,
> Who wrote bad verse on Magellan (ugh!)
> The moral of this story is
> Don't let your genius spout and fizz!
> Don't aim for something too sublime!
> Don't cast pearls before swine, next time!

Once, for entertainment on the cruise, a three-person panel sought out exotic words no one had heard of. Two panelists gave false definitions, a third a partially correct one. One of the words was "farding," used for obvious cheap comic effects. You know, a *d* for a *t*. But when a panel member said she was *farding* in an elevator while putting on lipstick, something clicked my mind. *Fard* in French is makeup, and *se farder* means to put on makeup. Apparently the word is buried somewhere in the *Oxford English Dictionary*.

On the cruise we visited Rio de Janeiro (January River), so named because it was discovered by Portuguese navigators on January 1, 1502. They asssumed the entrance of Guanabara Bay was the mouth of a huge river. We also made a port call at Ushuaia, Tierra del Fuego (Land of Fire). The latter owes its name to the early natives' campfires and also to the many active regional volcanoes. Finally, although Montevideo, Uruguay, does not come from a possible "I see a mountain," it may come from *Monte VI*, Mountain 6.

Putting My Best Foot Forward

Rather than put my foot in my mouth I shall put my best foot forward

— an expression used by Shakespeare's King John, "Nay but make haste, the better foot before" (4.2), and in 1855 by Robert Browning, "Put forward your best foot!" — and remind you that our word *pedigree* comes from the French *pied de grue*, meaning literally a crane's foot. In old documents tracing family trees, the three-line graph of lineal descent looked like the imprint of a crane's foot. From a 17th-century Spanish play I once translated the following:

> I shall be like those birds that streak
> through the wind, one stone in their beak
> one in their claws, a proof to you
> that I'm alert, faithful, and true.

I traced this animal legend to the *erudite* (*e* + *rudis*, out of, or free from rough; *i.e.*, educated, polished) Greek biographer Plutarch, who claimed that geese, fearing an attack by eagles, carried stones in their beaks to maintain silence in flight and a crane assigned to night watch would stand on one foot, holding a stone in the claw of the other, to keep him from falling asleep. Talk of killing two birds with one stone!

Confusion may arise from the fact that one group of words originates from the Greek *pais, paid* (child, boy), while the other derives from Latin, *pes, pedis* (foot). Medicine uses both forms; hence pediatrics deals with children, but podiatry with feet. A synonym, chiropody, has the identical meaning, although the Greek root *chir, cheir*, means hand. Once, before specialization, chiropodists treated both hands and feet. *Podagra*, better known as gout, literally means to trap the feet, which it does in a most painful manner. Back to hands: *chiromancy, palmistry* if you prefer, is divination by looking at a person's hands. *Necromancy*, from *nigro*, black, on the other hand, is black magic, achieving its purpose of divination by communicating with the dead. The Greek root of *chirurgeon*, now a *surgeon* (*chir*, hand, and *ergon*, work) shows us he works with his hands. If someone is at the directly opposite point on the globe of the earth, the soles of his feet facing yours, he is an *antipode* dwelling at the antipodes of the earth. A *podium* or foot base through its plural *podia*, meaning balcony, yielded Old French *puie*, which, with essentially the same meaning, finally gave us our word *pew*.

Latin *ped* (foot) yields pedometer, pedestrian, impede (hinder, literally, with *im* or *in* meaning not, and *pes*, foot; disable or trap the foot), expedite (here you move the foot out instead and get things going), expedient (helps move the foot or any other business along), expeditionary force (gets going, if not always on foot). However, pederasty, again from *paid* (child), is sex with boys as is pedophilia, which contains the Greek roots for child and love. Pedodontics concerns itself with the dental care of children. Peddler comes from Anglo-Saxon *pedde*, a covered basket, which is his main tool. A pedagogue, from Greek *paid* (child) and *agein* (to lead), was a slave who led his young master to his lessons. The rather rare *pedion* is a crystal with a single face, from Greek *pedon*, or flat surface, also a flat oar blade. The latter produced Italian *pedotya*, a helmsman, and eventually our *pilot*, also a guide of sorts, especially on ships.

On a less pedestrian note (here meaning prosaic, unimaginative), the city of Tempe, home of Arizona State University, was named after a valley in Thessaly, through which the Penneus River escapes into the sea. It once was a lovely glen where Apollo purified himself after slaying the Python, a monster serpent living in the caves of Mt. Parnassus. This is also where he chased Daphne, whose metamorphosis earned him the bay-leaf crown. Remember this (without the serpent!) when enjoying Tempe's new Rio Lago restaurant and eating steaks or lobster at Monti's *La Casa Vieja* (The Old House)!

Left Up a Pole

Please forgive the pun, but never allow a Pole at either pole with a pole to confuse you! Depolarize yourself from the first one, which comes from Poland. The second one signifies axis or pivot from Greek *polos*, through French *pole*. The third from Latin *palus* means pole, stake, and, with this meaning, is a so-called doublet of pale. If it is green, thorny, and grows in the desert, it is a paloverde, literally green wood, pole, or tree. The paloverde is any one of three thorny trees or shrubs of the family *Leguminosae*, which grow near the Mexican border in the American Southwest. The Latin *palus* also gave us the expression "beyond the pale." We accuse a person or judge an act to be beyond the pale when either appears uncouth or uncivilized. In the 12th century, when the English first went into Ireland and opened a can of worms that is still squirming today, the region around

A Treasure Trove of Word Origins

Dublin was known as the "pale." English authority was confined to "within the pale." Local kings and clan chiefs considered rough and uncouth governed the rest of Ireland. "Beyond the pale" grew to mean outside the civilized British zone and, by extension, just plain uncivilized and gross. With enough pales, poles, or stakes you can build a palisade.

Related to *palus* was Latin *palatium*, which through the French *palais*, gave us our *palace* with the same meaning. In Rome, *palatium* originally designated dwellings on the Palatine Hill, a choice real estate location by the standards of the period. No lesser luminaries than the first Roman emperor Augustus Caesar and such successors as Tiberius, as well as the debauched fiddler and arsonist Nero, built their palatial homes there. These homes were, of course, fenced off, hence the connection with *palus*. If one of them pierces you, you find yourself "impaled." Attendants of the palace, champions of the prince, legendary heroes, were paladins, especially the twelve peers of Charlemagne, including his nephew, Roland. According to the old French epic poem *The Song of Roland*, he was ambushed and killed at Roncesvalles in the Pyrenees by the Saracens. Actually, he may have been waylaid by a bunch of Basque robbers. But that is hardly epic or heroic.

Pale, pallid, pallor are all from Latin *pallere*, to turn gray. Now, I once told you about Grimm's and Verner's laws, whereby, among other consonant changes, Latin *p* becomes English *f*. Thus *pater* gave us *father* and *pallere* also produced *fallow*, a kind of gray. This brings me to *paleface* and another interesting linguistic subject. The term paleface, allegedly a name given to the white man by American Indians, may actually have been of non-Indian coinage. One of its earliest occurrences was in George A. McCall's *Letters from the Frontiers* (1822): "[At a masquerade ball, a man dressed as] an Indian chief thus accosted him, 'Ah, Paleface! What brings you here?'" Authors like James Fenimore Cooper and Washington Irving also coined many apocryphal Indian expressions, such as "happy hunting grounds" for the afterlife and "heap" for plenty, a lot, as in "fight a great heap." Mark Twain once ridiculed the expression: "Mph! Stove heap gone!"

I have just reviewed for the *Journal of the West* (the illustrated quarterly devoted to Western History and Culture) an extremely interesting and well-researched book by Charles L. Cutler, *O Brave New Words!* The author has written a quite scholarly and yet surprisingly absorbing account of the Native American loan-words in the English language. Cutler does not merely provide us with three lists of loan-words (over 1,000 from the North American Indian north of Mexico, four pages from the Eskimo and Aleut, and finally some 1,500 from Latin American languages). We participate in a historical exploration and witness the thrilling circumstances, and the cultural setting, in which these loan-words entered our American speech. Cutler convincingly shows how the linguistic borrowing process and its rate generally reflect and parallel the nature, quality, and extent of cultural relations between Native Americans and newcomers. In most cases we are given an etymological insight into the image within the words and thereby into how their Indian users perceived their world. More of this in another essay.

Silence Can Be the Cornerstone of Character

How many of us realize that at the time of Columbus (and according to researchers like Charles L. Cutler in *O Brave New Words!*) the Indians in the New World had possibly as many as 2,000 different languages? That is about one-third of the estimated 4,000 languages spoken in the entire world today (and, as noted earlier, some 6,000 dialects — 2,000 alone in the Americas)! The number of Indian languages spoken in North America (north of Mexico) is estimated at 350 to 500. The largest of these language families probably was the Algonquian. This impressive number of tongues made communication among Indians difficult (remember the tower of Babel!), hindered efficient cooperation between tribes, and prevented their uniting successfully against white encroachment. The so-called Plains Indians developed a very sophisticated and effective sign language with complex flowing gestures.

As is the case with any language, for the knowledgeable sensitive student and observer of Indian languages, the latter are a treasure trove (from the French *trésor trouvé*, treasure found) of past culture; in fact, they are fossilized poetry. Indian languages reflect how their speakers perceived the world around them, incorporating into their words the sounds of nature through onomatopoeia and the realities of life through graphically vivid metaphors. Just listen to the neighing sound effect of the Narragansett word for horse, *naynayoûmewot*, or the mimicking quality of the Ojibwa word for chickadee, *jigjigaaneshiinh*. Visualize the evocative power of the Cheyenne designation for nightingale, literally "all night-hollering," or for nut, "crack-with teeth."

Generally, Indians were sparing in their use of language, strongly condemning garrulity. When unsure of effectively communicating their intended meaning, they, much to their credit, opted for silence. Silence preceded important discussions and was even considered sacred. The Sioux defined it as the Great Mystery — patience, endurance, dignity, the very cornerstone of character. What a lesson for today's media, talk-show hosts, and politicians! Still, when the occasion warranted, the Indians could display fiery oratory and moving rhetoric.

To truly appreciate the original beauty of Indian loan-words in the English language, one must be made aware of their precious literal charm. The Algonquian *moose* is derived from a verb meaning "he strips, shaves," referring to the animal's habit of stripping bark and lower branches off trees. *Wampum* was shortened from another Algonquian word meaning white string and referred to strung beads made of shell. *Squaw*, now often considered disparaging, was from the Narragansett *eskwaw*, the Delaware *ochqueu*, and the Chippewa *ikwe*, but applied to the Algonquian, to whom it was not native. It simply meant *woman*.

Stogie, the slender, cylindrical cigar, can be successively traced to an Iroquoian tribe by that name extinct since 1763, to a Pennsylvania town named after them, and to the Conestoga covered wagon first made there and used by pioneers. Then there was a Philadelphia tavern named "Conestoga Waggon," [*sic*] no doubt frequented by those not traveling on it. Eventually, the inexpensive, not cheap, cigar smoked by the drivers of Conestoga wagons was called a stogie. A certain John Smith, soldier and adventurer, introduced the word *roanoke*, a wampum from smoothed

Thyroid	Shaped like a shield, it comes from a Greek word meaning just that.
Tit for Tat	Once "tip for tap," from French *tant pour tant*, or "so much for so much."

shells. *Roanoke*, the geographical designation, is from Virginia Algonquian *rawranoke*, meaning smoothed shells or curved, bent. And *Ugh!* is a grunt of assent.

Indian Words in English

As I prepared to write this essay on words that English has borrowed from American Indian languages, I happened to glance at "The Far Side" calendar with its daily "far-out" joke, and remain stunned by an amazing coincidence. Today's calendar page shows a picture allegedly of the no-longer dashing Lone Ranger in retirement, reading an Indian dictionary and mumbling, "Oh! Here it is, Kemosabe: Apache expression for a horse's rear end. What the hey?"

Seriously, though, some Indian loan-words have found their way into our English language. *Wapiti*, meaning literally white rump and tail in Shawnee, was the name given by the scientist B. S. Barton, around 1806, to the American elk to distinguish it from its European relative. *Sasquatch*, a human-like creature, known by many other names including Bigfoot, standing over eight feet tall, covered with hair, endowed with a fetid odor, was named by the Salish Indians. It has never been captured or distinctly photographed. It is sometimes called the Abominable Snowman or *Yeti*, a corruption of *Yeh Teh*, which in some Himalayan tongues means "man in the rocks." *Yeti* also means hermit in Sanskrit. The German Reinhold Messner, arguably the greatest mountain climber of our time (he scaled all fourteen Himalayan peaks rising above 8,000 meters, mostly without oxygen), tracked the creature for almost two decades in Nepal and Tibet. He is convinced that it is nothing but a large bear viewed distortedly through myth and legend.

One of the gentler, almost romantic Indianisms is *Indian summer*, mentioned by American author and agriculturalist J. Hector St. John Crèvecoeur in 1778 as a "short interval of smoke and mildness" before winter. In Europe it has been called St. Martin's Day, All-hallow summer, or Old Wives summer. In 1832, the *Boston Transcript* wrote that the term was coined because at this time of year Indians break up their village communities to prepare for their winter hunting. Other explanations may be the

Indians warning whites about the short-lived respite before winter or that Indian summer occurs mainly in regions inhabited by Indians.

We owe the Hopi Indians a few loan-words. The *kiva* is an underground room where the Hopi hold religious services and important meetings. The word is derived from Hopi *ki* meaning house and an unidentified suffix. The Kachina Cult highlights Hopi worship. *Kachi* in Hopi means life or spirit and *na* means father. *Kachinas* refer to supernatural beings that visit the Hopis at the beginning of the year, control the weather, and are the intermediaries between gods and people. They also represent the masked spirit-impersonators at religious ceremonies. Kachina dolls portray the Kachinas.

A Navajo loan-word from about 1871 is *hogan* from Navajo *hooghan*. It designates a dwelling made of logs and sticks covered with earth.

Apparently, *Texas* is derived, through Spanish, from a Caddo Indian word meaning friend or allies. After Texas was admitted to the Union in 1845, the name was used to designate certain manmade objects. Mississippi steamboat cabins were labeled after states, and the "Texas" is the structure on a riverboat that contains the pilothouse and officers quarters. We also have the Texas fever tick and Texas bluegrass. In 1628, William Levett in *York and Portland* mentioned words such as *wigwam* or house, from Eastern Abenaki, and *sannup*, a married male Indian. *Tomahawk*, a light ax, is from Virginia Algonquian. *Ugh!*

Research Can Be Overrated

I think most of you will agree that sound science should never exclude any data pertinent to the object of its inquiry, merely because they do not conveniently fit in with a desired outcome of the research in progress. Yet, occasionally, that is how American linguistics appears to proceed in its studies of language. The reason for this may be twofold: first, American linguists often by-pass semantic (dealing with meaning) considerations — that is, they focus more on form and structure than meaning, because the latter varies slightly with each individual and cannot be easily standardized; second (and this is related to the first), much of linguistic research operates with the ulterior motive of finding solutions primarily applicable to computer binary logic (something is either one thing or another) and artificial language rather than human language, which is much more complex with many more nuances of interpretation. An oversimplification, at best!

Take the example of the word *medicine*. Depending on the circumstances or context, it could refer to an art or profession, which, as practiced by some snake-oil hustlers, might appear more like quackery. To an Indian brave, the word might evoke thoughts of magic and the miraculous. We do not really know how each individual brain processes these infinite potential variations in the meanings of words; it depends on training, education, interest in or concern with language, and even talent and artistry. Could a computer program do it? Hardly! John L. Casti, mathematician and chaos/complexity pioneer, author of *The Cambridge Quintet: A Work of Scientific Speculation* (1997), has publicly expressed the opinion that we are a long way from any computer duplicating human thought. If artificial intelligence should eventually be able to "think" (however this is defined), it will most probably have evolved into something of its very own. It will still always be machine, not human, intelligence.

Now, here is a concrete example of why I remain skeptical of the work done by some linguists. Steven A. Pinker, professor of cognitive sciences also working with linguistics at MIT, in 1999 published *Words and Rules: The Ingredients of Language*, an ambitious, if controversial, study purporting to establish how and where the brain stores certain linguistic data. Based on tests administered to English and German speakers, he claims that irregular and regular English and German past verb tenses, which have much in common, are respectively stored in two different parts of memory, some as words, others by the rule of merely adding "*-ed*" to the root or infinitive (in German *ete, eten, este, et* to the verb root). In essence, he reduces to "words and rules" an arguably quite intricate process of interpretative and associative neural firings, impulses, and exchanges occurring in the brain and varying with each speaker as a result of factors enumerated above.

Pinker seems to deny a role to meaning in distinguishing between such pairs as *sang a song/singed her hair, bore fruit/bared her arm, hung a picture/hanged a thief, sold goods/soled shoes, stole money/steeled himself, met friends/meted out justice, knit socks/knitted his brow, abode his turn/abided by the rules, worked days/wrought a masterpiece, lay down/lied like a criminal, put it there/putted a golf ball, flew a plane/flied to left field.* Countless other cases prove that connotative and associative memory guides us through a veritable maze of semantic nuances in zeroing in on verbal subtleties. If you know foreign languages, meaning plays an even greater role: *singe* means *monkey* or to ape in French, and *See* means *ocean* or lake in German. Lest you forget, *Ausfahrt* on the *Autobahn* indicates an exit, nothing indelicate or scatological, as earlier noted. And by the way, *scatological* is from the Greek *skato* (to discard) and *logos* (science). Meaning is essential, a *sine qua non* — literally, without which nothing.

Columnists Affect Each Other

Recently, one of my esteemed fellow columnists trespassed on my linguistic domain, thereby providing me with material for a column. Miffed (origin of this word is unknown; it means offended and is slang, used since about 1935) by a high school valedictorian (from Latin *vale*, farewell, and *dicere*, to say) confusing *effect* and *affect*, he corrected the hapless creature, but not as "effectively" as he might have. Allow me first, however, to deal with the word *trespass* from Old French *trépasser*, from Lower Latin *transpassare*, from *trans* (across) + *passare* (to pass), which itself is from Latin *trans* (across) and *pandere* (past participle, *passus*, to stretch). This word demonstrates how one linguistic seed can sprout a multiplicity of quite different meanings. Essentially signifying to cross an established physical boundary or one of permitted behavior, to *transgress* (this one from Latin *gradire*, *gradus*, step, and mentioned in "The Loom of Language"), *trespass* ranges in meanings from committing offenses of varying seriousness, even sinning, to entering without permission another person's land or domicile.

No need to list the numerous words that sprang from the same root, such as a pass, to pass, passage, make a pass at someone, a mountain pass, etc. Of interest, however, is that in French *trépasser* means to pass across into the next world, to die. Few Spanish speakers probably know that the Spanish word *pasas*, meaning raisins, comes from the same root, because the grapes are stretched out to dry. But back to *effect* and *affect.* Very simply put, *effect*, which can be both noun and verb, from Latin *ex* (out) and *facere* (do, make), is to make something out of something, to bring about, and also the result brought about. *Affect*, from Latin *ad* (to) and *facere* (make, do), is to do something to someone, or something. It too can be a noun. The noun *affect*, with an original, now obsolete, meaning of feeling or emotion, is still used in modern psychology to mean the conscious subjective aspect of an emotion considered apart from bodily changes. Once again, we are on fertile linguistic ground.

Latin *facere*, *factus* (to make, to do, made; in combination with prefixes and suffixes it changes to *ficere*), yields many English words. *Faction*, originally the act of doing, then a group of Roman contractors to prepare circus entertainment, now means a political party or clique. *Factitious* means made by human art, and a *fact* is a done thing. An *artificer*, from *facere* and art, is a skillful craftsman. A *factor* contributes to making things happen: the possible gain was a factor in and affected his decision. A *factotum* (from *totum*, all) is one responsible for many, if not all, tasks. *Fiction* and *fictitious* are from another root, *fingere*, to fashion, shape, hence to feign or simulate. Formed with the Latin prefix *ad-* (against, to), the verb affect means to act on, influence. The meaning of *affection* came from the idea of influencing with feelings, eventually evolving (linguists call it sliding) into solely positive kindly feelings.

The *effect* is the result of an action being carried out, the result of a cause from Latin *ex*, meaning out. The verb *to effect* means to produce, bring about, make something out of something, as in "genes effect changes in humans" and "affect, or influence, bodily characters" or "the Romans effected the unification of Italy and affected its development." The effect of the misuse was to affect my colleague adversely, from Latin *ad* (against), and *vertere*, *versus* (to turn), which "in effect" he did by writing a column against the valedictorian. He became the valedictorian's adversary. There is another verb "affect," from the Latin frequentative *affectare*, to do something many times, to assume as an air or a characteristic, even a false one, hence *affectation*. He affects knowledge he does not possess.

With the prefix *de-*, meaning from, away, we have *defeat*, literally an undoing, and to *defect*, to undo a bond or duty, is to desert your county or abandon a cause. Facile, facility, are something that can be easily done and the ability to make it look easy, respectively. Even the word "affair" has the same root. Faculty comprises various shades of meaning: the power to do, what one can do; a field of knowledge; the individuals, usually teachers, engaged in teaching various fields of knowledge. *Suffice* comes from *sub* (under, in place of), and means, together with *facere*, to place under or provide enough. *Profit*, from *pro* (for) and the same *facere*, is to make or do for one's benefit. *Prefix* is a particle made or put ahead of or before a word, whereas *suffix* one that is placed under or at the end of it. *Benefactor* with *bene* (good) is one that does some good. I trust these explanations will also be beneficial.

Common Sense Is Always Useful

To consider another aspect of language, have you ever thought about how profoundly the emergence of writing and literate activity some 5,000 years ago transformed human life? For the first time, speech could be preserved, hence knowledge developed, accumulated, managed, and used more efficiently. Societies blessed with such an advantage could thereby gain power over cultures based on purely oral traditions. Common sense and our own mature reflection can help us realize the *power of the written word*. It is helpful, however, when an anthropologist and professor of cultural history like Jack Goody from St. Johns College, Cambridge University, in nine essays collected under that title and published by the Smithsonian Institution, explores all the aspects of writing as a transforming technology.

And, indeed, a technology it is, just like agriculture, electronics, and all the other technical advances that fundamentally altered our lives. Changes in the modes of communication are as influential as those in the modes of production. Restricted to speech and an oral tradition, a society is very limited. Memory can only go so far. Our forefathers developed "the art of memory," in some instances to an extraordinary degree, and philosophers like the Italian Giordano Bruno (1548-1600), severe critic of scholasticism and Aristotelianism, burned as a heretic by the Inquisition, even wrote a book with that very title. However, any knowledge not written cannot be preserved verbatim. Anthropological research with African tribes dependent on oral tradition has amply proven this point. Troubadours, minstrels, and, with much more important consequences, those responsible for prescribing and carrying on a cultural heritage with religious rituals and ceremonies, if limited to speech, are unable to guarantee perfect recall. Without writing, record keeping, the telling of time, and the preservation of vital data are seriously compromised.

Written storage and retrieval and its oral counterpart are not the same. The impact of the difference on social groups may have consequences ranging from bad to good. Take canonical texts controlled, preserved, and transmitted by the priesthood. If written, their historicity may be suspect, since they may be altered, with the newly selected text representing the ulterior motive of the selector rather than the teachings of the Master or the interests of the community. Writing does not always insure authenticity. In 1946-1947, when I produced a critical edition of a 17th-century Spanish play using the basic 1632 and 1637 printed texts, I found 499 lines in the first text not in the second, and 206 lines from the latter not in the first, not to mention a thousand or more trivial variants.

A source of power, books are also subject to and victims of power. Greek-born anthropologist Dr. Anastasia Karakasidou did ethnographic research on the northern part of Greece known as Macedonia, bordering on the Republic of Macedonia, which is predominantly Slavic. The Greek government opposes the right of this republic to that name. It denies the existence of Slavic Macedonian minorities in the country and seeks to Hellenize the region linguistically and culturally. Greek extremists threatened the researcher. Thus, when Karakasidou's manuscript was recommended for publication, the senior management of the publishing firm consulted British authorities. Predictions regarding the effect of publication ranged from public criticism to protests, demonstrations, violence, or threats of violence against the author or publishers. Pecuniary damage was also expected to hit the Local Examinations Syndicate, which holds about 800,000 English examinations in Greece every year. The *London Evening Standard*'s headline read: "Cambridge bans new book over terrorism fears." Writing can and does invite censorship!

Even Geniuses Need Rules

Who today worries about faulty diction when using the English language? Not many! There are other more important and pressing factors to consider in our hectic lives. Making money is much more valued than speaking and writing correct English. However, in the good old days, in this instance 1915, the Funk & Wagnalls Company, responsible for the *New Standard Dictionary of the English Language*, published a booklet designed "to aid those who consult it in the correction of many of the faults of speech and writing common among English-speaking people of some, or even considerable, education." Dublin Archbishop Richard Whateley (1787-1863), in the preface to his *Rhetoric*, wrote: "It has been truly observed that genius begins where rules end." But to infer from this that, in any department wherein genius can be displayed, rules must be useless, or useless to those who possess genius, is a rash and regrettable conclusion.

Besides, there is more at stake than rules. Good grammar often guarantees accurate, logical, articulate thought. Following are examples of faults to avoid! "Acoustics" *is* good, not *are* good, as the word is plural in form, but singular in construction. Beware of "admit" and "admit of": this gate *admits* visitors to the grounds, but this vehicle will not *admit of* its passing through. Emerson wrote: "Every action admits of being outdone." "Allude" should not be used in the general sense of to mention. Allude means to refer delicately or incidentally to something. Don't say "the speaker alluded at great length to our foreign policy." You may say: "In his lecture he did not venture *to* do more than allude to Shakespeare."

In correct style, "and" is used to add the action of one verb to that of another. It is wrongly used when, in connection with a following verb, it is substituted for the simple infinitive. "Try *and* do it" should not be used when the meaning is "make an attempt *to* do it." Say: "Try to write the letter yourself!"

Do not use "and" when "or" is required. Say "a language like French or German may be easily learned," because there is no language that is at once French and German.

Say "men of quite another caliber *from* those we saw yesterday," not "*than* those we saw."

There is a shade of difference between "as . . . as" and "so . . . as." In "John is not as tall as James," the speaker regards James as taller than John. In "John is not so tall as James," the speaker suggests something uncommon in the height of James as compared with the stature of John and other men or boys. "So . . . as" is usually used in negative sentences only, something I remember being taught when I had to learn English again in French schools, having left the United States at age five. It may be used in affirmative sentences that carry a negative suggestion: "So good a cook as Polly is hard to find" — that is, "It is not easy to find so good a cook as Polly."

Comparisons can be very tricky. The object designated by the superlative must be included in the class of things compared. Don't say: "Of all others he was the greatest." Omit "others"! Say: "He was the greatest of all." However, in "the molting season is vital for both birds and bipeds" you must add "other bipeds," lest you imply that birds are not bipeds.

"Rather" is superfluous with adjectives ending in *-ish*, like warmish, coldish, implying rather. We may say "rather foolish," because here *-ish* expresses quality, not degree. And there was a time when, except in Southern and Western states, only cattle were raised, but human beings were brought up or reared (see Introduction, p. xiv).

Historical and Unusual Word Sources

To the best of our knowledge, in contrast to animal language, human language is infinitely flexible and creative. Man can talk about anything, as politicians have amply proven to us by now. He is, therefore, most probably the only animal capable of lying. I always wonder, as I listen to speeches given by presidential candidates at their respective national conventions, how the speakers reconcile their minds to the gulf — nay abyss — that may separate the words uttered by them, and purporting to express their innermost and sincerest thoughts, from the actual belief patterns stored in their brain. Dare I mention the present debate about Iraq and Weapons of Mass Destruction? One would expect some physical damage to result, some breakage due to stress, as when one forces two incompatible objects, which are not intended for each other, to fit together. Yet the politicians in question move on unscathed. It is called *resilience*, from the Latin *re* (again) and *silire* (spring, another form of *saltare*), hence to rebound.

However, a good and productive side is also evident in this miraculous interplay between brain and language. To it we owe the wealth of shades of meaning of which languages are capable and the fertile inventiveness with which languages can alter, refine, and hone the current meaning of words to satisfy the need for new ones and forge them into perfected tools of communication. These may result not quite synonymous, but endowed, with added semantic nuances in order to express new concepts born in the human mind to reflect ever-diversified real life experiences.

I have previously mentioned that in 1066, after the Battle of Hastings, when the Normans invaded England and brought with them Norman French, the latter was added to the existing Anglo-Saxon tongue, and English resulted, with both languages eventually fused into one. Thus we have a great number of words coming from the Germanic Anglo-Saxon or the Romance (from Latin) French that overlap in meaning. In such cases it was natural and useful to have such words of almost the same meanings acquire differentiated ones, which usually mirrored the respective realities

Rile	A form of *roil,* to make turbid; may be related to French *rouille* (rust) or even *brouiller* (mix, confuse, jumble).
Sawbuck/Sawhorse	From Dutch *zaagbok* (the wooden frame used for sawing); German *sägen* (to saw).

and interests of the two disparate social classes that used them. By the way, *disparate*, from Latin *dis* (apart) and *parare* (to make ready), together mean to separate, make distinct. Thus, stool from German *Stuhl* was the object used by serfs, whereas *chair* from French *chaise*, which had a back, was what nobles sat on. Animals served as meals were designated by French terms — veal, pork, beef — but when cavorting in a courtyard they had Germanic names like calf (*Kalb*), swine (*Schwein*), or steer (*Stier*).

The differences between current English words coming from Anglo-Saxon and those of French origin can be quite subtle. *Thin* from German *dünn* is applied to physical people or objects, whereas its French counterpart, *maigre*, gave us *meager* of more lofty a style and used in a more abstract sense. *Fat* from German *fett* and *gross* from French *gros*, meaning fat or thick, present us with a similar case. Thousands more of such pairs can be found (*sight* from German *Sicht* and *view* from French *vue*), giving English possibly the largest vocabulary of any language, as it contains two tongues.

In some instances, especially in advertisements, the hidden meaning of words is so subtle as to escape the public. The Edison Mazda light bulb dates from *circa* 1912, providing 50 watts at 115 volts. The Edison Mazda "Frost Top" lamp, operated at 60 watts and 120 volts, was patented in 1904. Then there is the Mazda automobile. Why the name? Men were so delighted with the improvement in lighting that they named it after Ahura Mazda, Zoroastrian deity, believed to be the source of all good according to the Avesta, the sacred book of the Zoroastrians and Parsees. The car makers followed suit. Now you know the *rest* of the story.

Modern Terms for Ancient Roots

Most of us are concerned with the physical aspects of our body. Let us look at the linguistic ones. The Sanskrit root of "to bind" is *bhandh* and of "body" (Anglo-Saxon *bodig*) *bandha*, because the body was deemed to bind, fetter, confine the soul. The suffix *-ig* being a diminutive, the original sense was thus "little bond." Now *bodkin*, the slender instrument for making holes, needs two explanations. From the Welsh, it meant a dagger. This explains Hamlet's observation, ". . . When he himself might his quietus make/With a bare bodkin . . ." (3.1). In the phrase "Odd's bodikins/Od's bodkins" it stands (euphemistically — you know, don't use the Lord's name in vain) for God's bodikins or God's little body. In England it is still used adverbially and metaphorically to designate a thin person in such phrases as "sitting bodkin on the crowded train" and "too fat to ride bodkin between two friends."

Parts of the body are usually named after their shape or function. This is obvious with eardrums and canals. The temple, however, has nothing to do with the building, but comes from Latin *tempus*, which gives us all our words related to time, temporal, temporary, etc. The time of the body can be taken by the pulse of the temple. *Tempus* also means season and the temple is also the seasonable spot to hit one's enemy. Temple as a place of worship, on the other hand, refers to the arch-shaped section of the sky, which an augur, a member of the highest class of official diviners in ancient Rome, would partition off with his hand to observe and "contemplate" (note the *tempus* inside the word) for omens, good or ill. Remember, if the omen, birds, or whatever came from the left (the Latin word for *left* is *sinister)*, it was bad. Hence our meaning for sinister. The word *temple* is *cognate* with tend (tendency, contend) meaning to stretch. Even *tennis* may come from Old French *tenies*, the stretched strings, now net, over which the ball is played. I say may, because it may well also originate with the French "*tenez!*" (Take!), a sportsmanlike warning called out by the server.

Pylorus, the opening from the stomach into the intestine, is from a Greek word meaning gatekeeper, from *pyle* (gate) and *ouros* (watcher). The star-cluster *Arcturus*, related to Arctic, has the same origin, from *arktos* (bear) and *ouros* (watcher), meaning literally the "bear guard." *Intestine* simply means the insides, from Latin *intus*. Artery comes from the Greek word *arteria*, meaning windpipe. The Greeks thought that when a person was dead, there was no blood in the arteries and that the arteries thus contained air.

Belly comes from Germanic words meaning bag or bellows (*Balg* in German is paunch; *Bälge, Balgen,* means bellows). Remember Shakespeare's "fair round belly with good capon lined." *Bowel* comes from the Latin *botulus* (sausage), because the latter was often encased in bowel lining — another case where the chicken came before the egg, as it existed before it was used to make sausage.

The *clavicle* or collarbone, which "locks the chest," comes from Latin *clavis* (key), and *claudere* (past participle *clausus*, to close). Words related to close all have the same root: enclose, cloister, claustrophobia (or fear of being enclosed), seclude (to close yourself somewhere), preclude (to close or shut before). *Duodenum*, meaning twelve in Latin, is so named for its length of twelve times the breadth of a finger. *Elbow* comes from Anglo-Saxon *el*, the length of an arm (German *Elle*, yard) and *bow*. *Finger* is from Germanic words meaning to seize or catch (German *fangen*). *Jaws* is from the French *joe*, and subsequent *joue*, and may come from Pre-Latin *gaba, gabota*, from which comes the French *gaver*, to force-feed. Chew comes from Anglo-Saxon *céowan*, German *kauen*. We also find the *k* sound in German *Kiefer* or jaw, and our *jowl* comes from there. *Joue* may also have played a part in jowl. The *jugular* is from Latin *iugum* (yoke), as it yokes the body and head. *Lungs* are so named because of their light weight (Gothic *leihts*, light), and the lungs of a slaughtered animal are still called lights — not a light note to close on.

Math and Poetry — a Good Mix

Psychologist and philosopher William James wrote in his *Collected Essays and Reviews* (1892): "The union of the mathematician with the poet, fervor with measure, passion with correctness, this surely is the ideal." Before him, the Roman poet Horace, who had studied under Rome's best grammarians as well as at the University of Athens, polished his poems over and over again, advising in his *Art of Poetry*: "*Saepe stilum vertas*," which literally means "often turn the stylus," to make erasures with the blunt end on the waxen tablets — or, in other words, correct freely, if you wish to write well.

I know that grammar has been a subject often avoided in most American schools, except perhaps in a few foreign-language classes, where it might be taught with misgivings about its usefulness. I now observe, both on TV and in newspapers, mistakes that are just as disturbing to a lover of language as a shrill note to an orchestra leader. Recently I heard a lawyer on TV's *The Practice* say, "I have went." My reaction: "His English was gone!"

No situation in English speech and writing causes more difficulty for more persons than choosing between "I" and "me," "who" and "whom," "whoever" and "whomever." Evidently the distinction between these forms is breaking down for two possible reasons. First, speakers do not have the basic concepts of grammar, which would allow them to determine whether the words play the role of the subject or the object of either the verb or preposition in the sentence. Second, some speakers, afraid of mistakes, unerringly pick the stilted-sounding wrong one.

After any preposition such as *between, to, for*, one has to use the object form "me." Say "between you and me (not I)," "for him and me (not I)," etc. In a piece about the disastrous 2000 presidential election count in Florida I read recently, "The winner will be whomever secures enough legal rulings. . . ." The choice is simple: find out what role "whoever" plays in the sentence. Here "whoever" is both the predicate of the winner and the subject of "secures." Think: "The winner is he (not him!) who. . . ." The second mistake in the same article was a little trickier: "Pity whomever ends up occupying the White House. . . ." It looks as though "whomever" [*sic*] is the object of pity, whereas it really is the subject of whoever is elected. Check the sentence by either omitting "pity" or inserting "him." The real meaning is "Pity him, whoever is elected." See, it isn't all that difficult.

Here are some further examples. "The question of who voted in Florida is important." Who is the subject of voted, although the entire clause "who voted in Florida" is the object of the preposition of. "This is the man whom we elected." (Here whom is the object of elected). "He asked me who I thought would be elected." (The case of the pronoun depends upon its function in the sentence; don't be influenced by words that come between it and its antecedent. Get rid of "I thought" and you find who the subject of "is elected"). "I voted for the man whom everyone suspected the secretary of state had chosen." (Forget "everyone suspected"; whom is the object of had chosen.) You can always substitute *he* or *him* to check yourself. "Who/whom are you voting for?" You are voting for him, so use whom. "This is the kind of president who/whom we need." We need him, so use whom. If you wish to play the odds, use the following "Las Vegas" rule (just kidding!): Unless you are reasonably certain that whom/whomever is required, use who/whoever. Jimmy the Greek says you'll be right more than half of the time. Would that the rules for voting were as simple as that!

Don't Ever Lose *Hoffen*

Henry David Thoreau stated: "The mass of men lead lives of quiet desperation. What is called resignation is confirmed desperation." Now, I do not know whether by "men" Thoreau meant members of the human race or males, and I shall not belabor the point. Far be it from me to exclude my female readers, if, feeling discriminated against, they wish to join the melee and be included in this pessimistic assessment. What is interesting from a semantic viewpoint is the subtle difference in meaning between despair and desperation.

Despair is the utter loss of hope, from Latin *de* (away from) and *spes* (hope) and the verb *sperare* (to hope). *Desperation* is not despair itself, but the state of being desperate. These subtle distinctions, of which our human brain is capable, cannot always find adequate expression with all nouns in the vocabulary of every language. The suffix *-ation*, which manages the trick in this instance (it can also be *-ness*, as in preparedness, hopelessness), is not available in all cases. I remember, during the Soviet Regime, the Russians had two words for "consciousness," one ending with such an equivalent Slavic noun suffix, in this case *-ost*, similar to our *-ation*. The Soviet authorities used it for propaganda purposes. When added to the Russian word for consciousness it designated "the presence in Soviet citizens of a consciousness inspired by and convinced of the truth of Soviet policy." The persistent use of this word almost had a subliminal effect, reminding the people to cultivate such awareness and act accordingly. English offers no exact equivalent.

The fact that *spes* (hope) has come into our language only in a negative form causes one to further ponder Thoreau's negative outlook. May we add, however, that the Germanic root *hoffen* (to hope) did produce the positive English word "hope." So, please do not lose hope. Should you lose it anyway and think of "forlorn hope," we are dealing with something else. This is from the Dutch *verloren hoop* (in German *verlorener Haufen*), by way of folk etymology, literally a military term for a lost band, actually a body of men, often volunteers, selected to perform a perilous task such as attempting a breach or scaling a wall in advance of the main force. Moral: don't volunteer!

Speaking of body, here are some more origins for body parts. *Nail*, Anglo-Saxon *naegel*, German *Nagel*, is related to the verb *nag*, which is to scratch, as with a nail, but verbally. It is also related to gnaw, as on a bone. *Stomach* is from the French *estomac*, of course, since this nation practices the cult of satisfying it. The word also has the meaning of appetite and, hence, the seat of feelings, the capacity to withstand a challenge to such feelings. You may need a strong stomach to stomach this column. The Greek root *stoma* (mouth) is quite productive, as in stomatology, the branch of medicine concerned with diseases of the mouth.

Thyroid, shaped like a "shield," comes from a Greek word meaning just that. The word tonsils is from Latin *tonsilla*, a pointed stake. The *uvula*, the pendent fleshy lobe on the soft palate, is from *uva* (grape), which it resembles. The *vertebrae*, from Latin *vertere* (to turn), are the turners in the spinal column. This root is found in advertise, to turn attention to, avert, to turn away, and even versus (vs.), turned against. Wrist and to wrest contain the same root (wrist, literally turner, from Anglo-Saxon; wrest, to turn). Once there was a hand-wrist and a foot-wrist, the latter replaced by *ankle*, from Sanskrit *anga* (limb) and Germanic *Angel* (fishing rod or fishing-hook). Ankle, in German, is now "foot knuckle."

Language Games

The great German naturalist Baron Alexander von Humboldt (1769-1859) wrote: "Whenever someone takes a journey, he has something to talk about." I recently drove a rented golden Renault 3,516 miles from Paris to Budapest and back, through France, Germany, Austria, a part of Slovakia, and Hungary, and could talk for days about some of my adventures. However, an article in a Viennese literary newspaper caught my special attention, as it told about children intent on inventing a new language, a topic pertinent to this column. The article dealt with "linguistic handicraft" engaged in by a young "foppish art duo." The two performers enthralled large audiences of young children, encouraging their participation in language games where new words were created with exuberant youthful enthusiasm (in no way as harmful as the past "irrational exuberance" exhibited by many of us in the stock market). I first dismissed this news item as childish gobbledygook, similar to such silly language games as Pig Latin played for fun or to invent a secret esoteric code; but, on second thought, I felt the piece might offer some slight insight on aspects of the origin and nature of language.

For ten months, the duo of Evelyn Blumenau and Walter Kreuz crisscrossed Vienna with their "rolling dictionary." A movable electrical prop, modeled after computer games, with a perforated board, blinking lights and buttons, allowing input from the audience, was erected and acted as a translation aid. Kids in the audience could thus add to the ever-growing vocabulary of this artificial language; more than 700 had already made use thereof. It all started when Blumenau and Kreuz observed, or rather overheard, in the parks of Vienna, children conversing freely in a mixture of languages, consisting of German, Turkish, Serbian, Rumanian, English, and many others. Speakers, without missing a beat, often jumped from one language to another in the same sentence. A veritable Tower of Babel resurrected as a children's Babel workshop in the 21st century! However, here, the metaphor Babel no longer stands for a negative confusion of tongues, but acquires a positive, constructive connotation as a creative children's art form.

A sample dialogue might have sounded like this: "*Tagot / tagot / ingi! / waigu kaucuk? / gubi! waigu bibib? / spokl morgu? / miii.*" In some cases there even were strange written signs or phonetic symbols. Translated, we have: "Good day. Good day. I am hungry! What do you want to eat? A luscious pizza! What do you want to drink? Sprite! Is it good? Mmm, yea man!" One of the events to be offered by the language workshop was at the Children's Animation Tent as part of the Vienna Castle festivities, with the slogan "Out of Babel."

Like so many other cities in the world, and as a result of unprecedented immigration, Vienna has been invaded by numerous foreign tongues, which furnish the roots for this New Language. Childish fantasy, fertile imagination, and a youthful propensity for engaging in word games, were other contributing factors. The process, at times, could be wild and tumultuous. One of the creative linguists, ebullient seven-year-old Clio, illustrated the phenomenon of language creation. She was fond of pizza with mushrooms, and after Walter Kreuz had pointed out to her that the dish already had the name *rundibano*, she often used it as a springboard for a torrent of irrational changes. Young Clio, motivated to by-pass adult logic and perhaps also historical linguistic evolution, clipping and altering the word in a crescendo of ever-accelerated speech, romped into a sequence evolving to *Lundi, rundi, rumpano, runzano, lumpano*. Clio eventually culminated with *gubi*. In her mind, the *gu* represented a derivation from the second syllable of the Italian *funghi* (*fungo*, fungus or mushroom) and *bi* in Clio's active mind, the feminine form of the first syllable of *pizza*. The "neo-Babylon" dictionary comprised some 400 words derived from a couple of dozen existing languages, as well as some man-made. Future events were to also feature poems and songs performed in the new tongue.

Could this reflect what primeval men did when they used their natural speech organs to utter the first human attempts at vocal communication? Anyway, it beats doing drugs and misusing guns!

The Meaning of Meaning

What is meaning? What does *to mean* really mean? We are reminded of a similarly puzzling thought. A tree crashes in the forest. No one is there to hear it. Can we establish that a noise was present? Likewise, does meaning exist without cognition thereof on someone's part? Don't even think of putting the question to philosophers, for they will overwhelm and possibly confuse you and themselves with a succession of complex statements, each refining the idea that you cannot know what something means unless you know what you would experience if it were true. See, I warned you!

In any event, meaning is always conditioned by human *interpretation*, and the very roots of this word, *inter* (between) and *pretium* (value or price), point to a progressive and highly subjective, hence not always predictable, evaluation process, whether between two communicating individuals or an individual and an object as the source of potential sense. In very broad terms it might be stated that meaning occurs when an impulse corresponds and bonds with someone's cognitive faculties, eliciting a response or reaction from them and, one might even hypothesize, leaving behind an engram or memory trace, *i.e.*, a protoplasmic change in neural tissue. I apologize! As Goethe wrote in his *Faust*:

> All theory, dear friend, is but a lifeless gray;
> life's golden tree alone sparkles in green array!

Turning to more solid ground, let us look at the origin of the homonyms (same word, but denoting different things) of *mean*. *Demean* and *demeanor*, referring to behavior, are from the French *de* (from) and *mener* (lead), originally from Latin *minari* (to threaten). The idea must have been that people when threatened behave as you want them to. The word was first used in connection with driving cattle. *Amenable*, with the prefix *ad* (to), means easily led. *Amenity*, however, has a different root. From the Latin, through the French *amenité*, it means calm, pleasantness, and contains the roots *a* (away from), *moenia* (walls, ramparts), *i.e.*, not threatened, as well as *amare* (to love).

Another homonym, *mean*, denoting medium, of medium value, mediocre, is a doublet of median, from the Latin *medius*, middle. However, *mean* denoting common, base, is from Germanic and Old English origin *gemaene* (German *gemein*) and related to the word community (German *Gemeinde*). This root produced the verb "to demean," here not to conduct one's self, but to lower in status or character. *Demesne*, the last syllable pronounced like main, an estate or legal possession, is a doublet of domain. In some future essay I shall return to this word, originally from *domus* or house, related to a large group of words like *Dominus* or master of the house and Heavenly Lord, dominate, domestic, and many more. *Dominus vobiscum* means "the Lord be with you."

Our first-mentioned verb, *to mean*, *i.e.*, to have meaning, is related to Latin *mens*, mind, and such words as mental, mentality. I challenge anyone interested in language to define mind, the counterpart of which cannot even be found in some other languages. In French and German it is *esprit* and *Geist*, respectively, which also denote ghost or wit. Food for thought is also the fact that *to mean* is related to the German *Minne* (love), hence the medieval *minnesingers*, singers of love songs known as *Minnelieder*

Delerium	From Latin *de* (off) and *lira* (furrow) — originally designated a farmer staggering over his field, unable to plow a straight line; now, "off his track," slightly crazy!
Depend	From Latin, through French, literally means "to hang from" (*de*, from; *pendere*, hang).

that, if clever and seductive enough, may have driven the ladies out of their minds. From here it is but a short step to memory, mnemonic (that which assists memory, like a mnemonic device), and even amnesty, which, from the Greek, means literally not to remember, in this case the deeds of guilty individuals. For this, those forgiven should be grateful; for amnesia, loss of memory, they need not be, if you know what I mean.

Chad Anyone?

> I think we should be very sad
> that this election proved so bad.
> But there is reason to be glad
> as we did learn a new word: "chad."

Possibly originating from Scottish, where it means gravel, a *chad* can wreak as much havoc with elections as gravel inside a shoe. The U.S. presidential election exhibited the stuff that legends are made of. Not surprisingly, election, legend, select, even legible and eligible, all boast the same linguistic source: Latin *legere*, past participle *lectus*, to choose, pick. Now, if you are able to pick the proper letters, you should be able to read, which produces the derivative meaning of *legere*, namely to read. What is legible, including ballots, is what can be picked out and made sense of. Elected and eligible, with the prefix *ex-*, often shortened to *e-*, meaning out of, signify what has been or may be chosen, respectively. The Latin gerundive ending in *-end* expresses obligation; thus legend is what must be read. Legends first referred exclusively to a saint's life, a must reading for a Christian. but the meaning was later expanded to include any story worth reading.

A legion was a group of men chosen for military purpose. A legation and legates are also selected. In this last word the prefix *sed-* or *se-* means "apart," in other words to choose by separating. What is chosen by a people tends to become imposed, hence "legal," again from the same root. Loyal is a doublet (one of two words derived from the same source) of legal, meaning faithful to the lawful authority or to the sovereign. The prefix *cum-* indicates together, and *collect*, from *cum* + *legere*, means to choose and assemble together. If you can choose (Latin, *legere*) wisely and discriminatingly from or between (Latin, *inter*) several options or things, such as electoral ballots, you display "intelligence" and might even be an intellectual. An elegant person is capable of picking out the right clothes. The prefix *dis-*, *dys-* means apart and sometimes among. Therefore, diligent, from Latin *diligere*, shifted in meaning from choosing among and, of course, delighting in your choice, to being constant and persevering in your application of choosing among and of accomplishing a task. Legumes are the vegetables most easily and frequently picked: those that grow in pods. Dyslectic and dyslexia, from the same roots, indicate an inability to read.

Would you believe *vote* and *vow* are doublets? When the ancients devoted themselves or an offering to a god, they made a vow. From the Latin *de* (from, away) and *vovere, votum* (to vow), French *voeu* (a vow), *vouer* (to vow), to devote (French *dévouer*) means to give from yourself and offer to someone else. In linguistics, aphesis is the loss at the beginning of a word of the unaccented vowel. Thus vow is aphetic for avow, which is the doublet of avouch, which in turn has the aphetic form vouch. Wow! Hang in there, readers! These are also linked to advocate, literally "to call for or on behalf of." Remember the devil's advocate or lawyer. To vote meant successively a solemn pledge, an ardent wish, later a formal manner in making one's wish or intention known. A tough job in 2000 in Florida!

The suffix *-cracy*, from a Greek word meaning power or rule, is added to *demo* meaning people, *aristo* meaning the best, *pluto* meaning wealth, *bureau* meaning officials supposedly working at a desk, to designate different types of government. *Bureau*, interestingly enough, is from a French word *bure* designating a coarse reddish-brown woolen cloth with which early desks were covered. The expression "red tape" came from England, where, for centuries, official documents were endlessly tied and untied by bureaucrats with such tape, causing frustrating delays.

Before closing, let us again pay poetic homage to the 2000 election situation in Florida.

> Floridians are a cautious lot:
> they say "it is!" but mean: "it's not!"
> Democracy, they will insist
> means laws you don't like to resist.
> In fact, the meaning of true grit,
> is bend the rules until they fit.
> Thus when for presidents they vote,
> first, what elsewhere was done they note.
> Then, with twenty-twenty hindsight,
> they change their vote until it's right.
> If you don't like this brouhaha,
> well! Welcome to America!

Different Languages, Different Rules

Since Aristotle, there has been no serious disagreement that language is a system relating sound and meaning. It is also useful here to recall Austrian philosopher Ludwig Wittgenstein's famous analogy between using language and playing games. In either case we find various sets of rules or conventions, and these determine what moves are permissible or impermissible, successful or doomed to fail. Each set of rules identifies a distinct game or language, and any given move or linguistic idiosyncrasy can be judged only according to the rules of the game or of the particular language under consideration. Focusing on specific words, their origin, the way in which their usage and meaning evolved over time, can cast a great deal of light on how the human brain processes, alters, refines, and plays with such original meaning by applying to these words various associations and connotations — or viewing them from different perspectives. This is understandable, since most words represent persons, objects, or situations that may be perceived under different aspects or from different angles.

To illustrate, we may liken language to a loom, where multicolored threads crisscross each other to weave a pattern. In lieu of threads, think in terms of words with different ancestors, whose ghosts, with uncertain, vacillating semantic shades or nuances, keep surging from the past and crowding into their semantic design. This may result, at times, in meanings that appear confused or even contradictory. A good example thereof is the word *liege*, which can trace its dual ancestry to (or at least be associated with) both Latin *ligare*, meaning to hold or bind, and Old High German *ledig*, meaning free, now in Modern German also meaning single, unmarried. As our brain deals with this word and its derivatives, it is constantly jostled by the entangled, yet related, meanings that keep surfacing, and we have the illusion of wandering and groping about in a semantic maze.

The above-mentioned *ligare*, to bind, has given us the League of Nations, ligament, ligature (thread or wire used to tie a blood vessel), ligation (the surgical process of doing so), *legato* (in music bound together, smooth, connected). Latin *alligare*, with the prefix *ad-* shortened to *a-*, meaning to, produces alloy, a binding of two metals, as well as ally and alliance. Lower Latin *allegare* is more complex. It once even meant to free a slave by "alleging" or citing under oath good reasons for such action. Here, in the minds of speakers, allege was contaminated by the Latin *legare* (to read, name, cite) and the French *alegier* (to acquit, *i.e.*, break a binding). The French *alegier*, containing the root *leger* meaning light, conjures up the idea of alleviating, even allaying, the slave's status.

With *liege* the trouble really begins, depending on which ancestor's ghost (be it *ligare* or *ledig*) favors us with its presence. From the French *lige*, it designates a vassal or liegeman, who renders homage to his liege lord, thereby obligating himself to render faithful service to the latter. Oblige and obligate display the same root implying binding. Thus in one word all these meanings (at times almost conflicting) come to mind. A liege lord is a free lord chosen freely by his vassals, who nevertheless are obligated to him, pledged to serve him faithfully, owe him allegiance, but, in turn, are free from other servitude. To complicate matters even more, the source of liege, *ledig* (free), is linked to old Anglo-Saxon *lidan*, to depart, travel freely anywhere one pleases. To push my liege readers to the edge, I end my column with *liege poustie*, the state of good health required under Scottish law to the exercise of full legal power, especially in the transfer of property. There is no legerdemain (literally light of hand) — sleight of hand or trickery — here, I promise!

Testing the Boundaries of Language

Let us test the boundaries of language, but first set the stage for the experiment. What do truth, tree, and Druid have in common? Linguistic genealogy, of course! Considering that English is of Germanic and Anglo-Saxon origin, with the addition of Norman French after 1066, we can expect to find in its vocabulary cognates of the German and French words for *tree*. German *Baum* meaning tree, shows up in our ship's boom, the name of various spars or poles used on sailing ships, and in beam. From the Latin, French *arbre*, meaning tree, surfaces in arbor and arboretum. And there is a third root for English tree: an Indo-European ancestor *dreu* (tree), hence Old English *treowe*, the latter meaning tree and true, not to mention Old Irish *daur* and Welsh *derwen*, both meaning oak tree. Surprisingly, even Russian *derevo*, tree or wood, is recognizable as a cognate.

The meanings of "true" encompass "not false, genuine (in New York speech the latter often rhymes with wine), in strict alignment, faithful, and loyal." By extension it means in strict alignment with a given statement. Such meanings were inspired by the idea of something being "straight like a tree." The Germans used this root, not their word for tree, *Baum*, to form the term *treu*, true in the sense of loyal, faithful. If you take Indo-European *dreu* (tree) and add the suffix *-wid,* meaning to see, know, understand, you get *dreuwid*, modern Druid, one who knows about trees, also a Gaulish word. Remember, the Gauls, ancestors of the French, like the early Teutons, were druidical tree worshipers and associated "true" and "tree" in their religious beliefs.

Now, using the word *truth* as an example, allow me to confront you with a serious problem inherent in language. As long as we keep things simple, they run smoothly. We perceive an object with our senses in the world around us and wish to communicate it by means of vocal or phonic signs, to which linguists assign the fancy name of signifier. Linguists call the semantic value or meaning of the signifier, to add further confusion, a *signifié, significatum,* or that which is signified. Now, if the perceived object is real, like a lion about to devour you, or an apple on a tree, the words representing them are clear, meaningful, and true. Furthermore, if you ask your mother-in-law whether she likes you and she replies "No!" her answer may qualify as truth.

However, if you lose yourself in perplexing mental quagmires, if forsaking all logic, or, as Ludwig Wittgenstein might put it, bewitched by language, you elucubrate (from Latin *e*, *ex*, out of; and *lux*, light), *i.e.*, concoct by lamplight, through sleepless nights, nonsensical verbal divagations, you might end up, as an acquaintance of mine, with a lecture title such as "Absolute Truth." True or truth must refer to something that can be evaluated, compared to a standard. Absolute, from Latin *ab*, away from, and *solvere*, to loosen, means free from any ties. Absolute truth thus stands by itself, referring to nothing in real life. It is an abstraction, distorted beyond any recognizable tie to our universe, meaninglessly hypothetical. At least "absolute zero," albeit hypothetical, is defined as a temperature characterized by complete absence of heat, approximately -459.67°F. A term like "absolute truth" represents a withdrawal of mind from sensible nature, an incarceration of language within the human skull, where it can no longer reflect what is perceived, but, as if confined in a hall of mirrors, reflects its own mental vagaries.

Gloom, Doom, and Fear

Bertrand Russell, in his *An Outline of Intellectual Rubbish* (1950), wrote: "Fear is the main source of superstition, and one of the main sources of cruelty. To conquer fear is the beginning of wisdom." He might have added that it is also the source of many semantic shifts, as perfectly neutral words, implying neither good nor bad, tend to evolve and assume pessimistic or negative shadings with expectations of the worst. Etymological evidence, indeed, proves that the folk mind, obviously motivated by fear, instinctively associates most pronouncements from higher authority, whether divine or human, with dread and evil. What is your first thought when opening a letter from the IRS? Is it a refund, or a penalty? I give you odds that penalty comes first to your mind.

Thus *omen*, originally merely meaning a sign of heaven, has, together with ominous, crossed into the realm of bad news. Similarly, *portent* and *portentous* have shifted from neutral to negative connotations. Even *foreboding*, now a dark foreseeing, once just meant advance news, from Old English *fore* (earlier) and *boda* (messenger), German *Bote*. *On the carpet*, perhaps referring to the rough cloth that used to cover desks, formerly meant under review with an as yet undecided outcome. Now, when we are in that position, we immediately view ourselves in deep trouble. *Doomsday*, once spelled domesday, is another example worthy of attention.

The Sanskrit root *dha* (Greek *thernis*) of doom or dome, related to the verb *do* (German *tun*), meant to set or place, and Old English *dom* was a judgment. Doom, a law set by custom or judicial interpretation, was synonymous with fate, something set up beforehand. The Old English Domesday Book was the "book of a preset day." Originally, the word was neutral. After all, even doomsday, for a few virtuous souls, could turn out rather well. This old Teutonic root *"do"* once had an ending *-moz*, eventually shortened to *m*. When used as a suffix with nouns, it added a meaning of office, realm, or character, as exemplified in such words as officialdom (officials as a class or as a body), kingdom, dukedom, earldom, wisdom, martyrdom, and the now archaic holidom. The identical process occurred in German, where equivalents of such words end in *-tum*.

All might have been linguistically peaceful in "doomdom," if another dome with a different root had not been doomed to crash the party and muddle the waters. From the Greek word *dema*, housetop, whence Latin *domus*, house, another productive vein mingled with the one described above. First the word referred mostly to *domus Dei*, the house of the Lord, the most striking feature of which was called the dome. From there sprang many other words: *dominus* or master of the house, originally the Lord, then any head of household. Domain was the realm of the master. Even the Spanish title of respect, *Don*, as well as *Dom*, the latter used before the name of Benedictine or other monks, share the same origin. Another *dom*, a member of a Hindu caste of untouchables similar to gypsies, originates from the Sanskrit *doma*, man of a low caste of musicians, and is not related. Social bias has been with us forever in both word and deed!

Derived, of course, are domestic, domesticate, and domicile, all relating to house and home, as well as dominant, dominate, domineer, dominion, and dominical (dominical letter or supper), relating to a master or the Lord. The Scottish *dominic* is a teacher. Would you believe that the idea of a dominating tower gave us, through the French *donjon*, our *dungeon*, at first meaning the vault of the tower? *Domino* in turn referred to a hooded cloak worn by cathedral canons and members of religious sisterhoods, masks worn at masquerades, and, finally, because the winner shouted "Domino!" or Lord and Master, to the well-known game.

For *What* Do the Bells Toll?

As we ring in the New Year and ring out the old, join me in taking a closer look at tolling bells to discover what they might tell us about a vital element of language — meaning — often neglected, if not ignored, by contemporary linguists. The word *bell* (Aryan root *BHAL*) probably comes from an Old English word *bellan*, signifying to bellow or roar. It is related to the verb *bawl* and the German *bellen*, to bark. A bull originally was a "bellower." From bell spring such expressions as "sound as a bell," *i.e.*, in perfect working order or vibrant health; "with bells on"; and, of more interest to our present purpose, "that rings a bell." Pronounced with some hesitation of voice, the latter means one is trying to arouse a responsive chord in one's memory, a chord that cannot be quite clearly identified. Intoned with conviction — "*That* rings a bell!" — it does elicit a familiar chord.

What is this strange quality of sounds, not just those emitted by bells, but also those resonating in words and language, that enables them to evoke meaning and memories? The French poet Baudelaire (1821-1867) paid a melancholic homage to their power in his sonnet "The Cracked Bell." Here is my version, although I transformed it from the Italianate style to Shakespearean:

> It is bitter and sweet, in the winter at night,
> near the flickering fire and rising smoke to hark
> the distant memories slowly rise clear and bright,
> as carillons are heard singing out in the dark.
> How fortunate the bell with a voice strong and spry
> that despite its old age, alert, well and intent,
> now faithfully casts forth its pious timely cry,
> just like some old soldier awake under his tent.
> My own soul now is cracked: and in its deep despair,
> its weakened voice oft may like a thick rattle sound,
> as it tries with its songs to fill night's frosty air,
> like some wounded soldier left behind on the ground,
> who by a lake of blood, under a heap of slain,
> dies now without moving, all his efforts in vain.

Dealing with words, we focus here mainly on the wealth of meanings and associated memories they may inspire in our minds. Transcending language, any impulse sent to the brain by one of our five senses — hearing, sight, touch, taste, smell — can summon up remembrance of "things past," pregnant with meanings rooted in previous experiences, recorded by and, undoubtedly, permanently stored in our subconscious. It is tantamount to having at our disposal a personal inner library, whose tomes provide on demand a great deal of information affecting our verbal identity, especially where it is shaped by our relationships within the linguistic community. To visualize more graphically how we process meaning in language, is it then so unreasonable to imagine the words we hear or read as resonating or flowing through one of these mysterious labyrinths — here, of course, a cerebral one?

Winding their way at lightning speed through the labyrinthine passages, the words cannot help but brush against, be impregnated by and fleshed out with, a myriad of related associations and connotations, all based on how and under what circumstances we used them in the past. Thus, under closer scrutiny, meaning is not a mere diagram, as many linguists would have it, but may be, when perceived beyond the trivial to its very limits, a live reflection of our spirit and soul. This explains the inspiration you may glean from a book, the tears, laughter, or deep emotion a deserving work of art may wring from you. It also is a valid reason for treasuring and respecting language as a precious gift to humankind.

Cash and the Almighty Dollar

Because money is of such crucial concern to so many people, let's talk money! The expression "almighty dollar" was first used by Washington Irving in *The Creole Village* in 1837 and "almighty gold," a possible pun

Panic	From *Pan*, Greek god of flocks and shepherds. Travelers, whom he often startled, dreaded him. *Panikon deima* = the panic fear.
Pedigree	From *pied de grue* (foot of a crane), the three-pronged genealogical tree drawn by French Monks and resembling the foot of a bird — evolved from 15th-century England, where it was spelled *pee-de-grew,* then *pedegru*, and finally *pedigree*.

on Almighty God, by English poet and dramatist Ben Jonson (1573-1637) about 1600. But, first, let us explain how *crucial* acquired its meaning of essential, decisive. From the Latin *crux*, meaning cross, where the ways cross, by extension crossroads, "the crux of the matter" designated a pivotal point, time, and place, where a decision must be made. The famous English scientist Sir Francis Bacon used *instantia crucis*, or crucial instance, as a metaphor for a fork in the road, where one must decide where to go. Remember Robert Frost's poem "The Road Not Taken": ". . . Two roads diverged in a wood, and I —/I took the one less traveled by,/And that has made all the difference."

In the early 16th century, about 1518, Joachimsthal, Valley of St. Joachim or St. Joseph, in Czechoslovakia, was the site of a mint where coins were manufactured from silver. The German *Thal*, now usually spelled *Tal*, is the equivalent of our English dale in "over hill, over dale." It was customary to call the coins minted there *Joachimsthaler*. From this came a generic designation for coins of similar value elsewhere as *Taler* in German. America, once it became independent from England, was not inclined to use the pound sterling as its currency and adopted the dollar with the Coinage Act of 1792. Canada, Australia, New Zealand, and other nations followed suit.

The dollar sign ($), often drawn with two vertical lines, most probably started as a "U" superimposed upon an "S," where the loop of the "U" was later eliminated. A cent, from Latin *centum*, is one hundredth of a dollar, and a *mill*, Latin *mille*, is a thousandth. *Nickel* comes from the German *Kupfernickel*, or copper nickel, and St. Nicholas, because superstitious miners blamed the goblin Nicholas, whenever they found metal without a copper content. Under happier circumstances, Nicholas evolved into Santa Claus. *Dime* comes from Latin *decima pars*, tenth part. Colonial America often suffered from a shortage of small coins, and the Spanish silver piece of eight (it was worth eight *reales*) was often used and even cut up into halves or quarters to make change, which triggered the use of two, four, and six bits for 25, 50, and 75 cents, respectively.

A *pound*, from Latin *pondus*, Anglo-Saxon *pund*, German *Pfund*, first designated a weight, from *pendere*, to hang or weigh. Think of all the derivations: a ponderous or weighty matter is pending or hangs in the balance. Actually, in Latin, the full expression was *libra pondo*, literally a pound by weight, where *libra* (French *livre*) means pound. That is why a pound sterling is designated by a "£." Shilling, one twentieth of a pound and a diminutive, like duckling, may come from an Old High German word, *Skilling*, designating a gold coin, or from an Old English verb, *scylian*, meaning to divide, to distinguish, and thus is "a little dividing." On the other hand, to distinguish implies knowledge, hence our word skill.

About 835 A.D., Offa, King of Mercia, an ancient province of Britain, introduced the penny into England. The word is also a diminutive from Anglo-Saxon *pening*, from *pand* (pledge), and thus means a little pledge or pawn. It was modeled after the European coin *novus denarius* (compare with old currencies like the French *denier* or the modern *dinar* still used in many countries) and explains why the British abbreviation for pence is "*d*."

How Meanings Evolve

Frankly speaking, because word meanings are not always rigidly confined within inflexible semantic borders, but are free to evolve and roam as the human mind plays associative games with them, it should come as no surprise to you that *frank* and *free* are related. A cousin to the Sanskrit *priya* (dear, beloved), free once meant beloved and is related to friend. In ancient times, a home included both those one loved as well as slaves. Thus, free came to mean "not enslaved." *Slave* comes from *Slav*, a central European race, whose people, once conquered, became slaves and servants to the Romans and Franks. In their own tongue, *slav* and, in modern Russian, *slava* mean glory.

The Franks, a German tribe, conquered Gaul, which later became France, in the early 6th century. A proud and conquering people, the Franks claimed as their own the human traits embodied in the word frank. Under Frankish law, they alone enjoyed full freedom. However, those that accepted them as their protectors could be enfranchised as free men. In Old French, *franc* also meant strong, free. That is how *frankincense*, both "volatile or free" and "of strong fragrance," acquired its name. The French monetary unit, the *franc*, has not always been as strong. I have seen it lose much value over the years owing to inflation. The Franks forded the Main River at Frankfurt, which literally means the ford of the Franks. Natives of this city as well as the genuine all-pork hot dogs originating there, bear the proud name of frankfurters, the former with a capital "F." Remember J.F.K.'s *"Ich bin ein Berliner!"* In Frankfurt, he might have said: *"Ich bin ein Frankfurter."* The funny thing is that in Berlin, a *Berliner* or *Berliner Pfannkuchen* is a jelly doughnut. J.F.K. conjured up an entire meal! In postal parlance frank is free, and a franking privilege is the right to send mail free with one's signature, a privilege some of us enjoyed while serving in World War II. A *lingua franca* is an international language (a hybrid) that is of free passage, as French was for many years.

The river *portage*, cognate with Latin *portus*, port, is Anglo-Saxon and English *ford* (remember, according to Grimm's and Verner's laws, Latin *p* becomes English and German *f*), and a place where people can *ford*, and where one can carry things across, a stream. Similarly we have: *pater*, father, *piscis*, fish. Ultimately ford is related to Latin *per*, meaning through, as does Old English *faran* (to travel, speed), and German *fahren*. In German, *fahren* now means to travel by vehicle, but once simply meant to travel. The medieval *fahrender Schüler* (traveling student; *Schüler* is cognate with our scholar), did not travel by Volkswagen. *Thoroughfare* is to travel through, and fare the amount paid for the trip. *Farewell* literally means travel well, which is what some may be able do while on welfare. Speaking of cities like Frankfurt, others in Germany and later in America end in "*-burg*" meaning fortress, manor house. Hamburg is a combination of *Burg* with German *Heim*, or home, and is tantamount to home fortress. This explains all our cities containing the root of home, like Hempstead, Hampstead, Hampton, just as *burg* is the root of borough and originally comes from a Germanic word, *bergen*, to shelter, protect.

Traveling east from Germany we come to Wien or Vienna, whose medieval name was *Vindobono* from the Latin *ventus bonus*, or good wind. Perhaps, not to confuse it with Chicago, we should rather say good air, in honor of the gay waltzes and spirited airs that brought the city fame. Vienna also created the Vienna hot dog, to which beaten beef is added. It is thinner, with a different texture from the frankfurter, and is not to be confused with our canned Vienna sausage. Some scholars like Joseph T. Shipley claim, in my opinion erroneously, that *wind* comes from Latin *venire*, to come. I rather believe it originated with an Indo-European root *WA*, found in Sanskrit and other languages, and means to blow. Even in Russian, wind is *vyetyer*, and German *wehen* means to blow. Latin *venire*, past participle *vent*, has, of course, given us numerous words: prevent (to come before); event (what comes out of something); circumvent (to come around something); convention, convent, convenient, conventional, all combine *cum* (together) and *venire* (to come). *Convent*, from French *couvent*, also occurs without the *n* in London's Covent Garden. *Intervention* is to come between, and an *invention* is something you come or stumble upon, as I do in my essays.

The Line Between Man and Machine

Futurist Ray Kurzweil, whom the *Wall Street Journal* labeled a "restless genius," believes that in this century we shall see the difference between man and machine blur, the line between humanity and technology fade, the soul and the silicon chip unite. But wherever language is concerned, I still place my bet on man. Can machine intelligence really compare with human intelligence in the realm of language, more specifically in literary translation? Can a computer perform as well as a competent human being when transposing a literary work from one tongue into another? You be the judge! Pierre de Ronsard (1524-1585), one of France's great poets, an ardent disciple of the Greek and Roman classical tradition, wrote some of the finest and best-known French love sonnets. I chose one from those dedicated to Helene and subjected it to a machine translation, freetranslation.com, on the Internet. Here are the results.

> When you will very be old, to evenings has the *chandelle*,
> seated *aupres* of the *devidant* fire and spinning,
> will say, singing my towards and you *emerveillant*,
> Ronsard me *celebrait* of the time that I *j'etais* beautiful.
> During will not have you serving, *oyant* such new,
> *deja* under the toil has half *sommeillan*,
> that to the noise of Ronsard does not go itself *reveillant*,
> *benissand* your immortal praise name.
> I will be under the earth, and *fantome* without bones,
> under the *myrteux* shadows I *prendraia* my rest.
> You *serez* to the home an old *accroupie*,

regretting my love and your to trust *dedain*.
Live, if believe some for me, do not await has tomorrow!
Gather today the roses of life!

Here is my translation:

When you are very old at evening's candlelight,
with skein and spinning wheel, sitting at the hearth's flame,
you'll say, singing my verse marveling with delight:
"When I was fair, Ronsard would praise my beauty's fame!"
You shall now have no maid hearing such litany,
though still drowsy with sleep from tending the day's chore,
who hearing Ronsard's name will not awakened be,
and bless you with her praise to last for evermore.
A disembodied soul I shall be in the earth,
under the myrtle's shade at rest I shall remain.
and you withered with age shall crouch down by the hearth,
regretful of my love and of your proud disdain.
Live now, do mind my words, don't wait another day!
Gather this very hour life's roses while you may!

As you can see, the computer did a horrendous, nigh illiterate job. It would have failed even more miserably if required to produce a rhymed translation like mine. A comparison of both texts clearly shows why it is virtually impossible, at least for this task, to program a computer to proceed like a knowledgeable and sensitive human brain. The process, whether engaged in by machine or human mind, can no longer be strictly linear. For each word and phrase the translator must constantly shuttle back and forth between them and the sonnet's entire context to evaluate the precise linguistic, semantic, and artistic roles they fill therein. Assuming even an improved, richer thesaurus, the task requires *heart*, *soul*, and *judgment* to select, as the French literary dictators always stress, "*le mot juste*" (the right word) to fit the specific occasion and, in our example, the added difficulty of rhyme. Here, the computer program could not even cope with common idiomatic French expressions!

Disregarding the awkwardness of the translation, let us merely focus on the crudest errors: "Singing my towards . . . noise of Ronsard . . . *benissand* [sic] your immortal praise name . . . your to trust *dedain* [*disdain*]." Evidently, the machine's computer program blindly forges ahead when faced with homonyms or identical words with multiple meanings, unusual word order, and structures that alter the normally expected sense — instances where the human mind might pause, eliminate the unlikely, select the more plausible, proceed by process of elimination, and, maybe, get it right.... Proof once more that meaning reaches beyond the spoken and written word! No wonder an Italian proverb refers to translators as traitors (*Traduttore, traditore!*).

Putting it more kindly, the machine cannot, like a human, view its handiwork and say, "Oops! Back to the drawing board, is it now?"

Like Games, Language Has Rules

Would you believe that writing about language might prove hazardous to your health? After road rage are we now threatened by "language rage"? An article I wrote in 1993, about how logicians often use (or misuse) language to put some of their arguments across, raised a Sun City logician's hackles. A logician, in case you forgot, is someone who dazzles and confuses you with such pearls as "heads I win, tails you lose." I was merely attempting to show that, like games, language has various sets of rules or conventions. These determine which "moves" (in language it would be stylistic constructions) are permissible or impermissible. Ignoring the rules may result in meaninglessness. I might add that I have no quarrel with logicians as such who use mathematics as their language rather than misusing the one made of words.

As noted in an earlier essay, "Using Language Skillfully," the rules governing mathematics are not always applicable to language; math symbols do not enjoy the same qualities as words. Expressing it as simply as possible, math describes reality abstractly, without any emotion, judgment, connotation, *double-entendre*, i.e., ambiguity of meaning arising from language that lends itself to more than one interpretation. It is one thing to say "all x = y, I am x, therefore I am y," and another to say "all Cretans are liars, I am a Cretan, hence I am a liar." As indicated previously, this latter statement, known in logic as the Epimenides or Liar Paradox, and carried to its logical extreme (if, indeed, the statement is true and the speaker a liar), means "I'm not a Cretan and I am not lying." On the surface, it is something a cretin [sic] might utter!

What is wrong here? In math the equation is perfectly rational. The language of the statement, however, raises many red flags. Who in the real world can afford and prove without a reasonable doubt a faulty generalization such as "all Cretans are liars." General semantics teaches us that no one knows everything about anything. Besides, unlike math symbols, words are quite slippery, open to many interpretations. Does a liar tell nothing but lies? The statement is amusing, perhaps confusing at first, certainly not semantically sustainable. Another version of the Liar Paradox is: "This sentence is false, and if it is false it is true, and if it is true it is false." Now such a sentence does not pass grammatical or syntactical muster. Logicians claim the sentence to be self-referential, which, in this case, cannot be since it has no significant meaning. A meaningful self-referential sentence would be: "This sentence has five words." The first sentence would only gain meaning if "this" referred to a previously cited or forthcoming sentence. Anyone's natural reaction to the sentence would most probably be, "Which sentence?"

Another favorite of logicians is the Barber Paradox. "A barber only shaves those men who do not shave themselves! Does he shave himself?" Logically, this may be unsolvable. Linguistically, it is not. When the barber shaves himself, he is still a barber. Actually, if he is pleased with his performance, he might pay himself his usual fee, a hefty tip to boot, and drop it in his piggy bank. All jokes aside, some languages like Russian, provide by morphological inflection for such eventuality. In Russian the sentence "he shaved himself and thus was his own barber" would be *"on pobrilsya i yablyalsya svoim parikmaxerom,"* where "he" would be in the nominative or subject case and "barber" in the instrumental case to show that he was being temporarily viewed as a barber servicing himself.

My critic and I had a heated argument. I was guilty of attempting to erase 2,000 years of logic with one stupid article. To end the dispute, I replied like a logician: "I shall let you have the last word. Game's over!" That is how I managed to have the last word! Confusing? You figure!

Migration and Language

One of my readers wrote to me, inquiring what might have led to the broad geographical distribution of the Indo-European languages. The answer: migration! Where might the original homeland of the Indo-European language group have been? Three words common to all the languages in the group may provide a solution to the puzzle: *beech tree* (German *Buche*), *turtle* (German *Schildkröte*), and *salmon* (or *lox*, German *Lachs*). The only geographical area where all three were found is in central Europe, between the Elbe, Oder, Vistula, and Rhine rivers. There are no turtles north of the Danish border, no beech trees east of the Vistula, and no salmon west of the Rhine. (Now, you New Yorkers, please don't insist that lox with cream cheese on a bagel originated in New York City!) The spoken language closest to the original Indo-European roots is Lithuanian.

I have noted that there was a time in the early 1900s when any research pertaining to an original primeval tongue (German *Ursprache*) was taboo. Such restrictions no longer apply. Merritt Ruhlen, an expert in historical linguistics, deals with this subject in *The Origin of Language: Tracing the Evolution of the Mother Tongue*. He believes that all extant languages share a common origin. He endeavors to classify languages to prove his point. Of course, he is unable to do so. Many experts believe that linguistic change is so rapid that after around 6,000 years all traces of earlier relationships have been obliterated by constant phonetic and semantic erosion.

Ruhlen is not the first to believe in an original tongue. The famous German Wilhelm von Humboldt readily assumed that there was a common primeval language, an assumption he took no pains to prove. And, as noted previously, the Swiss scholar Adolphe Pictet was the first to mention the concept of linguistic paleontology. We know how accurate a science that is, since archeologists keep on discovering ever-earlier skulls lying around, thank heavens, mostly in Africa. I have mentioned that Russian philologist Nikolai Marr, one of the world's greatest authorities on Caucasian languages, nevertheless exhibited questionable scholarship with the New Theory of Language, claiming that ultimately all languages derived from the Japhetic language family. We'll forgive him, for "*aliquando dormitat bonus Homerus*" ("even Homer nods at times").

Then there was Richard Fester (1910-1982), also mentioned in an earlier essay, an authentic paleolinguist. Although merely a gifted amateur, not an academic, he wrote many valuable books. Fester had dared propose a primeval vocabulary, the first six archetypes of human language: *BA, KALL, TAL, OS, ACQ* (also mentioned by Ruhlen), and *TAG*. I have no quarrel with some of this. As noted, almost every town or village in French Provence has a name ending in "*ac*," signifying a nearby source of water. My opinion on his subject? Once again, the Italian proverb, "*Se non è vero, è bene trovato*" — if it's not true, it is well imagined.

I believe one can trace many linguistic influences. However, I am convinced that language, an inherent genetic ability of humans to coordinate sound, perception, and the skill of communication, sprang up simultaneously in all parts of the globe. Countless migrations enabled languages to borrow from each other. Linguistic evolution, while following some natural rules, was often random, depending on the races involved. Thus the spoken language of Roman legionnaires, evolved into French, Spanish, Italian, Portuguese, Rumanian, and other Romance languages, in contact with the speech of local tribes. One Siberian Finno-Ugric group, splitting into three and dispersing toward the west, evolved into Estonian, Finnish, and Hungarian. Metaphors and images in various languages do not follow rules, but are formed by popular imagination and myth. Sorry, Regis Philbin . . . even I don't have the *final answer*!

A New Look at Old Words

Let us look at some words that have been bandied about lately by the media such as *apology* and *holocaust*. Incidentally, *bandy* comes from the French *bander*, to bind, tie up, and *bande*, a strip, hence our *bandage*, BAND-AID. Subsequently, the same word was applied to a game, *bandy*, similar to present-day tennis, played with a ball and racket. The idea of tightness, no doubt, came from the racket. Bandy is even the name of another old game, reputedly the prototype of hockey. Hence, of course, the idea of bandying or batting either balls or words to and fro.

Words like *apology*, from the Greek *apo* meaning away and *logos* meaning word, and *excuse*, from Latin *ex* meaning out of and *causa* or cause, evidently all contain the idea of using words to explain away some regrettable act or statement. A fancier word, apologia, is a written defense

> **Old Fogey** A variation of *fogy*, probably inspired by the Old English *foggy*, meaning fat, bloated, moss-grown. The Scottish adopted it as a disrespectful term for an old man behind the times.
>
> **Pagan** From Latin *paganus*, villager, rustic — hence considered ignorant, or "living on the other side of the tracks," and likely an "unbeliever" in Christianity, which had spread into cities of the Roman Empire more rapidly than the outlying districts.

by a writer of his conduct. Apologue, on the other hand, is an allegorical narrative, as a beast fable, intended to convey a moral lesson. Thus, the Greek author Aesop and the French poet La Fontaine were masters of the apologue or fable. Every French child knows La Fontaine's fable of the fox and raven, the former praising the latter's voice and inviting him to display his singing talent, thus tricking him into dropping a cheese held in his bill.

Holocaust originally meant a sacrifice, not a massacre or slaughter. The Bible speaks of a sacrifice as a "burnt offering" to the gods and that is the literal meaning of *holocaust*, from the Greek *holos*, whole, and *caustos*, burned. Normally, a holocaust should designate a wholesale destruction by fire, but now frequently refers to the massacre of Jews by the Nazis.

An encaustic picture is produced by using paint mixed with melted beeswax and, after application, fixing it by heat. Encaustic tiles are tiles decorated with colored clays, inlaid and fired. Caustic and cauterize are from the same Greek root and contain the meaning of burning. Caustic may be used both literally in caustic lime and figuratively in caustic remarks.

Another word containing the root *holos*, whole, is *catholic*, which literally means concerning the whole or universal. If you have catholic taste, you like almost everything, including my essays. Of, course Catholic was soon applied to the church universal. First it referred to the entire body of Christian believers, then to the "universally" accepted orthodox doctrine and to the historic Catholic Church. Now, being a Catholic does not by itself guarantee a place in paradise. Usually, all words beginning with the

Greek prefix *para-* include the meaning of beside, near, beyond. Parallel literally means beside one another and paradox beyond belief. Paradise came from the Persian through the Greek and meant a walled garden or enclosure, literally around a mound, where Islam's faithful went after death. The ancient root *dis* meant to form and is related to Anglo-Saxon *dig*, to knead, which gave us our *dough*, German *Teig*. I earlier noted that the word *lady*, before the feminine revolution, evolved from *hlaf* or loaf and *dig* or knead, which once may have been her principal occupation. *Hell*, the final hiding place for some (not Arizonans, who would not even notice the heat), and *helmet* come from the same root, which meant to cover or hide. The French *heaume* was a large Medieval headpiece or helmet. In German, *verhehlen* is "to conceal," and *Hehler* is a receiver of stolen goods. A German proverb states: *"Der Hehler ist so Schlimm wie der Stahler."* ("The receiver or conceiler is as bad as the thief.") An early English verb, *hele*, means to cover, hide, and the final hiding place is Hell.

No Rigmarole Here!

I am certain that some of my readers may (of course quite seldom) find my essays somewhat rigmarolish, which, of course, they are not. *Rigmarole* (sometimes rigamarole), designates a series of foolish, meaningless, confused statements, and has a curious history. Edward I wanted Scotland as a vassal kingdom and the Scottish kings and nobles were in no position to refuse. In the year 1291, they presented Edward with a *hodgepodge* of diverse documents of allegiance with difficult-to-decipher signatures called *ragman roll*. The ragman, not to be confused with its present meaning, was an officer who made up the tax or feudal allegiance lists. But wait, there's more! As used in *Piers Plowman*, a 14th-century allegorical moral and social satirical poem, ragman was also an old name for the devil, who resides in the dungeon of Wrong, down in a valley, unlike God, who dwells in the tower of Truth, up on a hill. By way of folk etymology, "ragman roll" became "rigmarole."

Allegory, from the Greek *allos* (something else) and *agoria* (discourse), is a kind of sensible, imaginative double-talk, one might say a story with another hidden inside. The parables of Jesus and many fables are allegories, hiding a moral lesson inside another plot. Incidentally, a fancy name for double-talk is *amphigory*, from Greek *amphi* (both or around; compare amphitheater, or theatre in the round) and the same *agoria* (speech). It may also have as root *gyros*, circle, whence to gyrate and gyroscope, all implying spinning around an axis. On the other hand, the Greek *agora* meant successively marketplace, then assembly. So how did paregoric come to mean a medicine that mitigates pain? As today's radio and TV broadcasts often purport to soothe the audience, raise its morale, or even brainwash it, speeches delivered in the Greek *agora* aimed at exhorting and comforting the public. The term *category* took a quite different semantic path. Aristotle used it as a technical term. For him it referred to ten classes that, together, covered all modes of being. The Greek root of the word, however, meant to speak publicly down at or against something. Thus *catastrophe* was a point in the Greek drama, now in all walks of life, in which the action turned against the main figure. *Catapult* literally means to hurl against.

What about *hodgepodge*? It started as *hotch-potch*, but, from the 17th century onward, the preferred spelling became Hodge, perhaps because it was a nickname for Roger. Further back, in the 13th century, it was *hotch-pot*, from French *hocher* (to shake), a shaking together in a pot. *Hocher* comes from the language of the Germanic Franks, the people who occupied Gaul at the time of the Roman conquest. Before becoming a culinary term, hotch-pot was applied in law to the commingling of property to insure a more even distribution. The culinary meaning referred to a stew of mutton broth and vegetables. The figurative usage, designating a jumbled assemblage of persons or things, began in the 15th century and is the one more familiar to us in America today as hodgepodge.

They Stole My Thunder!

I noticed that a colleague was writing a column about language and word origins in another local paper. I might in jest state he was "stealing my thunder." The expression, by the way, dates back to about 1700, when a playwright named Dennis claimed to have invented a sounds-effects machine capable of imitating the noise of thunder off-stage. He also complained his rivals had appropriated his contraption, "*stolen his thunder,*" without his permission. The phrase is now used in a wider, more general, figurative sense. I do not wish to engage in a polemic (meaning "relating to war"; Greek *polemos*, war) with someone who shares my love of language. However, a few comments on his column may produce a combined effort benefiting our readers. He quibbles about the meaning of "indeed." The adverb "indeed" does mean "in very fact, truly, assuredly," my colleague's opinion to the contrary.

My friend also writes "nothing is so humbling for a wordsmith than [*sic*] to read these histories of words." The text would be improved if "than" were replaced by "as," or if it read "more humbling than," for "than" is a function word indicating that what follows is the second member in a comparison expressive of inequality. My colleague's column reads "from whence," a redundancy or tautology. "Whence" already contains "from," as it means "from where."

But back to words and their origins. *Yacht*, like many words with such a guttural sound not found in English, comes from the Middle Dutch. During World War II, the Dutch could detect Nazi spies by their mispronouncing the name of the sea town of Scheveningen (pronounced S-h-eveningen). Yacht originally was a speedy ship used by privateers to hunt prey. The German equivalent is *die Jacht*. The additional German words *Jagd*, *Jäger*, and *jagen*, mean the hunt, hunter, and to hunt, respectively. The root is probably related to German *jaehe*, meaning sudden, lively, and — believe it or not — to our own "to go" and "gay."

Tariff (Modern French *tarif*, not *tariffe*; Spanish *tarifa*; Italian *tariffa*), as my friend rightly states, comes from the Arabic *ta'rif*. It means inventory, from *'arafa*, to make known. Its first archaic meaning in English was a multiplication table, hence a rate schedule. The fact that the pirates occupied a town named Tarifa at the foot of the rock of Gibraltar is irrelevant here. Indeed, Turkish and Arab pirates regularly raided the Spanish coast, where *atalayas* or watchtowers (a Spanish word from the Arabic) were built to guard and sound the alarm against them. Atalaya is the name of a mountain overlooking Santa Fe, New Mexico, its original meaning unknown to most Santa Feans.

True, originally ordeal was a primitive torture test by water, fire, or the like, to determine a person's guilt. Overcoming the test was proof of innocence with divine approval. However, the word is related to "deal," is similar to the German *Urteil* (judgment), and once meant judgment, verdict (the latter from Latin *veredictum* literally means "told truth").

My colleague, in his column on language, took a shortcut to explain the relationship between *travail* and *travel*. The longer scenic road is more spectacular. The Romans had an instrument of torture known as the *tripalium*, literally "three poles." I do not really want to know how it worked. It later produced the French word *travailler*, which, when transitive, means to fashion (compare our own work iron, wrought iron) or to torment. Intransitive, it now means in French to work, labor. It evolved through many spelling changes into travail and travel. The latter can at times be an ordeal, as all of us who travel know well

Slang

Within any one language may be found many linguistic subgroups such as dialect, slang, argot, jargon, etc., based on regional or social variations. Let us focus on their precise meanings, which actually contain a great deal of information. We do not know for certain the origin of *slang*, which at first referred to a special and often secret vocabulary used by a class such as thieves or beggars. No doubt that is why some thought, albeit in error, the origin of the word to trace back to the Dutch *slang*, German *Schlange*, meaning snake, and later, in the 19th century, chains and fetters. Who knows? Perhaps someone once jokingly played with the words "language, slanguage."

Patois, from the French, earlier *patrois*, comes from the Latin *patrius sermo*, native or local speech. To the French ear, *patois* has a distinctly condescending, contemptuous flavor. This is not the case with vernacular, which is quite neutral. From the Latin, it means native or domestic, as *verna* refers to a slave born at home, a household slave. In Europe, the vernacular literature of the 13th century was written in the native dialects rather than in the learned scholarly Latin. The German equivalent, *Mundart*, is even more politically correct in that it literally just means "a way of speaking," literally "a way of the mouth." The Germans have a saying: "Everyone speaks according to how his or her beak or snout has grown." (*Wie ihm der Schnabel gewachsen ist*.)

Argot is definitively from the French. In the 13th century was heard "*gergons vulgare trutanorum*," the vulgar jargon of vagabonds or truants (you can recognize the root of the word). Thus *argot*, or *gergo*, ultimately may trace back to the Greek *hiero*, sacred (compare hieroglyph or sacred writing). *Circa* 1628, *argot* meant the practice of begging or *mendacity* (mendacity, on the contrary, from French *mentir*, to lie, refers to the practice of lying). In 1645, we read these lines (my translation):

> In short, with begging I desire
> to spend henceforth my life entire;
> a happy trade to which aspire.

From the world of beggars the term was gradually applied to their language. *Lingua gerga*, meaning sacred language, eventually evolved into *jargon*. To both the French and English ear, the sound of the word jargon recalled or imitated the chirping, warbling of birds, as does garble.

The Greek root *dia*, meaning through, is a very productive one. It gave us diabetes, which literally means to flow through (in this case an excessive flow of urine), dialogue or talking across back and forth, diameter or measuring across, and, more to the point, dialect. From *dia* (through) and *legein*, *lek* (to speak), it means to speak through the tongue of a special region. Any one dialect is usually not strictly confined within precise borders. Changes are gradual to enable communication between neighboring communities. *Pidgin*, a corruption of "business" as pronounced by a Chinese or Oriental speaker, effectively means trade language, a means of communication between people speaking different languages, yet desirous to trade with each other. Developed in the 16th century by sailors and traders, it was a language with multilingual lexical roots and with a highly simplified grammar and syntax. If a *pidgin* becomes the only language of a linguistic community and is passed on from generation to generation it is called a *Creole*. A *sabir* is a French-based pidgin language from North Africa. *Sabir* is the word for "to know" (compare Latin *scire*, French *savoir*, Spanish *saber*, all meaning to know) in a concocted *lingua franca* used by the French comic playwright Molière: "*Se ti sabir, Ti respondir.*" ("If you know, you answer.") The Latin *sapere*, however, meant to taste, know from taste. You can see how the human mind associated both meanings. Molière's real name was Jean-Baptiste Poquelin. The origin of his pseudonym is unknown.

Accuracy in "Signature" Phrases

"Now, here is the weather where you are, even as we speak!" When I first heard this turn of phrase spoken by a TV weatherman I dismissed it as inherently redundant. Evidently, it was intended as a distinctive "signature." Upon further analysis, my first reaction is confirmed. As an adverb, *"even"* can in turn mean: *without change*, as in "work even without increase or decrease in pay"; *precisely, exactly*, just as in "even as you and I need love, others do too"; *to a degree that extends*, as in "even unto death"; *at the very time*, as in "even as I threw the crumbs into the pond the ducks swooped down on them;" *an intensive*, as in "even we do it" or, in extreme and unlikely cases, "corruption is so widespread no one even protests," or "even if help arrives, it's too late." Strictly speaking, none of these justify the weatherman's usage, but he has a first amendment right to be cute and imperfect, *even* as he often is in forecasting the weather.

Issue is another word that has evolved a great deal in modern parlance. By way of Old French *issir*, from Latin *exire*, to go out, it referred to anything that came out, ranging from outflow, to outlet or exit (the latter is the doublet of issue, as French *issir*, which gave us issue, came from *exire*, which in turn came, not translated, directly into English as *exit*), to offspring. Barnum's Circus barkers used to shout "This way to the egress!" which comes from Latin *ex* and *gradire*, to step out. The latter produced *grade* with all its various meanings: gradual or step by step, graduated, centigrade and degrees (steps on a temperature scale), to progress, literally a stepping forward. Degrade is to take down a step, digress to step aside, transgress to step across permissible boundaries, moral or legal. Aggression is stepping toward and against. The Sanskrit root meant greed, then desire, hence moving toward the desired object.

Congress signifies a physical stepping together, which, of course, does not necessarily imply a meeting of the minds. *Congregation* derives from another Latin source, *grex, gregis*, a herd or flock. Thus, they flock together to pray together. Speaking of flocks, Latin *pascere*, through its French equivalent *paître*, to feed, lead to pasture, gave us *pastor* and *pastoral*, the latter with or without religious meaning (a pastoral landscape or poem).

Remembering the root *grex, gregis*, may help you better understand such words as *egregious*, from *ex* (out of) and *grex* (flock). Thus, literally out of the flock or herd, standing out from the flock, its meanings range, both good and bad, from conspicuous, to notorious, extreme, and flagrant, as in egregious error or behavior.

Speaking of flocks, the word has a double origin. As a tuft or *flock* of wool, its origin is Germanic, German *Flocke*, and it is related to *flake*. If, in Germany, you order *Haferflocken*, you will be served rolled or porridge oats, oatmeal. Now *flake*, on the other hand, since it represents a thin slice, is related to flay, to strip off skin. Other meanings of flake, such as a tray or platform for drying fish, relate it to Dutch *vlak*, or flat. You can easily see how flaky acquired its slang meaning of unreliable, since flaky means not firmly united in a stable mass, cleaving off in flakes. To flake out is World War II Navy slang for "to go to sleep or rest." As to the flock of sheep, its root is found only in the Scandinavian languages. Would you believe that it actually is, by way of *metathesis*, or transposition of letters, a variation of folk, where "*l*" and "*o*" are interchanged? Whenever you see *meta*, the meaning of "after" is present. *Metaphysics* was so designated by the editor of Aristotle's works, because this section came *after* physics and dealt with things not relating to external nature. *Metalanguage* is a language used to express data about or used to discuss another language. Well! There's nothing after metaphysics, so let's quit for now!

We Don't Have to Learn Anglo-Saxon!

After the departure of the last Roman legions, England was speaking Anglo-Saxon, a highly inflected Germanic language with three genders (masculine, feminine, neuter), a singular, even a dual (still found in our word "both" from German *beide*, and also found in languages like Russian), a plural, and verbs with complex conjugations. However, in 1066 William the Conqueror and the Norman French conquered England and French was added to and later blended with the local tongue. Thanks to William, we don't have to learn Anglo-Saxon. Today, at least half of the

English vocabulary is of French-Norman and Latin-through-French origins. The presence of both languages gives English arguably the world's largest vocabulary. At first the upper class was French, the lower Anglo-Saxon, a fact reflected in our language. Words of Germanic origin designate those used by the serfs; French words belong to upper-class society.

The names of domestic animals in the field and under the care of Anglo-Saxon serfs are all of German origin, as earlier noted, here given in parentheses: steer (*Stier*), swine (*Schwein*), calf (*Kalb*), sheep (*Schaf*), hen (*Huhn*), goose (*Gans*). Prepared for the dinner table, the names are all from the French: beef (*boeuf*), pork (*porc*), veal (*veau*), mutton (*mouton*), chicken or pullet (*poulet*). The story of deer is more complex. When served as a meal, it is venison from the French *venaison*. Old English *deor*, whence deer, came from the German *Tier* and was a generic term designating any animal (see *King Lear* 3.4.135: "But mice and rats, and such small deer,/Have been Tom's food for seven long year."). Then it was restricted to designate members of the Cervidae family (*cerf* in French is deer). The Germanic *Tier* also became the more specialized Spanish *toro*, or bull or steer. The reason? There were other general terms for animal, like the Latin and French *animal* now used for domestic animals and French *bête*, now designating beasts or wild animals.

Most English words related to food preparation are of French origin: boiled, roast, toast, fry, sauce, pastry, soup, jelly, etc. If it is plain chow, we "cook" it, from German *kochen*. If it is highfalutin cooking, we use two French terms: *haute* or *gourmet cuisine*. (There is also *haute couture*, fancy sewing, for fancy dressmaking, and *haute école* for fancy riding schools.) Often restaurant menus use French terms not used in France with the meaning we give it. Thus *entrée*, in France, is an appetizer, not our main dish. I can name you a long list of words that the Normans introduced into English, some of which would today have been considered politically incorrect: peasant, trespass (the original French now means to die), punish, oppress, prohibit, discipline, tax (the French also use *impôt* for tax, which we find in our "to impose"), judge, penalty, prison, torture, supplication, exile, treason, rebel, dungeon, execution, and thousands more. Other examples of two words, one Germanic (more basic), one French (more elegant): smell (the root is the same as smolder, the smell of something burned) versus *odor* — both stink (Germanic), but the second, from the French, "more gracefully"; *sweat* (German *Schweiss*) and

> **Fabric**　From Latin *faber*, one who can make, fabricate; also related to Latin *facere*, to make.
>
> **Denim**　Cloth from *de* (from) + *Nîmes*, the Roman city in southern France.
>
> **Gauze**　Fabric from the ever war-torn Gaza strip in Palestine.
>
> **Jersey**　Cloth from Jersey, England.

perspiration; *eat* (German *essen*) versus *dine*; *dead* (German *tot*) and *deceased*; *go away* and *depart* (German *weggehen*); *stool*, without a back (from German *Stuhl*), and *chair*, with a back (from French *chaise*). The French have two words for "to come back": *revenir* and *retourner*. The first is to return whence you departed, *i.e.*, to come back. You'll see it in "revenue," for the money issued by the government acts like a homing pigeon and returns to it with an IRS Form 1040. On this jolly note I bid you *au revoir*, much more elegant than *Auf Wiedersehen* . . . or don't you think so? *Ciao!*

Bible-spawned Bird Names

What do parrots, sparrows, and the stormy petrel have in common? If we include one of the French familiar names for sparrow, which is *pierrot*, or "little Peter," they all lead us back to the Bible and St. Peter, one of the disciples of Jesus. Incidentally, the regular French word for sparrow is *moineau*, or little monk, probably so called because of the color of its plumage. The reason for naming the parrot after St. Peter is that the apostle reportedly talked, perhaps even jabbered, a great deal. Sparrow itself has a Germanic root and is *Sperling* in German. By the way, jabber is an imitative or echoic word, like chatter, gibberish. Chatter is abbreviated and assumes a milder meaning in chat. It is reduplicated in chit-chat, which is lighter, less serious talk.

The petrel, of which there are many kinds, such as the Giant Petrel, the Diving Petrel, Mother Carey's Chicken, and the Storm or Stormy Petrel, is a small deep-sea bird. Petrels usually fly in flocks, quite close to the surface of the sea, their legs dangling, so that they appear to be walking on water. Some sailors believed their presence was a warning of an approaching storm, hence the qualifier "stormy." According to the gospel of Matthew 14:29, St. Peter was observed to be walking on the Sea of Galilee, and thus the Italians called the bird *Petrello*, or little Peter, which in English successively became pitteral, pittrel, and finally petrel.

The name "Mother Carey's Chickens" for the Stormy Petrel comes by way of folk etymology and the corruption of the Latin name *mater cara* (cherished mother), given to the Virgin Mary as the patroness of seafarers. Superstition had sailors believe that the virgin sent "her chickens" to warn them of a coming storm. As all of you no doubt know, the name Peter is Latin and Greek for "rock." This gave rise to the pun that founded the Catholic Church (Matthew 16:18): "On this rock shall I build. . . . " Both petrify and petroleum reveal the root "rock" and mean "to turn into stone" (the "*fy*" is a contraction of Latin *facere*, to make or turn into) and "stone oil," respectively

Peter, referring to the male organ, is purely American slang. The origin of the expression "to peter out" is actually unknown, but we can hazard a few guesses. It is definitely of American origin. Lincoln used it, when he said: "a store he was a partner in had petered out." Originally a mining term, it meant that the vein had run dry. This expression has two possible origins: it may come from French "*péter*," to fart, to blow wind, or more likely from "petrify," to turn back into stone. It may also have been inspired by the actions of the apostle Peter, as recorded by John, Chapter 18. When Jesus was seized in the Garden of Gethsemane, Peter first rushed to his defense. Hours later, his fervor "petered out." Before the cock crowed, Peter had thrice denied that he even knew Jesus. Now "to peter out" means to diminish gradually to nothing, to run out of energy.

Pet, from a different root, is probably a back-formation of "petty" and the French *petit*, meaning small. You see it on menus as "petite (should be *petit*, the masculine gender form) filet mignon." *Mignon* already means delicate, dainty, so please remember this next time you take a big bite out of one! "To be in a pet" is to sulk at not being petted. Petty, first meaning to have secondary rank or importance (compare Petty Officer in the Navy), evolved into small-minded. *Pettifogger*, a lawyer with petty, underhanded methods, comes from *petty + fogger*, actually *Fugger*, the famous 15th- to 16th-century banking and merchant family in Augsburg, Germany.

With these words I bid you *Auf Wiedersehen!* and *Guten Appetit!*

Different Views of Reality

I have in my research found many parallels between language and other fields of human endeavor, even science. Thus, the observer-created reality principle of quantum physics equally applies to language. The inventors of the quantum theory found (in contrast with the Newtonian world view) that what an observer decides to measure influences the measurement. What is actually going on in the quantum world depends on how we decide to observe it. The world just isn't "there" independent of our observing it. What is "there" depends in part on what we choose to see. The same holds true of language and meaning.

When we signify, express, denote a certain event, a natural phenomenon, even an object, we may choose to do so by referring to them either by different metaphors or as viewed from different points of view, different angles, and still come up with identical meanings. This may be illustrated by showing how different languages "choose to view the same thing differently." Thus, from the cliffs of Dover, in English, the white-crested waves of the English Channel are described as "the white horses," while the same spectacle in what the French designate as "the Sleeve" (the English Channel in French is *La Manche*, literally the sleeve) becomes "sheep." In French, the sea "acts like a sheep" (*moutonne*). A French horsefly is a *taon*, straight from the Latin *tabanus*. An English horse-chestnut traveling in France denies any equine ancestry and claims its origin from India (*marron d'Inde*). You may eat like a horse in London or New York, but at a four-star restaurant in Paris you eat like a wolf.

All this, in English, may not make any horse sense to you, but to a Frenchman it simply makes "big common sense" (*gros bon sens*). A praying mantis in French may not pray, but still is a "religious mantis." Other words are viewed from different, at times opposite, angles. A *lifebelt* becomes in French a *ceinture de sauvetage*, a *salvage* or rescue belt, and in German a *Rettungsgürtel*, a Salvage belt. Mortal danger remains *mortal* in French, but, in German, it is viewed from the opposite pole as "danger to life" (*Lebensgefahr*). I suppose the Germans do not wish "to talk of the devil" and mention the word death. In German they say, "paint the devil on the wall (*den Teufel an die Wand malen*).

We always try to save time, assuming we have it to save. The French, always ready to gamble and looking at it more positively, call it "gaining or winning time." Talk about observing nature from opposite viewpoints! In the United States patrons ride "at their own risk," but in France, with less lawyers than we have, "the management is not responsible for any accidents."

When dealing with proverbs, we witness the very identical overriding meaning expressed with the help of an entirely different scenario. Although allegedly less obsessed with food than the French, we insist "the proof of the pudding is in the eating." The French, old cathedral builders that they are, prefer "it is by the foot or foundation of the wall that one recognizes the mason." Some metaphors, for which we have one single word, must be described at length in other languages. The Germans, to express the phrase "with arms akimbo," must detail that "the arms are pressed against one's hips," whereas the French use "press their fists against them." This body posture, arms akimbo, indicating impatience, hostility, or contempt, comes from Old Norse and literally means a "keen (sharp) bow."

No Matter the Origin, Buxom Is Good

The word *idea* means "look" in Greek, from *idein*, to see. With the Greek philosopher Plato (427?-347 B.C.), its meaning evolved into "a conception of what is to come." (Plato's name is said to have been Aristocles, but, because of his broad forehead and physique, he was called Plato, from Greek *platys*, broad). In other words, we look something over and see — thereby developing an image — a pattern in the mind. I believe that thinking may arise first of all from perception through our five senses. Then we begin to form images of space and time. Later, we abstract these perceptions and images into verbal thought and build them up into higher and higher logical structures. Of course, present thinking is continuously affected by past thought. I shall now show you how certain complex meanings evolve from one simple one; they are built up by the games our imagination plays and the series of related, almost dreamlike, images it generates.

Why do the meanings of our English word "buxom" range from obedient to jolly, plump, and good to look upon? First of all, the word, as such, does not exist in French or Spanish. However, although to my knowledge linguists have not pointed this out before, the word has a counterpart in German, *biegsam*, which even sounds vaguely like our word and means flexible, pliable, supple, lithe, and, in a figurative sense, yielding, tractable. Both words possess the same Aryan root, *BHUGH*. In Middle English *to bow* is *bowen*, *bogen*, *bugen*. In German, *Bogen* is a bow with which to shoot arrows, *beugen* is to bow down from the waist, and *biegen* is to bend. Furthermore, *buxom* was once spelled *buhsum*, conjuring an association with *bosom*, thought to be akin to Sanskrit *bhasman*, blowing, hence a bellows.

Considering all these associations and connotations, which a bow (bending, flexible, supple, round shaped, and elastic) produce on the mind, not to mention the extra ingredient "bosom," no wonder a vivid human imagination wrought the rest! When a British bride, in early times, promised to be "buxom and bonny," she did not commit to gaining weight. The idea of "bending" implied being pleasant, and pliant. In those days, one was expected to be "buxom," that is obedient, "to the judges and even the pope." It is easy to see how, eventually, especially when thinking of a pretty girl, the meaning expanded to include blithe and gay, even full of health and vigor. Thus, we find George Borrow's quote, in the literature, "They are disposed to be buxom and obedient to the customs and laws of the republic," and in *Piers Plowman*, "and buxom to the law." Edmund Spenser, in *The Faerie Queen* has Neptune command, with reference to young castaways, "His mighty waters to them buxom be." John Milton writes about "winging silently the buxom [*pliant, unresisting*] air." Elsewhere we have: "how jovial it is and buxom," meaning blithe and lively. Burl Ives writes of a "buxom, warm, friendly woman." Of course, Mae West was a "buxom" or full-bosomed blonde. Shakespeare uses buxom with the meaning of lusty, sprightly, and buoyant. In *King Henry V* (3.6), we hear from Pistol's mouth:

> Bardolph, a soldier, firm and sound of heart,
> And of buxom valour, hath, by cruel fate
> And giddy Fortune's furious fickle wheel. . . .

In *Pericles, Prince of Tyre*, Gower, in the role of beginning chorus (line 20), says:

> I tell you what mine authors say:
> This king unto him took a pheere (peer),
> Who died and left a female heir,
> So buxom, blithe, and full of face,
> As Heaven had lent her all his grace;
> With whom the father liking took,
> And her to incest did provoke.
> Bad child! Worse father! To entice his own
> To evil, should be done by none.

Perhaps you'll gain from this a new insight on how language works.

What's in a Name Indeed?

The study of the provenance and evolution of family names is a separate field from word etymology. I am not particularly knowledgeable in it, but some colleagues of mine are members of the American Name Society. The name of former California Congressman Gary Condit was prominently featured in the news in recent years. Without any intent to incite new rumors, I merely wish to bring to your attention some curious, purely linguistic facts. No doubt they are just coincidences, what the Swiss analytical psychologist Carl Gustav Jung labeled synchronicities in his study of the "collective unconscious." Look up in Cassell's *Latin and English Dictionary* the word *condere*, past tense *condit*(*um*), meaning to build, found, compose, put away safely, store, hide, and, when speaking of corpses, to bury.

Those of us who toiled on Latin in our younger days are familiar with the Roman equivalent of our B.C. and A.D. to establish a date. The Romans used *a. u. c.* to date events. It stands for *ab urbe condita*, meaning in the year from the founding of the city — here Rome, approximately 753 B.C. Thus, 10 *a.u.c.*, designated 743 B.C., ten years after the founding of Rome. The Latin verb *condere* was formed from *cum* + *dare*, to put together. However, we can put together things in many different ways; therefore, the word, besides meaning to found, establish, also signified to store them, to preserve them. There is an Old English term, *to condite*, meaning to pickle, put away. We still find this root and meaning in *condiment*.

When we store things, lay them away, we often wish to safeguard them, even hide them. Eventually *condere* came to mean to hide and *conditus* secret. The next step in the word's evolution was to add the prefix *re-*, which means back or repetition, as in return, recur, rebound, and the more familiar word "recondite" appeared. Now we use it to express the idea of concealed, difficult to understand, uncommonly abstruse or profound. With the added prefix *ab(s)-*, meaning away, we have abscond, to put together and away, or to withdraw, to depart secretly, or even, specifically in legal terms, to evade the legal process of a court by hiding within or secretly leaving its jurisdiction.

With all this heavy linguistic baggage, no wonder Congressman Condit had the public looking at him askance. Did he have anything to do with his girlfriend's mysterious disappearance? The word *askance*, of essentially unknown origin, means sideways, with a side glance, with disapproval or distrust. It may originally come from sconce, a screened lantern or candlestick with a handle, which in turn probably came from Old French *esconse*, a hiding place, a screened lantern. The latter, no doubt, was inspired by the Latin *abscondere*, to abscond or hide.

I should probably stick to language. However, as an interrogator of German POWs in World War II and later of Soviet and other defectors, I might hazard the opinion that Condit, had he come under our scrutiny in this capacity, would have had a hard time obtaining *bona fides*. For defectors, it was the first stage to which we subjected them on their arrival to ascertain whether they were spies or agents and, if not, credible and potentially suitable for interrogation. With respect to POWs, we mainly screened them at the end of the war to determine whether they were SS or Nazi Party members. If they were clean, that is neither SS nor Nazis, we sent them home with our blessings, for we had so many of them. Congressman Condit, under similar circumstances, might have had a hard time convincing us.

The French Academy, Guardian of Language

A writer named Tibor Machan, whose column occasionally appears in my local Arizona newspaper, was recently fulminating against the venerable French Academy and its forty "immortals," as its members are called. The Latin root of *fulminate* is *fulmen*, a bolt of lightning, and I thought Mr. Machan was outdoing Zeus/Jupiter himself, the original Greek/Roman Fulminator. He was berating the Academy for "illiberal and collectivist measures" (quite a mouthful) in matters of language policy. Now collectivism is a pretty strong word, implying extreme control of the economic, political, and social life of its subjects by an authoritarian state. I suppose one might apply it to national language policy.

I have a soft spot in my heart for the forty immortals, especially since 1932, when I was a student in a Parisian *lycée* and the Academy published its first *Grammar* to almost universal condemnation and ridicule. The Academy, initially a private club in 1934 then in 1935 formally recognized by the parliament in Paris, was charged by Cardinal Richelieu, its founder, to make the French language "pure, eloquent and capable of treating the arts and sciences." The august body of men of letters was to implement this by publishing a *Dictionary*, a *Grammar*, a book on *Rhetoric* (description of styles and manners of speech), and a *Poetics* (description of literary rules). Today, having found the last two tasks impractical, and still smarting from its disastrous *Grammar*, the Academy continues, at snail's pace, to revise its dictionary, eight previous editions of which have appeared from 1694 to 1935, the latter the year I received my Bachelor of Letters degree from the University of Paris. By the way, the Larousse and the Robert are much better dictionaries!

In an e-mail, I tried to point out to Mr. Machan, perhaps not gently enough, that the French language situation was much too complex to cast all blame for its policy offhandedly on the forty immortals alone. The entire French system — the civil service and the administration of the state — are the legacy of the Napoleonic reforms of 1805-1815 (subsequently Gaullism), the French-Tunisian crisis of 1958, the student revolts and national strikes of 1968, and finally of Mitterand's long presidency. One must remember that the powerful institutions of France's public administration are staffed with career civil servants, who at the highest level are the top graduates of the National School of Administration. These in turn are all selected by competitive entrance and exit exams. In France, such an elitist system persists in all fields, from engineering to education. Engineers, chosen by the same competitive system from the *École Polytechnique* (Polytechnic School), as well as teachers, competing for the "aggrégation" (a nationwide competitive exam), gain employment for life and the feeling to have reached the summit of intellectual competence.

Overall, language policies are closely related to other types of policy: cultural, social, and economic. It is only possible to examine and evaluate them in relation to the concerns of a nation: regarding its social identity; the way that identity is projected abroad; the satisfaction provided by that identity; ways it affects social cohesion. The French are proud of their language. Not averse to borrowing words from other countries, even mispronouncing them, they do object to using foreignisms wherever French already has a perfect, often better, term for the same meaning. Perhaps Mr. Machan is envious of the splendid "green uniform" (*l'habit vert*) the members wear on special occasions.

Picketwire River, Colorado   From *Rivière du Purgatoire* (Purgatory River), so named by the French — formerly *Río de las Ánimas Perdidas* (River of the Lost Souls), as named by the Spanish explorers.

Pique   Directly from French, meaning prick or sting.

Roots Anchor Meanings in Language

Parsley is quite rich in vitamins. Today, however, although a seasoning, the plant serves mostly as a garnish, left uneaten on the plate. In ancient times, the Greeks also used it as decoration, but not of the culinary type. They preferred to make chaplets or "crowns of glory" from its richly green leaves for their victors in competitive games. Words like *chaplet*, *chapter*, *capital*, *cap*, all have the Latin word *caput*, or head, as a root. The Greeks must have associated the parsley plant with rocks, because the Greek name for it, *petroselinon*, contains the prefix *petro-*, which, as you know, means rock, as in petroglyph, a carving or inscription on a rock, and petrolithic, constituting a firm rock-like road surface. Through the French, *peresil*, later shortened to *persil*, it became English *parsley* and German *Petersilie*.

William Safire has punned that without the Greek prefix, the English word "parsley" might have become "*silly*" and our spice shelves would have displayed "sage" and "silly." *Silly*, once spelled *soelig* in Norman times, was identical to German *selig* and meant blessed or even happy. Later it included the meanings of innocent, plain, rustic, simple. Some societies — for example Indian tribes — deemed simple-minded individuals as "touched by the Lord" and treated them accordingly with more compassion. Because the Norman conquerors had little to do, silly came to mean not only blessed, but also idle. This explains Coleridge's "silly (here "idle" or "empty," because of the drought) buckets" on the deck of the Ancient Mariner's ship. Germans, especially Jews, refer to a dead person as *selig* or blessed ("my mother *selig*").

Obsessed with words and playing its usual tricks, my mind jumps from parsley to the verb "to parse." This comes from Latin *pars orationis*, or part of speech, and it signifies to resolve a sentence into its parts. In 1963, Susumu Kuno of Harvard developed one of the first computer-based sentence-parsing systems, which found it difficult to parse a simple sentence like "Time flies like an arrow." To the human mind it simply means that time passes as quickly as an arrow. The computer, however, found the sentence puzzling. Could it be a command to time or clock the speed of "flies," the same way as an arrow might time flies? Or did it mean to clock the speed of flies like one might clock that of an arrow?

Then again the sentence might be a command telling us to time or clock only those flies that are similar to an arrow. The computer, evidently not endowed with a gift of tongue, then surmised it might even refer to a special type of flies, like horseflies (here "time flies"), and that such flies had a predilection and fondness for arrows. I mention all this because I think it will be a long time before computers can translate impeccably somewhat complex literary texts, a subject I have treated elsewhere. Incidentally, *impeccable* is always negative and comes from the Latin *in*, or not, and *peccare*, to sin. So impeccable means "no sin" and implies, therefore, perfection. The root of the word sin reveals something about the workings of the primitive human mind and its constant struggle with feelings of guilt. *Sin*, the Latin *esse*, or to be, German *sein*, all go back to the idea of original sin, where to be and to exist implied being sinful. Biblical Adam's fall triggered the belief: that we all sinned. Merely to exist, to be, is to be a sinner. To be exempt from sin in our minds was so rare that we preserved and treasured the negative form in impeccable.

Attack and Violence in Language

With the September 2001 terrorist bombings of both the World Trade Center in New York City and of the Pentagon in Washington, D.C., we suffered a national calamity. This last word, and other related terms it suggests, make for some rather interesting etymological material, providing an insight into the metaphors our human mind conjures to express in words sorrow, damage, and misfortune. The word *calamity*, no doubt, comes from the French *calamité*, which again is derived from Latin *calamitas*, a disaster. However, the story does not end here. Many more specific mental associations further flesh out the meaning of "hurt." Greek words similar to calamity like *klan* (to break), *kolos* (docked, with the end of a body part cut off, as the tail of a dog or horse; hornless), *kolobos* (docked, curtailed), as well as Lithuanian *kalti* (signifying to beat), all contribute nuances to the larger canvas depicting a disastrous event.

The fact that Latin *calamus* means *reed* has led to other associations, even puns. The notion of reed may suggest to us plants ranging from leaves of grass to cornstalks. In late 19th-century England there was a "cult of the Calamus" among poets like Swinburne, Rossetti, and others, in admiration of the American Walt Whitman's *Leaves of Grass*. The ancients even speculated that damage to cornstalks from hail or mildew inspired the word calamity itself. Francis Bacon (1561-1626) had punned that "drought, when the corn cannot come out of the stalk, turns calamus [*the reed*] into calamitas [*calamity*]." Any student of Latin, of course, knows that *lapsus linguae* and *lapsus calami* mean a lapse of the tongue and one of the pen, respectively, not always calamities. Pertinent to what happened in America in 2001, Francis Beaumont and John Fletcher in *Four Plays in One: The Triumph of Honour* (1647), wrote: "Calamity is man's true touchstone."

Compassion is derived from Latin *cum* meaning together with and *patior*, to suffer, and from an old French word *pâtir*, to suffer. Thus, compassion means to suffer together with the person stricken by calamity. German and French speakers need not know Latin to catch the literal meaning of their words for compassion: *Mitleid* in German and *compassion* in French translate into native words the literal meaning. In this case we have the German *mit*, with, and *Leid*, suffering; the French *con* (*com* before a *p*), with, and *pâtir*, to suffer. This process of adopting foreign words by means of translation is referred to as loan translation, a practice English shuns, thereby depriving English speakers of the image behind the word, unless they are Latinists. *Retaliation* comes directly from the Latin *talis*, of such kind, and *re*, again, meaning you are doing to others such as they have done to you.

Slander was once considered the greatest of all evils. *Devil*, from Old English *deofol*, Greek *diabolos* (compare diabolical) meant slanderer, literally "he who throws across," from the Greek verb *diabollein* meaning exactly that. Depending on the myth invoked, what he threw across might be souls and where he threw them might be Hell. Anyone trying to relate *deofol* to "fallen God" possesses an overheated imagination. Imitating such words as centrifuge (literally fleeing the center) and febrifuge (chasing away fever), Oliver Wendell Holmes coined the term diabolifuge (from Latin *fugare*, to flee) as something that drives away the devil. In Hebrew, Satan meant adversary, from a verb meaning to plot against. Feud, feudal, foe, and Satan, the "fiend," are all related and derive from a root meaning enmity, German *Feind*.

I'll close, wishing everyone peace.

Astronomy Terms Not Always Extra-terrestrial

Did you ever consider the extent to which astrology (literally knowledge of the stars) is present in our language? Take the very verb consider. From the Latin *cum*, meaning with, and *sidus* (irregular plural *sidera*), signifying star, the verb reflects the fact that the ancients consulted with the stars in order to come to a final decision when considering a matter. Even today many believe that how the stars appear and join together (conjunction) at a person's birth may indicate his or her future. Of course, someone who has pondered carefully and thoughtfully an issue is likely to be considerate, which first merely meant giving thought and later more specifically giving thoughts to others. The scientific term sidereal is used in astronomy. A sidereal year is the time in which the earth completes one revolution in its orbit around the sun, measured with respect to the fixed stars (365 days, 6 hours, 9 minutes, 9.54 seconds of solar time).

The prefix *dis-* means apart, opposite, etc. Therefore, disaster implies that the stars are against you: you are "ill-starred" and apt to be at the wrong place at the wrong time. The word sinister, although not directly based on astrology, comes from a Latin word meaning "left," as the ancients believed that the left was bad. When priests probed the future, if they observed birds flying over from the left side, they concluded it portended evil. Another Latin word from the Greek for star, *astrum*, gives us the star-shaped flower, the aster, and the star-shaped printing sign, the asterisk. The motto of Kansas is *Ad astra per aspera,* to the stars through difficulties or hardships. In Shakespeare's *Julius Caesar*, Brutus is reminded that our fate lies "not in our stars, but in ourselves." Today, astrologers would be tempted to sue the Bard.

As noted earlier, astronomy comes from the Greek *nomos*, custom or law, here of the stars, and the Romans paid a great deal of attention to the heavenly bodies, using a third term for star, *stella*. This yields the name Stella, a stellar performance, stellular markings, constellation, meaning a group of stars together, and to stellify or turn into a star. The latter fate befell the twins Castor and Pollux, now stellified as Gemini. I have previously noted, in "Star-spun Words," that *star* is common Teutonic, *Stern* in

German; and consternation is from a different source, from the Latin *cum*, both an intensive and meaning together, and *sternere*, signifying to strew or strike down (originally to dumbfound in surprise and terror). Then again astrology may also have played a role in its meaning by referring to scattered and unfavorable stars.

Lately we witness much rhetoric. We coin words, the idea of which we cannot truly grasp, like infinity. President George W. Bush referred to Operation Infinite Justice. It literally means no *finis* or end. Think about it! In the range of the infinite, the whole is no greater than any of its parts. Add any number you please to infinity, subtract or add infinity from or to infinity, multiply it by itself, and you still have infinity. Justice is justice simply by its own little self.

Some great writers have managed rhetoric impressively. The great French scientist and thinker Pascal wrote (my translation):

> What does man represent in nature? A nothing with regard to infinity, an all with regard to nothing, a middle between nothing and all. . . . Man is but a reed, the most fragile in Nature, but he is a reed that thinks.

Pascal was not only a great scientist (at age eighteen he invented a calculating machine and later conducted famous experiments on the vacuum and atmospheric pressure), but a great writer in his *Thoughts*. As a Jansenist, whose theology was based on the teachings of Cornelius Jansen, bishop of Ypres, he debated the Jesuits.

Language Can Be Tantalizing

Recently, I read a tantalizing article on the front page of the *Arizona Republic*, which stated that a newly discovered gene might play a crucial role in human language and offer insights on speech. The findings are based on the study of a rare speech disorder known to affect only sixteen individuals worldwide. If successful, such research could shed light on the molecular basis of language and on what scientists suspect is one element of language ability, which, in combination with key social and environmental cues, has allowed the human species to talk. I almost thought my days as a newspaper columnist on language were numbered, but thank heavens for the above key factors, which saved me.

I call the article tantalizing, as it teased my expectations, only to frustrate them by revealing nothing earthshaking about my favorite subject. I have earlier written about *tantalize*, which comes to us from Greco-Roman mythology, where the gods punished anyone who sought to equal them in power. They condemned Tantalus, king of Phrygia, for his rebellious activism to stand in Tartarus (a place beneath the earth, reserved for the rebel Titans, as far below Hades as heaven is above the earth, and closed by iron gates) up to his chin in water that receded whenever he stooped to drink. Above his head hung branches with delectable fruit tantalizingly withdrawing from his reach, when he tried to grasp it. Sisyphean (that is, continuous yet ineffective), efforts on his part could not assuage his thirst or still his hunger. What's with Sisyphean, you ask? Sisyphus, the cruel king of Corinth, was sentenced in Hades to roll up a hill a heavy rock that constantly slid back down again. As prisons go, a tough act to follow for our local Arizona Sheriff.

Even if in the next decade or so we learn more about how our five senses enable us to perceive reality and transform such perceptions into manageable verbal metaphors and logical constructs communicable by sounds, writing, body motions, gestures, and grimaces, much will remain unanswered. Shall we ever know to what extent linguistic ability is "hard-wired" or programmed into the brain? The multidimensionality of everything in our universe makes it almost impossible for language and meaning to signify more than one property or aspect of anything at any one time. Different languages, for random cultural and traditional motives now irretrievable from the misty past, select such aspects differently. You will recall the praying mantis, which becomes a religious mantis in French, and our firewood, which is metamorphosed into French heating wood, the German burn wood, and the Russian fuel wood.

As exemplified by countless expressions, adages, and proverbs in various languages, the fundamental meaning may remain essentially identical, but is displayed in different window dressings — as though a primary semantic spark connected with our intellect to yield the same semantic imprint or lesson. However, the semantic "stage setting" varies with each expression. As the stage turntable rotates to the Spanish set, our "better a bird in hand than two in the bush" appears as "better a bird in hand than two flying," or, even more emphatically, "than a flying vulture." Our "you could hear a pin drop" becomes in French "one could hear a fly fly." The French equivalents of horse race, horse show, horse butcher, horse drawn, horsefly, horse chestnut, horse sense, never once contain the singular word "horse." And, of course, you will remember that to eat a napoleon in Paris, you should not ask for the Emperor — they'll lock you up; ask for a "1,000 leaves" (*mille-feuille*).

Terror Derivatives from Latin and French

We have lately been inundated from all sides with references to terror and terrorists. Before we consider the derivation of the word *terror*, a few comments on *inundate*. This word signifies "to cover with waves" from the Latin *unda*, or wave. We speak of undulant fever, because the temperature goes up and down, wavelike. When authors or speakers are verbose or prolix, they might be accused of being redundant, from the Latin prefix *re-*, which here indicates repetition, and the same Latin word for waves, here of words, that keep on coming at us like waves and break down over us mercilessly. Such criticism does not redound (same root as redundant, despite the different spelling) to their credit. In Alexander Pope's time, redound meant to surge up or billow, as in "waves [*while*] redounding roar." Now to redound rather means to have a good or ill effect. Prolix comes from Latin *pro*, meaning forward, and *lixus* or *liquere*, to flow like a liquid. But back to terror!

Terror comes straight from the Latin and French. To deter (from *de* + *terrere*) is to frighten away, as *de* means away from. The extremely productive Latin root *facere*, to make, gives us terror + *facere*, literally "to make terror" — in better English, "to terrify." A related word, albeit from a different Latin root, is *trepidation* from a word meaning to tremble and be anxious. Of course, our *intrepid* firefighters at the World Trade Center Ground Zero in New York City did not tremble and were not terrified, as *in-* here indicates the negative "not." Unrelated is the word *terse* from the Latin *tergere*, to wipe. It gave us detergent, which wipes away or gets rid of stains. Terse once meant clean, burnished, but is now used with the idea of devoid of any superfluity, concise. Take the *g* out of *tergere* and you get *terere*, to rub, which is more vigorous than wipe and gave us trite, something rubbed so much it lost its freshness. Hence come also our attrition and even detriment. This last word implies wearing away, impairing, and the damage resulting from it. Incidentally, what is left after rubbing off is detritus, loose material resulting from rock abrasion. Only one English derivative has a gentler meaning: contrite. Originally signifying rubbed together (*cum*, together), crushed, bruised, it evolved into crushed by one's sense of sin and, therefore, repentant.

Terrorism is causing many nations much agony, and intense physical or mental suffering. *Agony* has an interesting history, Can you believe that pleasure, rather than pain, was first intended when using this word? From the Greek *agon* or assembly, the word came to be applied to the great assemblies gathered to watch the Greek games and dramatic contests. Eventually it grew to mean contest for a prize. The main actor, whose soul's inner struggle was the focus of the play, was the protagonist, from Greek *protos* (first) and *agonistes* (contender). Milton wrote a poem entitled *Samson Agonistes*, about the captivity of the blinded Samson and the destruction by him of the Philistine temple.

Agonia came to be applied to both physical and mental struggles. The antagonist is the one against whom the protagonist struggles, and to be antagonistic is not to be kindly disposed toward others and ready to fight them, or, more crudely put, "a pain in the arse." However, Greek *gone* means knee, which through Latin *genu* gave us our genuflection or flexing of knees. It probably also came into English from the French *genou*, or knee. To finish this column with a flourish, an *agonoclite* was an unbending person, specifically a 7th-century heretic who prayed standing up: *a*, not, + *gone*, knee, + *klitos*, bent. Take a deep breath now and relax!

Rats! Dreaded Scoundrels Came from the East

In Act 1, Scene 2 of Shakespeare's *The Tempest*, Prospero reveals to his daughter Miranda how they came to be marooned on their forsaken island. Once Duke of Milan, Prospero was deposed by his treacherous brother and his accomplices, who

> Bore us some leagues to sea, where they prepar'd
> A rotten carcass of a boat, not rigg'd,
> Nor tackle, sail, nor mast; the very rats
> Instinctively have quit it. . . .

The above lines may well illustrate how words and metaphors originate and evolve.

The Spanish applied the word *cimarrón* (wild animal) to the escaped slaves of the West Indies. The French, through folk etymology or the use of like-sounding words in their own language, turned it into *ces marrons*, literally "these chestnuts." The color was right, so, while now politically incorrect, they also used it to designate runaway slaves. As these slaves roamed the desert islands, the English applied the term "maroon" to anyone put ashore on such islands. Folk etymology has yielded many English terms, most of them at first nonsensical, then accepted just like any other word, but their origin forgotten. Thus, as noted, the familiar Key West comes from the Spanish *cayo hueso*, literally little islet in the form of a bone, hoosegow (jail) from Spanish *juzgado*, judged, indicted.

Rats came from the East with the migration of other hordes before Roman times. The word was even imported from the Teutonic by Lower Latin as *ratus*, Anglo-Saxon *raet*, German *Ratte*, French *rat*. A little rat was *raton* in both French and Middle English, as people spoke a fairly similar language on both sides of the Channel after the Norman invasion of 1066. The common notion that rats desert sinking ships spread to those who deserted or betrayed a cause. Hence rat designated a scoundrel. A pun, particular to Ireland during 1921-1922, applied the term to those favoring *rat*ification of the treaty with England. To ratify, from the Latin *ratum facere* through the French meant to make valid. The Latin verb *reri* (past participle *ratus*) also meant to think, judge, calculate. Hence all our expressions *pro rata* (exactly calculable proportion), rate (agreed-upon amount), and, of course, rate of speed.

To *rate* or *berate*, meaning to scold, may be from the Scandinavian. The prefix *be-* has various functions: in berate it is an intensifier; in behead it is privative or negative; in bemoan or befoul it produces transitive verbs

> **Hoosegow** A jail or lockup — formed by folk etymology from the Spanish *juzgado* (judged, or sentenced).
>
> **Key West** The elongated islets were named *cayo hueso* — islets shaped like a bone — by Spanish conquistador Cabeza de Vaca.

(they take a direct object) from intransitive ones or other words; in bedeck (adorn gaudily) it expresses ridicule; as it does in bedizen, to dress like a harlot or meretrix (with meretrix from Latin *merere*, to earn), who was only despised because she took money. Bedizen originally meant to put *diesse* or flax on a staff, and distaff, relating to a woman or mother (the distaff side of the family), has the same origin. Rat, referring to a pad under a woman's hair, no doubt originated from the fact that it reminds us of the color and shape of the animal. The exclamations "Rat! Rot!" are shortened from Drat! Drot!, again shortened and euphemistic forms of "God rot it!" If you are still with me, you are now halfway through to a Ph.D. in linguistics! You may also be certain Sinatra's Rat Pack never knew all this.

Chemistry and Language

To study the origin of words is to gain insight into how we think. Thus the French chemist Lavoisier, one of the creators of modern chemistry, who was executed during the French Revolution in 1794, named hydrogen to show that it "produces" or "gives birth to" (*gen*, as in genetics) "hydro," or water. When observing foreign-language teaching in the United States, I have always been surprised that most of our educationists, or educational theorists, if you prefer, are so averse (may I hazard "allergic") to the use of grammar or anything remotely hinting of it. In general, Americans like to know how things work, how systems operate to accomplish certain tasks. So why not be curious about how languages utilize certain grammatical forms, varying, of course, with each one, to achieve specific semantic results, in this case extremely accurate shades of meaning? Grammar is a roadmap or blueprint to language! Let us illustrate!

Many verbs that express the beginning of an action have an "inchoative" or "inceptive" form. Both these words indicate *beginning*. Inchoate, from the Latin, literally signifies hitching the strap fastening the plow beam to the yoke, *i.e.*, to commence plowing. Inceptive and incipient are from Latin, to take hold or begin (*in*, here meaning to start in, and *capere*, to seize, take hold — note our word capture from the same root). Examples of inchoate English verbs include begin, set out, get, beget, awake. Many have the distinctive *-esce* Latin (*escere*) ending: adolesce (we normally only use the present participle adolescent), incandesce (become incandescent), coalesce (coalescent, becoming coagulated), acquiesce, evanesce, obsolesce. Some inchoate verbs, from the French, also end in *-ish*, like vanish, to begin disappearing. I am going to show you how, much as our senses perceive and our mind analyzes the singular elements that result in a complex action, language mirrors this process by having various sounds or parts of speech, each with its own singular meaning, combine to form the entire picture or scenario. It is like chemistry, where several elements combine to form a compound, or a like a Tinker Toy we assemble for a new construct.

Latin *alere*, to nourish, had an inceptive form: *alescere*, to grow. Add the Latin preposition *ad* (to) and we have adolescent, the growing individual, who, once grown, is in the past participle indicating completed action or "adult." When things vanish into thin air, they leave a vacuum or empty space. If an individual is "short a load of bricks," he may have a vacuous mind and a vacuous expression on his face. Hence also to vacate, vacant, even vacation, all indicating emptiness of space or work. The earlier word for empty was *vanus*, our vain, which indicates emptiness of purpose, substance, and usefulness. Hence, with the addition of Latin *ex*, *e*, or out, we have "to evanesce," to disappear gradually like vapor, to begin to empty out. In French the word was *esvanir*, which ultimately produced the more usual to vanish. The French *esvanir* is now obsolete, but there is *s'évanouir*, a reflexive meaning to faint, a form of vanishing, in a way. This has nothing to do with "vamoose," another form of vanishing, from the Spanish *vamos!* meaning "let's go!"

Does acquiesce truly mean the same as agree? Perhaps not quite! From the Latin, it literally means to begin to be at rest or *quiet*. In my view, to agree is active, to acquiesce is merely a passive, silent assent. Literally, one remains silent; one allows someone else to win, without endorsement. To obsolesce, to fall into disuse, has three original Latin components: *ob* (against), *solitus* (what is usual), and the *-esce* marking the beginning. You are now all CLCs, Certified Language Chemists.

Learning a Foreign Language: Bilingual Method vs. Total Immersion

Occasionally I am asked for my opinion of bilingual education. My response: It depends on your purpose. If bilingual education is only a political expedient to cater to immigrant voters, and you do not care how proficient these students become in English, by all means go for it! If, on the other hand, you want motivated students, with their families' support, to master English and become English-speaking citizens, forget about any watered-down bilingual approach and go for proven total immersion programs. Bilingual education is the choice of self-styled experts whose experience with foreign language learning or teaching is vicarious, not firsthand. Incidentally, Spanish has a delightful label for such would-be experts: *eruditos a la violeta*. Difficult to translate, this phrase means people that have acquired their erudition or expertise by merely sprinkling some violet-scented perfume on themselves; their competence is not even skin deep. Read the following and judge for yourself!

I have mentioned earlier that in 1922, at age five, I moved to Hamburg, Germany, with my parents. Faced with getting along in a country that had just lost World War I and was not overly fond of the foreign victors, I realized it would be to my advantage to blend in with the landscape. At that age, with my parents away all day at the office, reared by a German maid, attending German schools, motivated to fit into my new life without losing pride in my native land, it was easy to "become" a German boy and forget English completely. At age thirteen, I experienced another culture shock, before such a concept was even known! Mastering only German, I had to move to Paris around Easter time, because of my father's job. I found myself in a French *lycée*, compelled to learn simultaneously French, Latin (in Hamburg we used easy Latin readers, in Paris students my age were reading Caesar and Vergil in the original), and English. A pragmatist, the French teacher had assigned me to a grade where, after automatically flunking in June, I might, with tutoring during the long summer recess, stand a chance of holding my own in the fall.

For three months I was a mere auditor of the class, aghast, almost suicidal, at the thought of the task ahead. I spent hours struggling with huge dictionaries, making myself believe in the popular European saying "a word looked up seven times, is remembered forever." The summer was spent learning French and Latin with a hired tutor and English with my mother. The next year, together with other students seeking good grades, I took homework preparation tutoring in Math and Latin. Two years later, flawless in French, I made "best in class."

In 1951, recalled to military service during the Korean Conflict and assigned to the Pentagon, I heard that the U.S. Army had decided to open to all officers its Russian Area and Language Training Program, hitherto available only to Regular Army officers. I was the first to volunteer. Reserve officers would spend only three years, one at the Monterey Language School, California, and two at Detachment R (for Russian) in Regensburg, Germany. Regular Army officers attended an extra year at Columbia University with a chance for an M.A. It was a total immersion approach. No English was spoken. Monterey taught Russian by rote. The course in Germany, conducted entirely in Russian by former Soviet officers and professionals of the highest caliber, covered every possible aspect of Soviet reality: military, economic, historical, legal, ideological. Socializing was exclusively with the foreign teaching staff. It was the closest thing to living in the USSR. Total hours for the three years, including homework: 6,000. Most of us graduated fluent in Russian and expert in the USSR.

Such results are not achievable by the bilingual method.

Fractured English

Once upon a time, language was respected, correct usage extolled (from the Latin *extollere*, to lift up, exalt), faulty diction reviled, and a column like mine handsomely rewarded. A thin book entitled *Faulty Diction*, published by Funk & Wagnalls in 1915, supports my statements. This jewel of a book points out that the use of *than* is improper where there is no comparison. In cases like "no sooner said than done," mistakes are rare. However, when other words intervene, one might encounter: "This is derived from a different source *than* the other." Here, good usage requires *from*.

Formerly, *than* was often, if not always, used as a preposition. The habit of putting a pronoun that ends a sentence in the objective case is a survival of the prepositional use and explains such inelegant constructions as "he is older than me (in lieu of I)" and "you are taller than him (in lieu of he)." Surprisingly, "Cromwell, than whom no man was better skilled in artifice" is supported by classical usage. In another example, we compare one thing *with* another to note points of agreement or difference. We compare one thing *to* another, which we think it resembles. In "as a writer of English, Addison is not to be compared, except with great peril to his reputation, *to* at least a score of men," the writer should have used "with" or left out "without peril to his reputation." Indeed, if comparing him *with* others is perilous, then don't do it. Never try to combine two incompatible ideas, here "to compare him *with* others is a bad idea" and "he should not be compared *to* these others."

I can hear Cicero, twenty-one centuries ago, exclaiming "*O tempora! O mores!*" ("Alas, for the times! Alas, for the manners!"). In this speech he was bemoaning the decline of classical Latin. I felt the same way recently, while in line at an emission-testing station. A prominently displayed sign for Spanish speakers, "*Ofreciendo soborno es criminal*," was translated to "Offering bribes is a crime." The only crime was the faulty Spanish. The English "offering," here the subject and a verbal noun, was translated literally into a Spanish present participle, making the sentence meaningless. In Spanish, the verbal noun form is the infinitive; the sign should read "*Ofrecer soborno. . . .*"

I am again reminded of other linguistic pearls I have encountered in my travels. In a Bucharest hotel: "The lift is being fixed for the next day. During that time we regret that you will be unbearable." In a Japanese hotel: "You are invited to take advantage of the chambermaid." In Austria: "Not to perambulate the corridors in the hours of repose in the boots of ascension." In a Swiss restaurant, quite up front, I confess: "Our wines leave you nothing to hope for." In a Leipzig elevator: "Do not enter the lift backwards, and only when lit up." In a Paris hotel:

"Please leave your values at the front desk." In Athens: "Visitors are expected to complain at the office between 9 and 11 a.m. daily." In a Moscow hotel: "You are welcome to visit the cemetery, where famous Russian and Soviet composers, artists, and writers are buried daily except Thursday." In a Hong Kong supermarket: "For your convenience, we recommend courteous, efficient self-service." A Rome laundry: "Leave your clothes here and spend the afternoon having a good time." In former Yugoslavia: "The flattening of underwear with pleasure is the job of the chambermaid." In a Hong Kong tailor shop: "Ladies may have a fit upstairs." In a Rhodes tailor shop: " Order your summer suits now. Because of big rush, we will execute customers in strict rotation." And Moscow praised a show of paintings by Soviet artists "executed over the past two years."

I rest my case!

China's Name a Misunderstanding

In 1982, I visited China as a tourist. From 1985-1986, I taught English at Yunnan Normal University in Kunming, in southwest China, from where, during World War II, General Chenault's Flying Tigers flew the Hump (the Himalayas) to Burma. A V-shaped monument high on neighboring hills now commemorates this achievement. I returned there in 1992 and 1998 to visit my many friends, help Yunnan TV with its English programs, and give some lectures on America to students and faculty. I spent Christmas 2001 there, to lecture and witness again the enormous changes in terms of progress and capitalistic modernization that have taken place in the past sixteen years. Development and new construction are so extensive that my friends who leave Kunming to travel abroad and return are lost in their own native city. When, using the Kunming dialect, they ask passersby for directions, they elicit the inevitable reply: "What's wrong with you? You speak the Kunming dialect and don't know your way?" But back to language!

The name Kunming, a city situated at over 6,000 feet elevation, originally meant "spring city" in Chinese, as it enjoys a mild climate. Yunnan means "south of the clouds." The word China owes its origin to a misunderstanding. The Romans bought so much Chinese silk for their ladies from Chinese traders in Persia that such excessive foreign imports provoked a public outcry and reproachful speeches in the forum. When asked where they came from, the traders, rather than using the correct name of their country, *Chung Kwo* (Chun Kwo), literally middle kingdom, would often refer to it by the name of the powerful reigning Ch'in dynasty (221-207 B.C.). In Latin, which avoids the *"ch"* sound, this became *Sina*, still found in such English words as Sinology. The Russians call China *Kitai* (Cathay), of Turkic and Tatar origin and referring to the Khitan dynasty (900-1100 A.D.).

Since 1945, Chinese has been one of the five official languages at the United Nations, along with English, French, Russian, and Spanish. All speeches are simultaneously translated into them. Our pejorative "Chink," designating a Chinese person, derives through folk etymology from the above *Chung Kwo*. In Chinese, "I am a Chinese" becomes *"wo chungkwo ren,"* where the *"r"* is pronounced *"zh."* Long ago, the Chinese occasionally referred to Westerners as *fankwei* (mountain ghosts or devils), as white is the color of death and mourning. They were also called *tabeetsu* or "the big-nosed ones." U.S. Marines serving in China may well have distorted this by folk etymology into the now seldom-heard slang for nose, "beezer," a far more plausible explanation than Webster's suggestion it might be a blend of beak and sneezer.

The Chinese word order appears at times primitive, but is quite logical. "How are you?" almost becomes a true or false question, as *"ni hau"* literally means "you good?" and is countered by either *hau* (good) or *buhau* (not good). One particular Chinese construction, sometimes referred as the yes-no syndrome, is rather odd. When we ask the question "Aren't you a teacher?" we expect in reply either "Yes, I am" or "No, I'm not." In Chinese, you get either "No, I am" or "No, I'm not" as the reply must reflect the negative slant of the question. "Go figure!" as they say.

Dzai jian! — Goodbye! — for now, with more to come about this 1.4 billion people nation.

Xie, Xie! Thank you!

◈ The Chinese Language ◈

The official language of the People's Republic of China (PRC) is now the northern variant *Kwo yu* or *Chun Kwo Hwa*, where *yu* and *hwa* mean language. It is often referred to as Mandarin, which technically was the language of the Imperial bureaucracy and ceased to exist in 1911. China has fifty-six different nationalities, twenty-six of which are in Yunnan province. They are not referred to as minorities. One main Chinese tongue, Cantonese, is spoken in Canton (*Guanshou*) and Hong Kong. The ideogram writing is the same for all Chinese variants. Grammatically simpler than many Western languages, Chinese (without case endings, verb conjugations, noun plurals) nevertheless is rich in specialized expressions used to refer to different kinds or categories of objects when preceded by cardinal numerals (persons, books, money, birds, or various domestic animals). They recall our English *pair* of shoes, *head* of cattle, *brace* of quail, but are more numerous. Chinese, like most languages, is rich in images. The word for kangaroo literally means "pocket rat." *Wo meikwo zhen* means "I am an American," where *mei* mimicks the "me" in American and *kwo* is "nation."

"When the cat's away, the mice will play" is rendered in Chinese by "cat gone, old rat comes out." "Something is rotten in Denmark" becomes "I don't know what kind of medicine is inside this melon." All Chinese words are formed by single syllables. Because their number is limited, oral Chinese resorts to four tones, Cantonese even to six. *Chun Kwo* has a short up tone, a rising questioning tone, a deep sinking then rising tone, and a short down tone. The word *chiang*, depending on tone or writing, can mean "shall," "command," "a river," "soy sauce," "mechanic," "to drop," "descend," or even a name, as in *Chiang Kai-shek*. The family name always comes first, the given name last. "*Ma ma ma ma ma*," each with a different tone, means: "Is mother scolding the horse?" "One woman under roof" means "peace," "two women" means a "quarrel," "three" means "debauchery" or "adultery." Chinese writing, like ancient Egyptian and Mesopotamian, evolved thousands of years ago from pictures or pictograms to more generalized ideograms.

Thus the sun, originally a circle, is now a square with a line through it. The moon looks like a Cyrillic "l" or a curved half moon with two lines through it. Written together, the two characters signify "bright." The character for good or happiness is a woman and child, the one for perfect a large ram. The character for horse still displays four legs and a tail. Combine fire and cart and you get locomotive. Cart with a sweeping enveloping line above gives us army. "Mouth in doorway" stands for "ask"; "ear" in "doorway" stands for "listen"; "horse coming through doorway" stands for "sudden interruption." In my own Sun City, this character should change into "automobile" crashing through a "storefront."

Chinese writing, like ours, is now from left to right. Every character has a radical that indicates the class of things to which the word belongs. Thus the heart radical designates an emotional state, the water radical the presence of water, the sickness radical matters of pathology, and so on. The original 214 radicals have been so far reduced to 189. In most cases the radical is positioned on the top or on the left of the character. To look up a character in a Chinese dictionary, you find it in a listing arranged first under its radical, then under the number of extra strokes beyond the radical. The radicals have a fixed sequence in ascending number of strokes.

"*Xie, xie!*" Thanks! Y'all are now certified Sinologists.

Sign Language

I recently reviewed for the *Journal of the West* a reprint of a remarkable book by Garrick Mallery on *Sign Language Among American Indians*, which was originally published in 1881 by the Smithsonian Institution. More than ever before, it made me realize how much those that preceded us already knew and that, when we ponder the origin of language, the possibility of man, at some time, having survived and managed without any oral language is quite likely. Mental images or representations do not necessarily require sound to be formed. Without the aid of sound, they may also serve for thought, if not for vocal expression. It is certain that sound is not the only way to express concepts. Even when highly sophisticated, concepts may be expressed by other modes, such as gestures, though absolutely no evidence suggests that gestures began as an interpretation of or substitute for words. Is it not more reasonable to theorize that language had its origin in and served to translate gestures? Much evidence points to gesture language preceding articulate speech as the earliest attempt of humans to communicate with one another.

Examples of the importance of gestures in communication abound in literature and art. Volumnia, Coriolanus's mother in Shakespeare's *Coriolanus*, advises her son that often "action is eloquence, and the eyes of the ignorant more learned than the ears" (3.2). Paraphrased it means that the hands and gestures of the ignorant are more learned or speak louder than their tongues. The classical author and Jesuit Ludovicus Cresollius favored gestures over speech when he wrote in 1620: "Man, full of wisdom and divinity, could have appeared nothing superior to a naked trunk

---

Tale From Anglo-Saxon *talu*, designating both speech and number; also from Anglo-Saxon *tellan*, to list in order, and thus English "tell" and "teller."

Tattoo East Island origin: Maori *ta* means "to scar" and Tahitian *tatu* means "pricking" — thus the colorful designs with pigments injected beneath the skin.

---

or block had he not been adorned with the hand as the interpreter and messenger of his thoughts." He goes on to say that language would be nearly useless without the hand: "Whereas the hand, without the aid of language, has produced many and wonderful effects." George Dalgarno, writing in 1661 in Latin, states: "Man finds it not less natural to communicate with figures than with sounds." Roman historian Livy (59 B.C.-17 A.D.) declared gesture speech to be of great antiquity, and Roman rhetorician Quintilian (35-97 A.D.) specified that "*lex gestus . . . ab illis temporibus heroicis orta est*" (the law of gestures originated from these heroic times), later providing elaborate rules for finger gestures in oratory.

Plato classed the practice of gesture language among the civil virtues. With appropriate terminology, it had its place in Greek education. Cordax was the class suited to comedy, Eumelia to tragedy, Sicinnis, named after its inventor Sicinnus, to satire, and a fourth one, *pantimimos*, meaning actor or mimic, to pantomime. Such digital gestures are still in use by modern Italians who appear to have inherited them. Even the Venerable Bede (672-735? A.D.), English monk, scholar, historian, and author of many works in Latin, including the *Ecclesiastical History of the English*

People (731 A.D.), wrote a book on *Speech through Finger Gestures.* The 16th-century French satirist Rabelais has one of his characters assert in all seriousness that "he will dispute by signs only, without speaking, for the matters are so abstruse, that words proceeding from the mouth of man will never suffice for presenting them adequately to his liking." If we know where and how to look, we find a great deal of evidence of body language in the graphic arts from the earliest times to the present.

Perhaps Roman philosopher (5th century) Macrobius's story about Cicero and the celebrated actor Roscius is not apocryphal. It relates that both vied as to which of them could better express a sentiment, the one by gesture and the other by speech. The victory went to the actor, who, convinced of the superiority of his art, wrote a book about it. Quintilian (35-97 A.D.), waxing eloquent in describing the fifteen emotions the hands can express, asserted that "body language aids the speaker, but the hands speak themselves." Writer and translator Johann Heinrich Voss (1751-1826) echoes him: "*Manus non modo loquentem adjuvant, sed ipsae pene loqui videntur.*" ("The hands do not merely help the speaker, but themselves almost appear to speak.") During Nero's reign, the cynic philosopher Demetrius despised pantomime. Prevailed upon to watch a performance thereof by a celebrated artist, he experienced a complete change of mind and exclaimed: "Man, I not only see, but I hear what you do, for to me you appear to speak with your hands!"

With all this in mind, I challenge you to scrutinize more carefully examples of graphic art, from ancient to modern times, and observe in the drawings and paintings how much attention is paid to the body language of the characters depicted, thereby providing us, in fact, with an articulate, if silent, commentary on their actions. Consider a reproduction from a vase in the Homeric Gallery showing a group of five personages, whose natural gestures, which I shall describe in detail, speak louder than a thousand words. From the costumes and attitudes we can recognize the protagonist and the general subject represented. The warrior goddess Pallas Athene (the Roman Minerva) stands in the middle of what appears to be a war council. The votes of each of the four other members of the council can be inferred from their body language. Athene, looking at the two figures to her right, her feet ready to move forward, her left arm and hand with fingers extended upward toward invisible opponents to her left, her right hand brandishing a spear aimed in the same direction, obviously exhorts the two to immediate action.

One of these, bearded, older, seated, holding two spears pointed in the opposite direction and not ready for action, his right arm with hand palm down in a calming moderating gesture, might as well be saying, "Easy, girl, let's not rush into this!" A female figure, standing behind him, her left arm raised high with palm vertical in a pacifying, gesture toward Athene, clearly warns, "Stop! Wait!" Evidently Athene faces a conservative "right-wing" opposition. Another warrior, seated to Athene's left, two lances at rest in his right hand, looks straight at the pacifists and extends forward his left forearm and hand, cupped palm up. He obviously requests more information from the two advising a temporizing policy. The fifth and final figure, to the right of the picture, a command staff signifying high rank in his left hand, holds up his right flat hand, indicating surprise and reproof of any delay. With such clear gestures, who needs a long commentary? By the way, the primary reasons for sign language among North American Indians were so large an expanse of territory, so few Indians, and so many linguistic and dialectic boundaries.

Indians carried out entire dialogues with gestures. "How old are you" was conveyed by clinching both hands, crossing forearms before the breast with a trembling motion (indicating cold-winter-year), then elevating the left hand as high as the neck and about twelve or fifteen inches before it, palm toward the face, with fingers extended pointing upward. Using the index finger, one finger after another was turned down slowly, beginning at the little finger, until three or four were folded against the palm. The speaker looked inquiringly at the person addressed, signifying "How many?" The answer, "fifty-six," was indicated by closing and extending the fingers and thumbs of both hands, with the palms forward, five times, signifying fifty, then extending the fingers and thumb of the left hand, closing the right, and placing the extended thumb alongside of and near the left thumb — six. *Ugh!*

Linguistic Origins of Evil

Pelted as we are almost daily since September 11, 2001, by both endorsements and criticisms of President George W. Bush's use of the word "evil," I recall the lines of Faulconbridge, bastard son of King Richard I, in Shakespeare's *King John* (2.1.457):

> Here's a large mouth, indeed,
> That spits forth death and mountains, rocks and seas,
> Talks as familiarly of roaring lions
> As maids of thirteen do of puppy-dogs!
> ... He speaks plain cannon-fire, and smoke, and bounce;
> He gives the bastinado with his tongue;
> ... Zounds! I was never so bethump'd with words. ...

Bastinado, corrupted from Spanish *bastonada*, related to our band leader's baton (from the French *baton*), designates a beating administered with sticks — in Asian countries on the soles of the feet. . . . Now, what about the word "evil" itself?

The word is of Germanic origin, *Übel* in modern German, and has lost much of its original force, perhaps owing to overuse. In German the word now most frequently refers to feeling sick or nauseous: *mir ist übel* (I feel nauseous). Even in English, the word once referred to a malady, especially scrofula, a swelling of the lymph glands of the neck. The literal meaning of scrofula (diminutive of Latin *scrofa*, breeding sow) is "little sows." This again led to a popular superstition known as the "king's evil." The disease did not especially strike kings. Rather, because the kings of France and England were anointed with consecrated oil, popular belief endowed them with Divine powers, such as the ability, by a mere touch, "the king's touch," to cure any individual afflicted with scrofula. In France, the power of so healing "*le mal de roi*" (the king's evil) was first ascribed to Clovis I (465-511 A.D.) and later in England to St. Edward the Confessor (1000-1066).

Historically, the practice of "touching" an afflicted subject for the "king's evil" can be traced only to Louis IX of France, known as Saint Louis (1214-1270) and Edward III of England (1312-1377), who started the Hundred Years War against France. The practice was abolished in the 19th century. King Saint Louis took part in the Seventh (1248-1251) and Eighth (1270) Crusades, leaving from Aigues Mortes (literally, in Provençal "dead waters"; compare Spanish *aguas muertas*). This walled city, once a seaport in the Camargue or Rhone River Delta in Provence, constantly recedes from the Mediterranean because of alluvium deposits, hence its name. Every crusader was required to travel with a long box, which simultaneously served as trunk, sleeping bunk, and, in case of death, coffin.

What are we to make then of President Bush's choice of language — the "axis of evil"? It may vary with those being targeted. Visiting the USSR in 1990, I asked Russians what they thought of then President Reagan's "Evil Empire." Those queried were rather amused, laughing heartily, and not taking this *imperia zla* (Russian version) seriously. Iran, North Korea, and, before our 2003 "preemptive invasion," Iraq may have lacked the right sense of humor.

Viewed stylistically, the phrase appears somewhat dated, almost medieval. It brings to mind such allegorical epic poems as Edmund Spenser's *The Faerie Queene* and the 13th-century French *Romance of the Rose*. All characters carry both a literal and an abstract allegorical meaning. In Spenser, the knights represent moral virtues: Temperance, Holiness, Friendship. In the French poem, the Rose is the Beloved, and we meet up with Danger, Slander, Lust, and others.

Would that our wars were solved by knights in shining armor, no matter the difficulty of getting them through airport security checks!

Radio and TV Language

The warning "waste not, want not" also applies to language, if our aim is precise, concise, effective, disciplined speech. What follows may strike you as picayune or overly critical . . . but really! Just as politicians provide an endless source of material to stand-up comedians, radio and TV offer a rich harvest of faulty diction. However, first a comment on *picayune*! It means of little value, concerned with trifling matters. The word is related to Italian *piccolo* (small) and Spanish *pico* (a bit, a tad: "*Son las dos y pico.*" — "It's a little after two o'clock."). From the French *picaillon*, a small copper coin worth one-half a *centime*, picayune once referred to the smallest Spanish silver coin used in Louisiana and the South, worth half a *real*, or 6.25 cents. A piece of eight, roughly comparable to our present silver dollar, was worth eight *reales*. In Provençal, *picaioun* means small coin (also little child), and *picaio*, coin or money. New Orleans had a newspaper called *The Picayune,* with a strong Creole flavor.

But back to the subject of nonstandard English, I have been noticing an ever more frequent use of *myself* instead of *me. Myself* should normally only be used as a reflexive pronoun directing the verbal action back to the subject, as in the following case: I hurt or wash myself. Although for emphasis we may use "I myself opened the door," there is no need for "The cop and myself (use *I*) witnessed the accident," or "He took my wife and myself (use *me*) to the theater."

Another pet peeve of mine is the redundant "general consensus." Consensus alone means a general agreement with regard to opinions and requires no further qualifiers. And why the cliché "at this point in time" in lieu of "now" or "at this time"? Einstein must be squirming in his grave: *Ach! Du lieber Gott!* It's a dimension, not a bunch of meaningless dots or spots in front of your eyes! "A period of time" is also superfluous, unless a specific length is indicated like "a short period of time." I miss the days when we sent telegrams and cables and paid for every word!

The ever-present "even as we speak," as earlier noted, and just plain "as we speak" are more subtle problems. The expressions attempt to convey the meanings of "already, at the same time," but should only be used to emphasize, beyond simultaneity, a very close interdependence between two events or actions. Don't waste them on events that are in fact not related or interdependent.

Here are, in my modest opinion, justified uses of "even as," to emphasize not only that the events occurred at the same time or successively, but were intimately connected and one would not have occurred without the presence of the other. "*Even as* the fish's head fell from the crocodile's munching mouth there was a swoop of white wings"; or "*even as* the hapless pedestrian was run over by the speeding car, the alert lawyer, who had honed his natural talent by chasing many an ambulance, rushed toward the victim calling card in hand." Yet, as noted, for a weatherman to expand into wanton verbosity "it is raining in Podunk (no offense intended toward a village of the same name in Worcester, Massachusetts; originally a *podunker* was a bullfrog and its name an echoic rendering of its croak *po-dunk, po-dunk*) *even as* we speak," is bombastic to say the least, because, if it is going to rain there, it will do so without the weatherman's frivolous verbal outpouring. Soon, he will announce, quite illiterately, "It won't be raining nohow!"

Language Is Fun and Games

Let's play a game today! In its early sense the word *game* had many connotations and embraced almost anything in the way of amusement, for the Old English term *games*, the forerunner of our word game, meant "fun." Now, in sports, game implies a contest, with perhaps a winning score and a trophy. From the Norse and Old High German *gaman* (mirth, amusement, pleasure), the word does not appear to have any cognates in modern German, unless, as some believe, *gaman* also meant taking part, from *ga* (together) and *man*. In that case, it might have something in common with the German word *gemein*, which itself means common, public, and, sometimes dialectically, friendly.

King Henry V, in Shakespeare's play of the same title, addresses his troops:

> I see you stand like greyhounds in the slips,
> Straining upon the start. The game's afoot;
> Follow your spirit; and upon this charge
> Cry "God for Harry, England, and Saint George!" (3.1.31)

You will all recognize Sherlock Holmes's "Come, Watson, come! The game is afoot." Here is a great opportunity to see how language operates. Having obtained from Germanic sources an adequate term for what pertains to sports, amusement, games, English was free to put the Latin words and their French derivatives for *game* and *to play*, *ludus* and *ludere*, respectively, to other more propitious use. The meanings of the Latin *ludus* ranged from play, game, sport, pastime, to the more figurative jest and joke. With the addition of various prefixes indicating different directions, English was thus provided with a rich source for new terms, which all contained the idea of game, play, and trickery.

Adding the prefix *in-* (it becomes "*il-*" through assimilation with the *l* of *ludus*) allows us to force our game on others, to create illusions, even deceive. Once our victims have fallen prey to such deception or illusion, they might disengage themselves (*dis-* indicates separation) from it, but possibly suffer from disillusion, since illusions, albeit often artificial and unattainable, offer faith, hope, and enchantment. With the prefix *de-* meaning away from, delusion means that we have been tricked into some game off the right, rational path. We were tempted into a game or deceit that led to a false belief. With the preposition *ad* (*al* by assimilation), the jest (game, play, reference) becomes allusion and is aimed at someone or something. With *cum* meaning together, collusion implies that several parties band together to "play" some, often sinister, game against another unsuspecting one. We also have ludicrous, which means that whatever is referred to is laughable, not serious — a mere game.

Although rare, *prolusion*, with the prefix *pro-* meaning before, is an exercise or trial preliminary to a contest or performance. We are more familiar with prelude, with the same Latin roots and similar meaning. It often refers to a musical movement introducing the theme of a fugue, suite, or opera. If you know all this, you should be ahead of the game, an expression common in business, because the latter may involve risk-taking and gambling. The English slang *gams* for legs is from heraldry *gamb*, leg, which itself is derived from French *gambe* or, in current French, *jambe*, also leg. The *viola da gamba*, a larger bass member of the viol family, owes its name to the fact that it is played while held between the legs.

Rest assured that I am not pulling your legs with all this.

Rhetoric Often Spells Deceit

The efficacy of a delicate tool depends on the skill of the user thereof. It is the same with language. To fully exploit the latter's strengths and avoid its pitfalls, we must recognize its almost infinite potential for both insightful reflection and nefarious distortion of reality. By the way, *nefarious* comes from the Latin and literally means "that what one does not speak of." *Ne* is not and *fari*, to speak. *Fari* also gave us our infant, where *in* means no and *fari* speak, therefore one that cannot as yet speak. The pernicious rhetoric we are constantly subjected to from the government, the media, or other means of communication, offers us a perfect illustration. Even as far back as the Greeks, rhetoric (from Greek *rhetor*, orator) was cultivated as the art of persuasion. As such it became endowed with a kind of fascinating, siren-like bewitching charm and power. The clever, artful speaker presented such an appearance of wisdom that he was given the name of sophist, which means master craftsman, or wise man. Socrates, aware of the danger, attacked the rhetoricians as trying to confuse the human mind instead of leading it toward a perception of truth. I choose the qualifier *pernicious* advisedly. From the Latin intensifier prefix *per-* (through, thorough) and the noun *nex, necis* (death), rhetoric can, indeed, "kill" any human attempt to reach a truthful, assessment of an event or a situation. Call it, if you wish, more kindly "sleight of tongue"!

Official agencies, businesses, the media, all humans using language, have the power to control whatever is represented publicly as prevailing truth. Words and images pervade the "mediascape" and the public's perception of the true nature of events may be based on how these representations appear. I have just reviewed an awesomely researched book, *Shifting Borders*, in which the authors Kent A. Ono and John M. Sloop provide a detailed study of how rhetoric affected the public view and passage of California Proposition 187 on Immigration and Illegal Aliens. At stake — and here is where language plays a crucial role — is what assumptions we can make about how humans come to understand the world and the relationship between "words and things." Alfred Korzybski's *General Semantics* (1933), popularized by Stuart Chase in *The Tyranny of Words* (1938), S. I. Hayakawa in *Language in Thought and Action* (1949), and others, addressed the problem of how words control, even tyrannize, our "every thought and action." Structuralism postulates the objectivity of knowledge: from the structure of things we may arrive at some fundamental truth. Poststructuralism assumes all knowledge to be "interpretive," subjective: it is or can be understood only in and through cultural discourse.

Things may exist outside of discourse, but not meaningfully. Everything in our world depends on how it is "talked about." Theoretically, material reality may exist; practically, our knowledge thereof is acquired by and dependent on cultural discourse. There's the rub! Even knowing all the facts behind a situation, we are unable to assign it a definitive evaluation. We are slaves to the language of discourse. Ludwig Wittgenstein stated: "Philosophy is a battle against the bewitchment of our intelligence by means of language." Thus, with one single conflict, one body of facts, like the on-going Middle Eastern crisis, we can witness both sides, the Israelis and Palestinians, being simultaneously accused of terrorism by two allegedly informed writers. Even mathematics and its branch, accounting, has its own "rhetoric," as we have experienced from contemporary business scandals. How else could different orators — here accountants — derive and represent two sets of entirely different realities of one mathematical body of data?

When exposed to rhetoric, beware of smoke and mirrors!

Words with Dark Roots

Would you ever dream of indulging in alcoholic beverages at a symposium, which is a meeting at which speakers address related topics or various aspects of the same topic? From the Greek *syn* (together) and *posis*

> **Teton Mountains, Wyoming** From French trappers who thought the gorgeous peaks reminded them of *tétons* (teats, breasts).
>
> **Thug** From Hindi *thag*, thief, and Sanskrit *sthaga*, rogue.

(drinking), a *symposium*, during Plato's days, was once a gay affair, where drinking wine was mixed with intellectual conversation. Today, a symposium may also mean a collection of articles on the same subject. Along similar lines, *collation*, from Latin *cum* (together) and *latus* (brought, carried; the past participle of *ferre*, to carry), once designated the collected *Lives of the Saints*, read aloud in the evening by the Benedictine monks. The term was then applied to the light meal that followed with a discussion of the readings. Still later, collation was a light meal eaten on fasting days instead of supper. Now it means a meal, at times even an elaborate one. In French, the same word still designates a light meal. Collation also refers to the detailed scholarly comparison of several texts, noting the differences or variants, to possibly establish dates or authenticity — perhaps even a critical edition.

Speaking of refreshments, ambrosia and nectar were the food and drink of the Greek and Roman gods, and both conferred immortality. Ambrosia literally means "not mortal" from *a* (not) and *brotos*, also *mrotos* and, by inversion, *mortos* (mortal). Nectar means the same, from Greek *nek* (death) and *tar* (conquering). Because of its good taste, it also gave its name to the nectarine peach, now simply nectarine. The root *nek* (death) is found in necrology, which is a register of the dates of death of persons associated with the church, or just an obituary. Necromancy has the same root joined to Greek *manteia*, divination, and means foretelling the future by communicating with the dead. Fortunetellers now do not stress the macabre aspect of their art. *Macabre*, from the French *danse macabre*, dance of death, ultimately from the Maccabees, 2nd to 1st century B.C., Jewish patriots associated with death because of some biblical writings.

Necropolis, or city of the dead, is a fancy word for cemetery. A famous necropolis is Alyscamps, located southwest of the Roman city of Arles, in Provence, southern France, on the Rhône River. *Cemetery*, from a Greek word merely meaning dormitory or sleeping chamber, is a euphemism, literally a "well spoken" word. It is much like substituting "he went to his reward" for "he died." We find this Greek prefix *eu-* meaning "well" in *eulogy*, an oration in praise of someone, in euphonious or well-sounding, eugenic or well-born, evangelist or good messenger bringer of good news. However, *eunuch* comes from another root, *eune* (bed) and *echo* (keeper). Speaking of euphemism, I strongly dislike the "killed by friendly fire" we hear so much of lately. Would you rest more peacefully knowing that whoever killed you was a well-meaning friend and did not intend to do it? I, for one, would find no consolation in having someone dear to me, including myself, killed by "friendly" fire.

Would you believe that once *giddy* and *enthusiast* had identical meanings. Giddy, now meaning dizzy, from *gydig*, literally meant "possessed by a god." People referred to the "giddy prophets" and the "enthusiasts," who converted the pagans. Enthusiast is from the Greek *en* (in or in the power of) and *theos* (God). Many of our words have original religious or ritualistic connotations. Thus *ashram*, now a religious retreat, comes from a Sanskrit word meaning "to get tired from religious exercises."

Well, enough of this merry-go-round, which the British call a "giddy-go-round."

🙢 The Images Behind the Words 🙢

Occasionally I am asked about the origin of words that contain an image or metaphor. Most of them do, if you can just learn to find them, especially when they are hidden behind foreign roots. As noted earlier, a metaphor is a figure of speech in which a word or phrase denoting one kind of object or action is used in place of another to suggest a likeness or analogy between them. People love to compare things, actions, and scenarios with others that produce similar effects on their senses. Examples: the ship plows the seas; he uttered a volley of oaths; a marbled brow. The word *windfall*, which suggests fruit being swept off trees by the wind, was actually first applied to fallen trees. Members of the English nobility were not allowed to fell trees even on their own estates. All timber was reserved for the Royal Navy. However, the nobles were free to use any trees blown down by the wind. A windfall thus brought them good fortune.

Our word *window* contains a very poetic metaphor. It comes from a Scandinavian word meaning literally "wind-eye," although earlier spellings, such as *windore* and *eagdura*, suggested such origins as "wind door" or "eye door" respectively.

Most, but not all military terms come to us from the French and Italian. The official U.S. Army designation for the four-wheel military vehicle known as a *jeep* was G.P., which stood for General Purpose vehicle. However, there is more. It is almost certain that the comic strip "Popeye," created by E. C. Segar and widely read by GIs, contributed to the word's formation. In the strip appeared a strange beast called "Eugene the Jeep," which made an odd noise spelled out as *"Jeep!"*

Our word *strategy* comes from the French, but is originally derived from the Greek *stratos* (army) and *agein* (lead). Strategy refers to the overall plan and the effective management of the armed forces. One story tells of a Chinese General who sent his advance guard through a wooded area. To avoid an enemy ambush he ordered each man to hurl a stone into the trees. If birds flew away, there would be no enemy troops. The birds scattered to be sure, but the opposing General, a more astute strategist, had his men capture birds beforehand and release them when the enemy threw stones. With such a stratagem the second General outmaneuvered and ambushed his foe.

The word *ambush* comes from a 12th-century French word *embûcher*, which in the 15th century, under Italian influence, was changed to *embusquer*. Both words contain the word wood (*bûche* is log in French and *bosco*, wood, forest, in Italian) and conjure the image of hiding in the bushes or woods. You might ponder this interesting Spanish proverb: *Más vale salto de mata que ruegos de hombres buenos*. It translates into: "Better to hide in the bushes than to rely on the intercession or pleas of good men."

The term *tactics*, similar, but not equal to strategy, comes through the French from a Greek word meaning "to arrange." It represents the art of maneuvering war vessels and disposing troops in an effective manner.

Logistics, the moving, supplying, and quartering of soldiers, is a French word essentially meaning to lodge or quarter. Our mountain lodge has the same origin. *Besiege* (the archaic term was *assiege*), from the French, literally means to "sit by" either an enemy town or a young lady. The synonym *beleaguer*, from the Dutch *leger*, German *Lager*, is to "camp by" a town until the enemy gives up. Latin had two words for enemy, one *inimicus*, the other *hostis*, which explains the two series expressing an adversarial relation, enemy, enmity, and hostile, hostility. *Grenade* also came to us from the French, inspired by *pomegranate*, a shell full of explosive seeds hurled by a *grenadier*.

Relationship Between Thought and Language

Many linguists and philosophers are convinced that all the thinking we do, be it about anything at all, must proceed in terms of language. For them, thinking is language spoken to oneself and, until language has "assimilated" experience, in effect made sense of it, such experience is meaningless. Philosopher Ludwig Wittgenstein, who taught at Cambridge University, strongly believed in the inseparableness of everything in the world from language and in the systematic misuse of the latter. Thereby he shared common ground with Alfred Korzybski's *General Semantics*. For Wittgenstein, "philosophy is a battle against the bewitchment of our intelligence by means of language," and "the limits of our language mean the limits of our world." Once *homo sapiens* had created and, over extensive periods of time, gradually developed a complex, albeit fragmentary, symbolic system of communication, codifying, either verbally or by other means, his perception of the universe, he understandably was tempted to substitute this newly acquired, infinitely more manageable tool (one is tempted to say restful), despite its possible shortcomings, for the previous much more demanding, much more active, perpetual cerebral interpretation and reinterpretation of reality. True, ever-increasing reliance on language, an almost knee-jerk reaction or standardized and stereotyped cognition and communication system, may cause fear of eventual intellectual apathy and control of thought by language.

I submit that, despite such fears, thought is alive and well. Verbal constructs do not necessarily either parallel or limit thought. At times they exceed cognition. We can coin the word "infinity," but can we truly grasp the idea? Carving up and representing reality by means of language, is not always determined by how it is perceived. There is a connection between the two, if only to communicate to one's self and others what is not actually or absolutely perceivable. Thought is not located in the linguistic units, but in the usage we make thereof. Syntactical analysis does not correspond to our analysis of reality. Consider a simple example. In "it is snowing" and "Peter beats Paul," the grammatical subjects are not the main focus of our thought. Word sequence and thought sequence may vary with the language. The Chinese say, "To Beijing the plane where?"

Language may actually obstruct thought. While teaching at Florida State University, I was translating for a colleague in chemistry A. S. Davydov's *Theory of Molecular Excitons*, from the Russian. At one point my colleague insisted that I had mistranslated the text, because the subtle meaning of the theoretical concepts eluded him. Finally, his thinking caught up with Davydov's meaning. The words no longer veiled the precise meaning of the text. Words could only hint at, but not replace thought. Words and signs do not contain meaning; still, enabled by a linguistic and cultural community, by convention and always subject to change, they trigger the volatile, unstable, and highly individualized mental semantic process. Only our ever-present capability of thinking can help us discern the *mental, not linguistic, common semantic denominator* in verbal expressions as varied as: "the proof of the pudding is in the eating," "actions speak louder than words," "actions judge or define the man," and "one can tell a mason by the foundation of his wall" — the last one a French proverb.

Cogito ergo sum — I think, therefore I am.

❧ This Information Is *Sub Rosa* ❧

Recently I was asked about the expression *sub rosa*. I have known this phrase from the Latin, literally "under the rose," since I was a very young boy, when my father explained it to me. I have often heard it used in Germany as well as in France. I would not expect today's high school students to use it to excess, if ever. It means "very confidentially, in absolute secrecy, in strict privacy." The phrase may be used adverbially and written in two words: "They convened the council *sub rosa*." As an adjective, it should be hyphenated: a *sub-rosa* report, a *sub-rosa* group. The origin of the phrase or word is attributed to Greek mythology, more specifically Eros, in Latin Amor or Cupido, our Cupid, the god of love, son of Aphrodite also known as Venus by either Ares, Zeus, or Hermes (without DNA the paternity is uncertain). The lady got around quite a bit, and thereby hangs a tale.

It is said that Eros, in order to keep the amorous affairs and indiscretions of his mother secret from the other gods and goddesses, bribed Harpocrates, god of silence, with the first gorgeous rose ever created, to keep him from blabbering them all over Olympus. In German the phrase becomes *unter der Rose*, in French *sous la rose*. Some believe that there is even more to the story. The Greeks noticed that the Egyptian god Horus was usually depicted seated under a rose with a finger at his lips. They falsely assumed from this gesture that he was the god of silence. Anthropology is, at times, a risky venture! Their assumption was, of course, inaccurate. The rose was really a lotus blossom and the infant god was merely acting his age and sucking his finger. Incidentally, Harpocrates is the Roman name for Horus. I mention again the Italians saying "*Se non è vero, è bene trovato*" — "Even if it is not true, the story is cleverly invented." Thus many accept this legend as the true origin of *sub rosa*.

However, we are language scholars, right? We cannot stop here. So, let's forge ahead! There are also reasons to believe that the origin of the phrase dates back to a much earlier Teutonic source and that, in Medieval times, it was translated into Latin and spread throughout Europe. Often, in ancient German dining-halls, a rose was carved upon the ceiling to warn those meeting there that whatever took place or was discussed should never be divulged to outsiders by anyone present, whose tongue was loosened by too much wine. The phrase was also known in England at the court of Henry VIII (still, evidently not that well, since records show that it required an explanation for some). We can read in a letter dated 1546 the following passage:

> The sayde questions were asked with lysence, and that yt shulde remain under the rosse, that is to say, to remain under the bourde, and no more to be rehersyd.

You can also notice from this citation to what extent present-day spelling differs from that used centuries ago.

Thus, ancient councils, as far back as the 5th century B.C., were wont to have a rose hanging from the ceiling, requesting all present to be tight-lipped about all matters discussed on the premises, to keep them *sub rosa*. I suppose that because roses were often either out of season, rather expensive, or hard to get, it became a measure of economy to carve a rose or rosette on the ceiling of halls and chambers where confidential matters were discussed.

So now you know the rest of the story!

Multiple Meanings in Different Languages

It is often surprising how the same word over time may span or acquire so many different, though often somewhat related, meanings. Consider *span* for instance. As a verb, "to span" is common Teutonic, the basic meaning "to stretch," and the idea of tension and stress. Thus in modern German, *anspannen* is to harness horses or yoke oxen to a carriage or plow, respectively. The adjective *spannend*, when applied to a novel or a movie, means gripping, absorbing, tense. I guess it is not too much of a stretch, if you'll pardon the pun, to accept that span once designated the distance from the end of the thumb to the end of the little finger of a spread hand. Figuratively, attention and memory span also make good sense, referring to how far either may reach or endure. In Scotland, span means a measure for butter. In Afrikaans, from the Dutch, span designates a pair of horses, mules, or oxen, matched in looks and action and driven together, which recalls the German meaning of harnessing or yoking.

Anglo-Saxon span or *spon*, referring to a chip of wood, gave us spoon. Because of its openness and shallowness, spoony was used in the 18th century to mean a fool, then someone foolishly fond — hence to spoon in the sense of making love. Spic-and-span, once spelled "spick-and-span," owes the change in spelling to the well-established trade name *Spic and Span* for the detergent. For the past 200 years, we have been using this expression to mean very trim, smart, neat and orderly, spotlessly spanking-brand-new clean. Previously, from the middle of the 16th to the middle of the 18th century, the phrase "spick and span-new" simply meant absolutely new. As early as the 18th century, "span-new" or "spannew" was clean and fresh as a newly shaven wood chip. Spick once meant nail, spike. Related is the 17th-century Dutch *spiksplinternieuw*, *i.e.*, new in every nail or splinter, also found in German *funkelnagelneu*, literally sparkling new like a nail. *Span* in German still means shred, chip, shaving, and splinter. When chips were still used as spoons, span-new really meant a fresh-cut, unused spoon.

Another interesting expression, the precise origin of which is unknown, but might have originated with some medieval animal fable, is "cock-and-bull story," a tale that stretches the imagination beyond the limits of credulity. Many American scholars, amongst whom the poet John Ciardi, have claimed that the French expressions *coq-à-l'âne* and *passer du coq à l'âne*, literally "rooster to donkey" and "go from rooster to donkey," have the identical same meaning as our cock-and-bull. I must disagree. The French expression, also possibly based on some long-forgotten medieval folk tale, refers to an illogical, unsubstantiated transition from one subject to another entirely unrelated one. The semantic nuance is quite different, with, in the French phrase, the emphasis on an unrelated transition from one subject to another.

Speaking of bulls, where do you think "bulldozer" and "to bulldoze" came from. This strictly American term, referring, since about 1890, to a heavy machine with tank treads and a large adjustable steel blade for moving earth or debris, as well as to the job it does, was originally "bull dose." At first it specifically referred to flogging slaves and administering a dose of whipping strong enough for a bull. Around 1880, the spelling changed to bulldoze and applied to powerful political coercion, similar to the related phrase to "steamroller a convention." I, too, may at times bulldoze, come on strong and overwhelm, but "that's no bull!"

Grammar Rules Must Make Sense

Today, if I do not allow myself to be distracted along the way, I wish to broach the subject of correct versus incorrect English usage, which somewhat concerns a certain Barbara Wallraff, a senior editor at *The Atlantic Monthly*, and known on the Web as MsGrammar@theatlantic.com. Darn! Why did I have to use "broach," which here means to "open up" and lures me off my subject like the Lorelei warbling a sweet song on her rock overlooking the Rhine? *Broach* conjures broker. After closing a deal, those participating in it were wont to broach a cask of wine, and the one to prick it open was the first broker, from Latin *broccare*, to tap a cask. The verb broach as well as brooch, the ornament affixed with a pin, are variants of the same word. From wine merchant, the term spread to any dealer, pawnbroker, or middleman in a transaction.

The idea of piercing comes from the Latin *brocca*, spike, and gave us the French verb *brocher*, to stitch, the French culinary term *à la broche*, on a skewer or spit. Noted earlier, from the Latin diminutive *broccola*, or stalk, we have the Italian *broccoli*, little stalks — the first President Bush's "allegedly not too favorite" vegetable. Our word brochure, a small booklet stitched together, originated from the same source. However, any suggestion that pamphlet, likewise a small booklet, is derived from French *par un filet*, held together by a small thread, is a stretch. No way! *Pan* and *philus*, is Greek for "loved by all." Pamphilus was the name of a 12th-century Latin writer of popular love songs as well as the name of the little book, *Pamphilus, seu de Amore*, literally "Pamphilus, or About Love." The

> **Gibraltar** Named after its Arabic conqueror, Tarik: *Jabalu't Tarik*, Tarik's Mountain, later *Jibal Tarik*, and thus Gibraltar.
>
> **Grenade** From French, inspired by *pomegranate*, a shell full of explosive seeds hurled by a *grenadier*.

suffix *-et* in Old French serves as a collective. Thus the book was called *Pamphilet*, roughly a collection from Pamphilus, just as a translation of Aesop's *Fables* by Marie de France was known as *Ysopet*, something like "Aesopery" and the medieval term *bestiary* (*beast* and suffix *-ary*) designated a collection of animal fables with a moralizing theme.

But back to Ms. Grammar! She defends the use of *anymore* in colloquial affirmative contexts as occurring at least since the 1930s and endorsed by the *Dictionary of American Regional English*. That may be so. However, I humbly suggest that more is at stake here than correct usage. There is logic, clarity, and style. Of course! If someone says, "I only throw small parties anymore," he may actually attempt to communicate the *negative* meaning, "I don't throw large parties anymore." I submit the faulty grammar reflects the thought sequence "I don't throw big parties, only small ones." Please note also that "*only*" is misplaced and should come before "small." *Anymore* means now, at present, from now on, if accompanied by a negative such as not, doesn't, or won't. Placed at the beginning or end of an affirmative sentence I contend it is mostly meaningless or ineffective. "Anymore they are coming to see us" or "They are picking apples anymore" compels us to wonder whether "They are still coming to see us" — or not, and whether "They are still picking apples" — or not. When you tell me, "We do all our shopping at the A&P anymore," I wonder whether there is an "Anymore" branch of A&P supermarkets, like the Scottsdale A&P. Perhaps there is an "Anymore A&P?"

John Ciardi does not mince words, calling such usage a barbarism defying all language sense. Hear! Hear! Unlike Ms. Grammar, I am no judge presiding over "Word Court." Let others commit crimes against language and make no sense. I am only concerned with saying what I mean correctly, simply, clearly.

I've done said all I care to on the subject anymore! *Whoa!* Scratch that last barbaric sentence!

Easy with These Neologisms

A comedian has said, "I can always count on material for my jokes, as long as there are politicians in Washington!" I might echo his sentiments with equal aplomb: "So can I, for my columns, as long as people try to speak and write in English!" By the way, *aplomb*, which means complete confidence or assurance in oneself, as well as a dancer's perfect equilibrium in a pose or movement, comes from the same word in French. It was originally made up from *à* (according to) and *plomb* (lead) and literally refers to a plumb line, which helps determine the perfect perpendicular. The word is now used figuratively.

As to material for my newspaper column, some helpful local writer recently regaled me with his article about "many seniors considering recareering." This last word almost "blew my mind," as well as the "spell and grammar check" on my computer. What an unfortunate word coinage! The prefix *re-* means either "back" or "again," and "to career" as a verb signifies "to make a short gallop, drive or run at top speed or in a headlong and reckless manner." It always carries with it the image of rapid motion with veering or sidelong rocking. Did this call for new speed limits, or were we merely dealing with what William Safire calls "Neologic Nellies." In this case, a full stop sign was in order.

A neologism refers to a newly coined word. H. W. Fowler in his *Dictionary of Modern English Usage*, a good source for would-be writers desirous to avoid crimes against English, has this to say about their coinage:

> Word-making, like other manufactures, should be done by those who know how to do it; others should neither attempt it for themselves, nor assist the deplorable activities of amateurs by giving currency to fresh coinages before there has been time to test them.

Just quoting, but heartily agreeing! Neologisms, indeed, may prove felicitous as well as disastrous. The one prompting this essay counts among the latter. Thousands of new words are coined every year as the need for them arises. Examples show that some could be avoided by using either existing terms close enough, if not identical in meaning, or by substituting sentences for single words.

Take "repurposing," a neologism purporting to mean "taking material designed for one medium and converting it to another format." Why not use "reformatting, converting, recasting"? I do not like basing a neologism on a non-existing verb or barbarism, here "to purpose." Some people try for the impossible. The editor of the *Atlantic Monthly* quotes a reader trying to coin a term to describe the children of a parent's live-in lover. Suggestions included the absurd "significant-siblings" and "quasi-step-siblings." Why not "my Mom's or Dad's live-in lover's kids"? The cascade of possessives allows one to savor step by step the tantalizing relationship. Better yet! Don't even talk about it! Why wash your dirty linen in public?

Words, even language, cannot always cover all aspects of anything. Why do you think Hayakawa entitled his journal of general semantics *ETC*, needed after most statements, since words never cover any subject completely? Imagine someone looking for one word designating vegetarians who, besides fruit and vegetables, eat nothing but eggs, fish, and chicken? Someone (I hope jokingly) suggested semi-carnivore. How about "fussy eater"?

Don't lick your thumb and index finger before turning pages or handling paper! You might be labeled "digilingus."

Tricky Problems of Correct English

You may find this hard to believe, but many among us are very much concerned with correct English usage. Witness thereto is Barbara Wallraff's book *Word Court*, in which she (the previously mentioned senior editor at *The Atlantic Monthly*), cites a surprisingly high number of inquiries she receives daily and sits in judgment on regarding English grammar, syntax, and vocabulary. I just read her book from cover to cover, relieved to find that there were no queries put to her beyond my ken. In fact, while I respect her vast experience and knowledge, my conclusion is that correct usage requires more than merely blindly adhering to rigid rules, leafing through a multitude of dictionaries, and consulting panels of allegedly foolproof lexicographers. We must complement rules with common sense and sound logic, as we search for the perfect style to deliver the precise meaning we wish to convey. Becoming "hung up" to the point of paralysis, while fixated at and agonizing over one sole particular way of saying something, then wondering whether it is correct or not, may trick us into overlooking more felicitous stylistic alternatives. Such blind attitude toward correctness may well produce a true case of not seeing the forest for the trees.

Allow me a few examples. Some purists believe that *obviate* only means "make unnecessary," thereby objecting to a sentence like "her phoning me *obviated the need* for me to call her" as redundant. Not so! Obviate comes from the Latin *ob* (against) and *vitare*, probably an intensive of Latin *viare* (to go), viare being derived from *via* (way). Thus, the word obvious, from the same root, literally means something that you run up against, meet on your way. The French say, "*Cela vous crache aux yeux*" — "It spits into your very eyes." Now *obviate* rather emphasizes "to meet on the way," hence, by extension, to take care of, dispose of: "Richard Nixon seems to be the last to understand how obviously he had been obviated." It is true that "disposing of" may "eliminate the need" for something. The word implies this, but does not spell it out or contain it in its root.

But back to the sentence objected to by the purists: it actually has two parts, first the need to phone, second the phoning. "Her phoning obviated my calling her," sounds terrible. No reason to object to "obviated the need or necessity for calling her"!

Another much trickier case is the use of the adverb "deceptively" with the verb "to be" and a modifier. What should we make of "This exam is deceptively easy"? Ms. Wallraff submitted the sentence to a panel of experts for *The American Heritage Dictionary*, who, to my utter disbelief, could not agree on the answer. With all due respect for these learned lexicographers, the sentence plainly and simply does not make any sense, mainly because of the use of the verb "to be." The statement "this exam is deceptively easy" is equivalent to a mathematical equation x = deceptively y. That is pure nonsense! It could also be worded, "This exam is easy, but my saying so is due to a deception" . . . or, "I am being deceived when I say this exam is easy." Why not just say the exam is not easy or difficult?

Please note, there is no problem if instead of "*is*" we use "sounds, looks, appears" easy. However, to define something and simultaneously admit the definition is due to a deception is an absurdity and in very poor style.

A final example is the expression "This is too complex for anyone not *to the manor/to the manner* born or bred." Which is correct, *manor* or *manner*? Shakespeare enlightens us in *Hamlet* (1.4.14):

> But to my mind, though I am native here
> And to the manner born, it is a custom
> More honour'd in the breach than the observance.

Never argue with the Bard. With lexicographers, you may risk it!

Oxford English Dictionary's Insane Contributor

In American English, "bedlam" means noisy disorder or a place where it occurs. In England, originating as a contraction of Bethlehem, its root sense of "madhouse" springs from the following historical facts. In 1247, the hospital or hospice of St. Mary of Bethlehem (pronounced Bethleëm) was founded as a priory in London, becoming, in 1402 a hospital for lunatics. In 1547, after the break with the papacy and the proscription of monasteries, it incorporated as the royal foundation for the reception of lunatics. How could a bedlamite, an insane person, become one of the greatest contributors to the *Oxford English Dictionary?* Here is the story, brilliantly told by Simon Winchester in *The Professor and the Madman* (1998).

The Scotsman Dr. James Murray, born 1837, a polyglot and polymath, was the first editor of the *OED*, which is known as the "great book." It was conceived on January 7, 1858, was seventy years in the making, and the completion of its twelve volumes was announced on New Year's Eve 1927. It was hailed by the *New York Times* on its front page as "one of the great romances of English literature." It defines about one-half million words and is characterized by its rigorous dependence on gathering quotations from published or otherwise recorded uses of English and using 1,827,306 of them to illustrate the sense of every single word in the language. Murray, who of necessity had dropped out of school at fourteen, nevertheless had a working knowledge of the languages and literatures of the Aryan and Syro-Arabic classes, most of the Romance languages including Provençal and Catalan, Anglo-Saxon, Moeso-Gothic, and Celtic, and was once turned down for a position with the British Museum. His motto was: "Knowledge is power."

Murray depended on numerous outside volunteers, who collaborated in the making of the dictionary by gathering quotations from published or recorded uses of English to illustrate the evolving sense and application of every word. The *OED*'s guiding principle was that a dictionary should be an inventory of the language and not a guide to proper usage.

In the early 1880s, a copy of a four-page appeal to the English-speaking and English-reading public for volunteer contributors reached Dr. William Chester Minor, Surgeon-Captain, U.S. Army (Ret.), born June 1834, inmate at the Broadmoor Asylum for the criminally insane at Crowthorne in the County of Berkshire. Minor, cultured member of a noted New England family, studied medicine at Yale University, excelled in painting water colors, played the flute, joined the Union Army, and witnessed many horrifying events in the Civil War: mutilated bodies, shattered limbs, broken heads. His participation in the bloody Battle of the Wilderness in Virginia, early May 1864, especially his being ordered to brand an Irish soldier on the cheek with a 1½-inch "D" for desertion, unhinged his sensitive mind and drove him gradually insane. He felt he had violated his Hippocratic oath. Suffering from paranoiac dementia, he was retired unfit for service on September 3, 1868.

In 1871, Minor moved to London where, constantly obsessed by feelings of guilt because of his dissolute sex habits and by fears of being pursued by Irish enemies, he shot, on February 17, 1872, in Victorian Lambeth Marsh, a certain George Merrett, married and with six children. The victim had risen at 2 a.m. to shovel coal at a local brewery. Minor admitted killing Merrett in error, thinking him an intruder, an Irishman out to kill him. Declared legally innocent of murder, Minor was to be detained as insane until Her Majesty's pleasure be known. Wealthy, Minor bought tons of books and from his cell contributed thousands of quotes to the *OED*, more than most volunteers. Freed in 1910, Minor died in the United States in 1920.

Caveat Lector!

Let the reader beware! You cannot take everything that you read in the newspapers as the gospel truth. Unfortunately misinformation is now often rampant in our media. When it concerns language, however, I can at least do something about it. Recently, in a letter to the *Wall Street Journal* editor, a reader, addressing the fact that the population of the United States is often labeled a melting pot, contended that diversity implies division and justified this assertion by incorrectly claiming that "divide" and "diverse" possess the same linguistic root. The editor should have caught this mistake and scrapped the letter. Now, before I dispose of "diverse" and "divide," allow me to return to the word *rampant*. The latter is related to rampage, which comes from the Scandinavian *ramp*, to rear up, but originates more directly from the French *ramper*, to crawl, climb, rear up. In my first sentence it means unbridled. In heraldry, a rampant beast is seen in profile, rearing up on one hind leg with one foreleg above the other.

Divide, from the Latin *dividere*, breaks down into *di, dis*, meaning apart, and *videre*, a lost verb probably meaning to know, from an Aryan root *WID*, but here "to separate." Indeed, the Latin *videre*, past participle *visu* (to see), has a long heritage. Thus "to divide, division" also means to "see apart or in parts." Devise is to see down or in detail. The changes in spelling devise-device, advise-advice, and prophesy-prophecy are artificial. An individual, from the same root, the prefix *in-* meaning no, is someone not divided. Provide, provident from Latin *providere* is to see before, revise to see again or anew. From *invidere*, to see into and desiring what you see, comes *invidia*, our envy. English even has a doublet where both mean the same: invidious and envious.

On the contrary, divert and diverse come from an altogether different Latin root: *di, dis* (away, apart) and *vertere*, past participle *versus* (to turn). Some day I shall return to this root, which is incredibly productive. Pervert is someone who is completely (Latin *per*, through, through and through) turned around. Even verse comes from it, since it indicates the turning at the end of the line, because originally prose was written continuously without any space between words. Verse turns and starts a new line after it has reached a specified number of feet or syllables. As noted, the Latin *vergere*, to bend, is a variation of *vertere*, yielding to converge or bend together, and diverge or bend apart. The "verge" from the same Latin source has blended with Latin *virga*, rod, possibly once a phallic symbol, carried as badge of authority, like a mace. "Within the verge," in England, meant within the boundary of the power of the Lord High Stewart, or twelve miles around the King's court, then became more general, as "on the brink of."

Albeit likening myself to an equine creature is both unflattering and presumptuous for a humble word drudge like myself, all this comes "straight from the horse's mouth." Just for the sake of this column, I claim my authority to be of the highest, which is the true meaning of this expression. The latter comes from horse racing and refers to the age of racehorses. You can infallibly tell a horse's age from the teeth of its lower jaw. The first permanent teeth in the center of the jaw do not begin to appear until the animal is 2½ years old. A year later, the second pair starts coming through alongside the first. The third pair appears when the horse is between four and five years old. So, just as you can tell a horse's true age from its mouth, you can tell linguistic truth from my column.

Acronyms — Not Always the Last Word on Word Origins

A posh finishing school is one that is elegant and luxurious to an extreme degree. Posh also means smart and spruce in appearance. At one of my lectures on language, someone, in a valiant attempt to display his knowledge of etymology, asked me if I knew the origin of the word posh. Before I could reply, he volunteered it was an acronym (a word formed from the initial letter of each of the successive parts of a compound term), in this case: p(ort) o(ut), s(tarboard) h(ome)." Acronym, incidentally, comes from the Greek *acr* or *acro*, meaning topmost or extreme, and *nym*, or name.

This has been a very stubbornly maintained, if dubious, folk etymology based upon the following ingeniously assumed facts. It purports to refer to the best possible location of staterooms on the passage to India via the Suez Canal on a Peninsular & Oriental (commonly known as the "P&O") packet boat, which, allegedly, would be on the lee and shady side of the ship, thus protected from both wind and sun. This is true with respect to shade on the east-west passage, since the ship sails north of the sun, although the time of year could make a great deal of difference. Protection from wind is more questionable. The lee side is determined by the monsoon winds, which blow into the Asian heartland all summer and out of it all winter. Therefore, only the right season determines which side is sheltered. I am always naturally skeptical of those who resort to far-fetched etymological explanations. A simple one, like SNAFU — for "situation normal all fouled (I am trying to be politically correct) up" — is more readily plausible.

A little research proved the word *posh* to predate this ingenious reference to an acronym. Besides, veterans of the Peninsular & Oriental Line had never heard of the meaning of posh in the sense claimed by the acronym. Although dictionaries list the origin of the word as unknown, I believe there are other possible explanations. In Romany or Gypsy speech, *posh* means half. Romany *shiv* for knife entered the English language, as did *rum go* for a Gypsy thing or a queer thing. The British underworld learned about *posh* from expressions like *posh-houri* or halfpence and *posh-kooroona* or half crown. Thus posh was always associated with money, which is exactly what it meant in thieves jargon from the 17th to mid-19th centuries. From "money" to "swank, fashionable, luxurious, expensive," everything that is available for money, is not such a big step, is it?

Although I do not claim that *posh* could possibly come from *plush*, I wish to draw attention to the fact that plush also means "notably luxurious, expensive, highly superior for its kind," and that the two words are only separated by one consonant, "*l*," and a change in the vowel sound from *o* to *u*. It just may be that the meaning of a like-sounding word helped to influence the meaning of posh. As earlier noted, *plush* comes indirectly from "pile," which is from Latin *pilus*, or hair, and *pilosus*, or hairy, and more directly from French *peluche* after a contraction eliminating the *e*. French *peluche* is a cloth similar to velvet that on one side has long shiny silken and recumbent hair. Contractions by means of eliminating vowels are frequent in language: *inamity* became enimity then enmity; *fourteen night* gradually evolved to fortennight, and finally to fortnight; *dirge*, through a similar contraction, was shortened from the first word of a Roman Catholic service called the Office of the Dead, *"Dirige, Domine, Deus meus, in conspectu Tuo viam meam"* — "Guide, O Lord my God, my life in Thy vision."

Those Pesky Pronouns

I am always delighted to hear from readers. One of them called me recently with a question about the correct usage of the relative pronouns "who, which, and that." I shall proceed to elucidate this problem. *Elucidate*, by the way, comes from Latin *ex* or *e*, meaning out, and *lux, lucidus*, meaning light and clear respectively, hence also the word lucid. Elucidate, therefore, signifies to bring out into the light and shine the latter on the problem in question. *Fiat lux* from Genesis 1:3 means "let there be light," which is also the motto of Switzerland. *Lux et veritas*, "light and truth," is the motto of Yale University, which most politicians graduating from there seem to forget. *Lux in tenebris* means "light in darkness" and *lux venit ab alto* tells us that "light comes from above." You are now certified Latinists.

Back to our relative pronouns! *That* may refer to persons, animals, or things; *which* to animals and things; *who* and its object case *whom* to persons only. The problem with dictionaries and grammars is that they often define adjective clauses introduced by "that" or "who" in all cases as restrictive clauses, *i.e.*, clauses so closely attached to the antecedent noun

To Boot	From Anglo-Saxon *bōt-profit*; we used to say: *bōt*, better, best: from Aryan *bhud*, good. In the English game "Hand in Cap," players were told by an umpire what each should get "to boot," or in addition to the other things gained or exchanged in their play.
Handicap	Evolving from the English game "Hand in Cap," which gave something "to boot" — an allowance — and also a golfer's weakness.

as to be essential to defining its meaning. For example, they may refer to both "the boy who succeeded, had worked hard" and "a boy that succeeded must have worked hard" as restrictive clauses. Confusing, isn't it? "That" introduces a more restrictive clause than "who" in that it provides information restricted to, limited to, and necessary for the full understanding of an antecedent — here "boy," which itself may be in question. Notice that when using *who* we introduce *boy* with the definite article *the*, which already nails him down, while with *that* we use the indefinite article *a*, which places in doubt his existence. A similar example would be "*a* man *that* pays his bills is liked by all" or "*the* man *who* pays his bills is liked by all."

Some of us have a problem with the difference between agnostic and atheist. The distinction becomes crystal clear once we consider the Greek etymology of both words. In both cases "*a*" negates or states the absence of something. However, *gnostos* means knowledge and *theos* God. Consequently an agnostic mainly disclaims any knowledge of a god or any god for that matter. A god for him is unknowable. He does not deny his existence. An atheist denies the existence of a god. He states there is none.

Some of you may label me a fuddy-duddy or an old fogy for being irritated by the use of aggravate in lieu of irritate or annoy. Aggravate from Latin *ad*, or to, and *gravis*, heavy, serious, means to make more serious, more grave, to intensify, to increase something unpleasant. If used at all in a figurative meaning it would mean to add to someone's burden or troubles. It is much stronger than annoy, which means to harass, to pester. Irritate, the milder term, is merely to excite to impatience. Language can be very precise; it is up to the user to select the right word corresponding to the intended meaning.

Fuddy-duddy, probably from a reduplicated Scottish word *fuddy*, signifying an animal's tail, refers to someone old-fashioned, ultraconservative. Old *fogey* (variation of *fogy*) was most probably inspired by the old English word *foggy*, once used for fat, bloated, moss-grown. The Scottish adopted it as *fogey*, a disrespectful term for an old man who is behind the times. Does this mean I am going to pot? That expression comes from blacksmiths who used to throw broken metal pieces from their work into a pot, to be melted down and used again later.

Language and the Dissecting of Reality

Those of us who search for the deeper roots of the hidden beauties and wonders of nature, of which language is certainly one of the more intriguing, can follow two approaches. We can either scrutinize the extraordinary intricacy of surface phenomena or search for evidence of general principles that explain fundamental aspects of such intricacy. Where language is concerned, the search for what physicists refer to as a "unified field theory," whereby language could be reduced to a few general rules and principles, has not proven too fruitful. It has continuously frustrated us with baffling exceptions. We often discover that a richer harvest may be gleaned by merely keenly observing the action of several different languages or tongues. By the way, as an example of how differently languages dissect reality, English has only two terms to refer to language in general and to its multiple manifestations: language and tongue. French has three: *langage*, or language in general, in the abstract; *langue*, corresponding to our tongue; and finally, *parole*, the spoken tongue. Basic principles may well rule, but, if so, in realms outside of (albeit connected with) language itself, such as our organic and cerebral functions.

While languages bear the imprint of how its speakers dissect and perceive the reality in which they sense and live, there is no uniformity in the resulting pattern. Take the Nakhi in China's northern Yunnan province. They have a pictographic script unrelated to any other in the world, made up of entirely recognizable creatures and objects. They run their society along conventionally patriarchal lines, yet there is an odd matriarchal aspect to their lives, which deeply penetrates their spoken language. Add a feminine suffix to any noun, and it makes it bigger, more powerful, dominant. Adding the masculine suffix denotes weakness, delicacy, and submissiveness. A female stone is a cobble or a boulder; a male, a pebble, gravel, even a grain of sand.

English has just one word for "to know." Other languages, like French, English, German, Spanish, and Russian, distinguish between knowing a fact, a field of knowledge, and recognizing (being able to distinguish) something. Greek is very subtle when it deals with such matters. *Gnosis* is knowledge pure and simple. *Epistemology*, from *epi* (over, above) and *histanai* (to set, place) is the study of the where, whence, and how of knowledge with reference to its validity. The second Greek word is closer to our "understand." Both these words are based on similar, albeit opposite, spatial metaphors, the Greek emphasizing the grounds on which knowledge is based, the English what stands under it and supports it. Different perceptions, different metaphors!

To *comprehend* essentially means understand, but views it from a different perspective. Latin *praehendere*, which gave French *prendre*, means to grasp, seize, and is the antonym of *rendre* (give back, render, as in "render unto Caesar the things which are Caesar's"). To comprehend signifies to seize together in your mind. Hence prehensile is what is adapted to grasping or seizing, like the tail of a monkey. To reprehend, with *re* meaning back, is to return with disapproval something you may have figuratively taken in or observed. To apprehend is to take unto oneself, and if you worry about having done so, you turn apprehensive. Every metaphor is apt to evoke different associations or connotations, and, consequently, produce different meanings. To comprehend, basically meaning to take together, may evoke on the one side the more figurative sense of understanding, on the other the element of "all inclusiveness" dominant in "comprehensive."

Mi capisce?

Language May Bewitch Our Intelligence

In 1922, Ludwig Wittgenstein published his *Tractatus Logico-Philosophicus*, in which he pointed out that most philosophical problems were the result not so much of difficulty or inadequate knowledge, but of the systematic misuse of language by philosophers. "Philosophy," he had said, "is a battle against the bewitchment of our intelligence by means of language." I, too, have repeatedly warned in my columns about the misuse of language, not merely by philosophers, but by speakers and users of language in general. Language, a symbolic system shared by a social community and capable of triggering semantic reactions in the human brain, represents but one factor in the complex process of establishing meaningful communication. Our senses and brain play the far greater role. Does this not allow us to logically conclude that the human use and handling of, respect for, attitude toward language may provide an insight into the personal characteristics of the speakers and even yield clues as to how they deal with other data?

Here is a case in point. A talk-show host's principal tool is language. The subject matter of the show, mostly opinions, cannot always be judged by "strict" standards. I avoid the use of "objective," because I believe human beings are, constitutionally, subjective at all times, except perhaps with scientifically verifiable matters subject to rules and laws. Recently I heard the rather brash, egomaniac, know-it-all talk-show host Bill O'Reilly (I cannot label him a windbag, because, contrary to the definition of that word, "he does not have little to say" and "does not talk volubly to little effect" as long as he has a fawning audience) read a passage from the *New York Times* containing the word "vituperatively." O'Reilly found it necessary to offer, unasked, a definition of this word, apparently believing it was beyond the intellectual grasp of his audience. He defined it quite erroneously as "hostile."

Hostile comes straight from the Latin *hostis*, a word combining both the meaning of stranger, outsider, and enemy, foe. Vituperate, adverb vituperatively, has two sememes or meaningful semantic units. From the Latin verb *uituperare*, comprising *uitium* (vice, fault) and *perare* or *parare* (to prepare, find), it essentially means to abuse in words, censure severely, heap blame on someone. Nothing in vituperatively *directly refers to hostility*. Once a pontificating talk-show host errs (*i.e.*, one who delivers dogmatic opinions), by proving "he does not know when he does not know," he loses credibility in all respects.

Pontiff and to *pontificate* are from Latin *pontifex*, high priest, itself composed of *pons* (bridge) and *facere* (to build). In Rome, the function of the five pontifices or bridge builders was to conduct the building and demolition of the bridge over the River Tiber. Latin *pons, pontis*, is from Greek *patos*, Sanskkrit *patha*, which also means path. Both the Romans and the medieval clergy were also great road builders, the church to encourage pilgrimages to sacred shrines. Noteworthy is that pontifex is originally a variation of pompifex, from Greek *pompe*, religious procession, from *pompein* to send, thus meaning one that directs the rituals. Hence pomp and circumstance! The change from *m* to *n* is common. Joseph T. Shipley points out that Pompeius, or Pontius, was the man who asked a pilot to steer him to the truth, to which a bridge has not as yet been built. Truth, it is said, is at the bottom of a well; but, when we look, we see only our own image.

The Origins of "Juke" Are No Joke

It never fails! A fellow columnist writes about language and, presto, I have material for a new column. One of my esteemed colleagues quotes a source as contending that "juke" means "to dance and act wildly." Well . . . maybe! However, that is not the only origin of the word, and there is a great deal more to the story. As a conscientious linguist, I would be in dereliction of my duties and subject to the wrath of Clio, the Muse of History, if I did not protest and bear witness regarding this matter. I have mentioned that *protest* comes from the Latin *pro*, come forward, and *testis*, a witness. As noted earlier, *testis* is also related to its diminutive *testicle* or little witness, for in olden times one pledged one's truthfulness by placing the right hand on the site of manliness. I shall forego this ritual, as I am sure you will trust me without it!

Oh, yes, *dereliction* is a magnificent triple hitter, which contains the meanings of *de* (away from), *re* (backing off), and *linquere* (past participle *lictus*, leave behind), thereby pounding into our head the idea of "forsaking" three times!

Mind you, it is not my colleague, but rather his source that has here committed a tad malfeasance (from Latin and French meaning to do evil) — a word resonating with medieval court splendor and reminding us of the motto of the British Order of the Garter, *Honi soit qui mal y pense* (Shame on him who thinks evil of it).

But back to *juke*! In the mountains of Tennessee and the Southern United States, many Elizabethan words that have died out in England were or are still preserved. There indeed was a word "jouk," meaning to dodge, move quickly, and it was often applied to the places where liquor was sold, especially during Prohibition. Eventually the word was used to designate any cheap drinking place. When the automatic phonograph became immensely popular and appeared in such bars, it was called a "jukebox."

However, there is still more. In Southern religious revival meetings, characterized by rhythmic "jumps" and "jerks," any person driven to such an ecstatic state was said to "juke," a combination of both words. Dancers stimulated by such hot or "juke" music will "juke." But hold on! We're not there yet! As several linguists — especially Lorenzo Dow Turner — have pointed out, "juke" is from Gullah, one of the few English Creole languages of African origin used by a group of Negroes inhabiting the Sea Islands and coastal districts of South Carolina, Georgia, and a small part of northeastern Florida. Many of its words can be traced to Africa. It means misbehavior, disorderliness, or riot. In the 19th century, a juke house was nothing but a brothel. The jukebox, however, only dates from about 1920. We know that in early 20th century New Orleans, "jass" house (whence jazz, from Charles — pronounced "Chas" — Alexander of "Alexander's Ragtime Band" fame, the 1911 Irving Berlin song) was the name given to a whorehouse, where Dixieland musicians found a convenient place to play.

Jukebox quite probably also owes its name to the same association of loud music with houses of ill repute. It might have been one way to muffle suspicious outcries and noises. Juke thus is a disorderly house. The word is encountered in dialects spoken in Senegal, French West Africa — in countries that constitute the ancestral lands of many of these Negroes and that possess in addition to a native literature another so-called black one of French expression. "Juke" thus has many sources.

You now know the entire story and Clio will let me rest in peace.

Style Defines the Man

English clergyman and scholar Robert Burton (1577-1640) wrote: "It is most true, *stilus virum arguit* — our style betrays us." I would rather translate this as "our style defines us." The Latin proverb literally means "a man's style shows him in a clear light." An assiduous (from a Latin verb meaning to sit beside, *i.e.*, applying the seat of the pants to the seat of the chair) student and lover of language, I write about word origins and various aspects of language. The latter changes constantly. Therefore, I accept new usage of words, but, without any implied condescension toward the parlance of others, choose mine to be grammatical, concise, and logical, avoiding the redundant and hackneyed.

I prefer not to use "hopefully" as it often is now, instead of "it is to be hoped that." Hopefully, meaning full of hope, is an adverb and normally should modify the following verb, as does merrily in "Merrily we ride along." When I hear "hopefully he will arrive on time," I have a vision of someone bouncing euphorically up and down — *I hope* mindful of traffic — in my general direction.

I select "all-round athlete" over "all-around athlete," because *round* provides the idea of completeness. *Around* rather suggests position with regard to a center. Now, I would say: "The dog walked around, not round, the chair," and "I walked all around (without hyphen) the park." Yes! Without considering myself pedantic, I do distinguish between lay, laid, laid, laying, meaning to place (lay a carpet) and lie, lay, lain, lying, meaning to recline (lie low). I would be lying down on the job not to do so. Ultimately, I prefer to dwell on language being fossilized poetry. As I have noted, a good geologist should be able from rocks to tell you much about what happened to the landscape over time, and a sensitive student of words can tell you how our ancestors perceived their reality and the world and people around them.

Language and Consciousness

The mystery of language and meaning may ultimately well be beyond the grasp of human intelligence, but this does not mean we cannot infer a great deal from the thoughtful observation of the linguistic data at our disposal. Some thinkers have argued that reality is a "collective representation" projected by an evolving human consciousness. We may safely assert that language is made possible first by the speech and auditory organs with which we humans are endowed and second by a collective force of consciousness, in which we all participate. This applies to language globally and to every individual language community. My late friend and colleague Mario A. Pei, formerly of Columbia University, used to speak of the loom of language. Indeed, the entire linguistic process might well be compared to an elaborately woven motley wall hanging, with a multitude of patterns. In our metaphor, the threads would represent the words, while the rest, artistic effect and beauty, would be the meaning of it all.

Meaning, as I shall show you, is in the mind, not in language, although the latter may trigger it. Consider, for instance, the original Aryan root *STA*, Sanskrit *sthá*, in Latin *stare*, to stand. This is a very productive root, to which we owe numerous English words, such as state, estate, status, and stationary, where the main idea is standing. Prefixes determine what additional spatial meaning we must attribute to words so formed. I emphasize "spatial," as space, time, matter, and number are all concepts human consciousness has developed over the ages. Consider the word "exist," at the very basis of life, the meaning of which humans have pondered for millennia. The metaphor or image behind the word could not be simpler. Made up from *ex*, Latin for out, and *istere* or *sistere*, another form of *stare*, the word thus means "to stand out from" some background. If you stand out from and do not blend in with the background, you evidently may be noticed and exist. Any additional meanings mankind may have added to the original root sprang from physical, psychic, and spiritual experiences, associations, and connotations, all of which took place in the mind.

Arrest is composed of Latin *ad* (to), *re* (a retrograde movement or repetition as in "return"), and *stare* (to stand in one place). The totality conjures the image of standing still, keeping from moving on, and fixed at one place. Assist, from *ad* (to, by) and *stare,* paints the image of standing by someone. Circumstance merely adds Latin *circum*, meaning around. Knowing Latin and asked to define circumstance, you might do so quite deftly by stating that it comprises all facts that surround a particular event. Latin *cum* means together, so that constant means to stand firmly together, and "to consist" means essentially the same thing, as all parts stand together. Constitute adds the element of causing to stand together. Desist, where Latin *de* means away from, literally means to stand aside.

The human mind took these primitive images and, as the need for expressing new shades of meaning arose, utilized the same linguistic building blocks to come up with them. Thus, destitute ultimately is similar to desist, but now "you stand alone and away from what you had." It's high time for me to *resist*, literally to stand back from, the temptation of persisting (Latin *per* means through, here keep standing) with this column, unless you *insist* (*in* here means stand firm in the same spot) otherwise.

The Power of Words

Any psychologists, psychiatrists, hypnotherapists *worth their salt* will tell you unequivocally that language provides valuable insight into people's thought and reasoning processes. Incidentally, "worth one's salt" and "earn one's salt" date back to the days when salt was the chief means of keeping meat from spoiling. The Latin *salarium*, salt money, was then the figurative word for what we now call literally salary.

Words can be powerful! Promise you will *try* to stop smoking, and a therapist will know you won't, because "trying" implies anticipated failure. Similarly, nefarious linguistic labeling, as for example telling yourself "I must have arthritis," instead of merely "a pain in my joints," or a doctor's diagnosis of "You'll be dead in a month," will most probably bring about the misguided verbalized effect. Nefarious, by the way, comes from two Latin words meaning "that what is not spoken of," hence bad, against divine command.

Those of us who write about language display quite different interests and styles. Prolific writer Dr. Richard Lederer (he once wistfully thought his name in German meant "rich tanner" rather than just plain tanner, until I disabused him and wrote to him that words do not change with one's tax bracket), a witty, clever language maven (from Yiddish *meyvn*, an expert often in minor matters, and Hebrew *mebhin*, wise man), plays word games, looking for palindromes (words reading the same backward) and other intriguing linguistic "collectibles." For instance, he will challenge you in "pin, nose, drag" to change one letter in each and find a triad of words often used together. The answer: win, lose, or draw. Or: identify a fourth word ending in *vous* besides nervous, grievous, and mischievous. The answer: rendezvous. Now, unlike Lederer, I would have recognized in this last example a unique opportunity to solve a problem in memory storage. A quick survey would show that speakers not versed in French are more likely to think of rendezvous as the solution, because to them the four *vous* endings seem alike. Someone familiar with French will, however, distinguish the first three as suffixes, but the fourth as a meaningful French pronoun, "you," direct object of the verb *rendez*, the literal meaning being "take yourself to" or appointment. This would be of immense interest to cognitive science and human memory data-storage research.

Sometimes even a famous wordsmith such as William Safire, Pulitzer Prize-winning columnist and erudite commentator on the state of the English language, "nods like good Homer" and "fails to see the forest for the trees." In his last book, *Let a Simile Be Your Umbrella*, Mr. Safire needlessly agonizes over whether the singular "is" is preferable to the plural "are" in such sentences as "The manufacture and distribution of cash is by far the Federal Government's biggest profit-making operation" and "I think drinking and driving is a really bad thing." He should have known that here the infallible grammar rules of syntactical agreement alert us to an ambiguous, undesirable construction, which should be shunned or eschewed (the latter from the same root as shy or shy away from). In both sentences the two actions are inextricably intertwined, a single unit. Why not obviate the awkwardness, improve the style, and say precisely what you mean. Reverse the first sentence, "The Federal Government's biggest operation is or consists of . . .," and in the second one write, "Drinking while driving is a really bad thing," which is what is intended. Safire failed to see that, as first written, the second sentence is nonsensical and flawed.

Colorful Word Origins

After reading Nadine L. Smith's column on colorful meanings in the Arizona *Senior World*, wouldn't you like to know how and why all these semantic color pigments show up on the palette of language? The origin of *bluestocking*, now designating a pedantic woman with literary pretensions, may be traced as far back as Venice in the 1400s, where a group of ladies and gentlemen formed a society known as *Della Calza*, literally "of the stocking," as they wore blue stockings. In 1590 the custom caught on in Paris, and in 1750 in England. English society women formed *Bas-bleu* (French for bluestocking) clubs. Members wore blue stockings instead of the formal black, creating a scandal — blue was the color of servants and lower-class people. Surprisingly the French word *bas-bleu* for a pedantic woman entered France in 1801 as a translation from the English.

The nobles of Castile were the first to use the term "blue blood" (*sangre azul*). Until 1492, when the Moors were expelled from Spain, Spaniards feared lest they be suspected of having the "darker" blood of Moors or Jews running in their veins, always protesting that they were *cristianos viejos* (old Christians), rather than converted ones of mixed blood. The official report of the British government is called a "Blue Book," because all reports of the British Parliament and Privy Council have a dark blue paper cover. Preliminary, less extensive reports, lacking a cover, are known as "White Paper." The New Jersey "Blue Laws," forbidding business on Sundays, are so called because such Puritanical laws were first devised by the New Haven colonists who considered blue as the color of the Presbyterians of the "true-blue" pro-Parliament party in England.

> **Bailiwick** From Lower Latin *bailulivus*, the man in charge of a fort; Latin *ballium* and *vallum*, a wall or rampart, castle wall, also giving us London's Old Bailey.
>
> **Bistro** Thought by some to derive from "*buystro*," the Russian word for "quick." It was said that Russian soldiers visiting Paris in 1814 were encouraged to go into local restaurants with the call of "*Buystro! Buystro!*" – "quickly, quickly!" Actually, *bistro* indeed designated a small wineshop or restaurant. The word first appeared in the late 1800s in a book authored by Father Moreau.

"Once in a blue moon," which was never expected to occur, originally meant never. However, they do occur as a result of volcanic explosions and smoke-filled fogs, causing the expression now to signify "rarely ever." The seafaring expression "hoist the blue peter" means ready to depart. A ship about to leave port hoists a blue flag with a white square in the center and the letter "P," known as the "blue repeater." "P" is the first letter of French *partir*, to leave. This signal alerts all seamen ashore to return aboard and all citizens with monetary claims against the crew to collect debts before it is too late.

Some word origins are more nebulous. The pink, a flower from the Dianthus genus, may have been named from pink eye, or little eye, as the

French *oeillet* (Dianthus and carnation) literally means little eye. On the other hand, because pink, prick, and peck are related, pink being merely a nasalized "pick," some thought the flower was so named because its edges are cut in and out. There are two reasons for such expressions as "the pink of perfection or courtesy": one, pink meaning tip or point made by cutting, hence peak; two, because pink was once a general term for flower, it is like saying the flower of perfection.

"Drawing a red herring," an attempt to draw attention away from the main issue, comes to us from fox hunting, where the herring was used, because of its strong odor due to curing, to mislead hounds. Red always was the color of blood, revenge, and revolution, a legacy of "the red cap" of the French Jacobins, the "red shirts" of Italian Garibaldi followers, and the Soviets, the "reds." However, in Russian, red (*krasniy*) also means beautiful, and Red Square (*krasnaya ploshchad*) also means beautiful square.

Do svidanya — good-bye!

More About the *Oxford English Dictionary*

Anyone passionate about the English language should be interested in the *Oxford English Dictionary*. When Shakespeare lived, there were no dictionaries; one could not "look something up," an expression first used in 1692 by the Oxford historian Anthony Wood. Word lists were available, but no full statement of the extent of the English tongue. In 1604, Robert Cowdrey published 2,500 words in *A Table Alphabeticall* [*sic*] *of Hard Unusual English Words* of 120 pages. Then came literature's "Great Cham," as Tobias Smollett called Samuel Johnson. (Cham, also Khan, in Medieval Turkish, Tatar, is a Mongol ruler or prince, a Chinese sovereign, here just a title of respect.) Johnson created the truly first quaint, pivotal *Dictionary of the English Language*, establishing the latter's limits and inventory; and, wisely aware that language changes, he never attempted to "fix it." For financial help he addressed himself to Lord Chesterfield, who induced England to adopt the Gregorian calendar, wrote the famous letters to his bastard son, and finally gave Johnson a measly ten pounds. When later the Lord claimed credit for the dictionary, Johnson wrote: "Chesterfield taught the morals of a whore and the manners of a dancing master."

Johnson, not relying on previous word lists, opted for recording words heard and printed, buying an abundance of books and recruiting a team of seven helpers to read them. He started with the writings of Sir Philip Sidney, from about 1580, but also included English poet Geoffrey Chaucer (1340?-1400). Johnson's entries are quaint: "Oats — a grain which in England is given to horses, but in Scotland supports the people." "Lexicographer — a writer of dictionaries; a harmless drudge who traces the origin of words." The verb "to take" has as many as 113 explanations. He finished his list in 1750, spent four years writing 118,000 illustrative quotations, and ended up with 43,500 "headwords." The work was published in 1753 and enjoyed four editions.

On November 5, 1857, Guy Fawkes Day (commemorating the 1605 plot by Fawkes to assassinate the King and Parliament), at the London Library, Dr. Richard Chenevix Trench, Dean of Westminster and Archbishop of Dublin, referred to as "Divine" in his obituary, staunch believer in the ceaseless dissemination of the English language around the planet, recommended to the members of the Philological Society the launching of the "big dictionary" to include the entire English language with every shade of meaning. It took another twenty-two years before work on the *OED* under the auspices of the Oxford delegation actually started.

Henceforth, the *Oxford English Dictionary* will only be published on computer disks.

Complexities of Language, a Wonder of Nature

We may never be able, with dry formulas, blueprints, or diagrams, to capture and explain the wonders of nature, which include language, in their richness and complexity. As Goethe's Faust tells his students: "All theory, dear friend, is but a lifeless gray;/Life's golden tree alone sparkles in green array." We can, however, learn from this semantic symphony constantly offering itself before our eyes and ears. Thereby we witness how, impelled by necessity, we humans manage to process and communicate, as best we can, the meanings provided by our sensory perceptions of the universe in which we live, making good use of what is already available for ever newly fancied figurations.

What, for instance, did language forge from the concept of leaping or jumping? By the way, in Shakespeare's time, "jump" could mean "just": "Thus twice before, and jump at this dead hour,/With martial stalk hath he gone by our watch" (*Hamlet*, 1.1.65). Now even if we believe in the jingle "Sticks and stones may break my bones, but words will never hurt me," both "insult" and "assault" once referred to a physical attack. From the Latin etymons *salire* (to leap), and its frequentative *saltare* (to jump or leap often, even to dance), through the French *sauter*, with the prefix *in-*, it meant to leap upon, with the prefix *ad-*, *ass-*, to leap at or against, both definitely physical attacks. This root gave us insult, assail, and assault, and, with the prefix *re-*, meaning backward, we derive "result."

Now that is where our mind or "figuration" plays tricks on us, distorting our notions of space and time. We visualize a result as being in the future, yet it always follows something from behind. The idea of a result being a by-product, of following along, is clearly illustrated in the close synonym consequence, from two Latin words *con* (together) and *sequi* (follow), which gave us sequence and the negative *non sequitur*, an inference or conclusion that does not follow from the premises and is not a logical result thereof. Somewhere along the line, as need dictated, the meaning of *re-* as "backward" stepped in again and appeared in *resaltare*, to leap back. You bounce a ball; it jumps back as the *result* of the action. Legal minds, availing themselves of the opportunity, used result in the literal sense of jumping back, reverting, in such sentences as "After the heir's death, the estate shall result to the trust." Result can be in the future, follow behind, or jump back at you.

Somersault does not come from summer, but may generate heat when it is done. It is a corruption of French *soubresau(l)t*, a word dating back to 1369 as an equestrian term, a horse's plunge, and to 1410 as a sudden bound, or start, from Latin *super* (over) and the now familiar *saltare* (to jump). In Wall Street a leap is an option, call, or put, valid for over a year. *A leap in the dark*, an action with unforeseeable results, dates back to a

1697 play by Sir John Vanbrugh, *The Provok'd Wife*. A dying man says, "So now I am in for Hobbes [*sic*] voyage, a great leap in the dark," words similar to those attributed to philosopher Thomas Hobbes on his deathbed. To jump Jim Crow, *i.e.*, to dance with a peculiar limping step, comes from a popular song and its accompanying dance, copyrighted in 1828 by Thomas D. Rice:

> First on de heel tap, den on the toe,
> Ebery time I wheel about I jump Jim Crow.
> Wheel about and turn about and do jis so,
> And ebery time I wheel about I jump Jim Crow.

Now "jump," or just tell me to jump in the lake!

The Politically and Historically Accurate *Squaw*

With the current controversy raging in Arizona about renaming the local Squaw Peak Mountain Piestewa Peak after the Hopi Private First Class woman U.S. soldier killed in Iraq, it might perhaps be useful to recall some hard linguistic data and bring to light, again as Paul Harvey would put it, "the rest of the story." After all, even Arizona State Transportation Board member Bill Jeffers was quoted as stating that "only one of about forty American Indians he spoke with objected to the word 'squaw.' When it was suggested that the term was offensive, [he] was greeted with laughter."

No serious dictionary will start off its entry *squaw* by defining it as offensive, pejorative, derogatory, derisive, words literally and respectively meaning "to strike against, make worse, ask down or lessen, and laugh down." They all define it as an American Indian woman and a term of Algonquian origin, akin to Natick *squa* female creature, *squáas* woman, and Narragansett *squaws*. Earlier forms were the Narragansett *eskwaw*, the Delaware *ochqueu*, the Chippewa *ikwe*, and Massachusett *squá* younger woman. Some dictionaries further state that non-Indians, to designate an effeminate person or a non American Indian woman, may use the term disparagingly. According to George B. Cheever's, *The Journal of the Pilgrim at Plymouth* (1848), a certain George Morton mentioned the term when he wrote: "Also the *Squa Sachim*, or Massachusets Queene was an enemy to him [another *sachem* or Indian leader]."

As a noun, *squaw* first occurred in William Wood's *New England's Prospect* (1634), published, as the front page states, for "the mind-travelling reader" and "the future Voyager." Wood spent four years in Massachusetts, returning to England in 1633. Among new Eastern and Western loan-words, including *squaw*, we count: squaw vine (1850); squawberry (1852); squaw huckleberry (1857); squaw winter, a brief period of wintry weather in autumn (1861); squaw dance, one in which women choose their partner (1864); squaw man, a white man married to an Indian woman (1866); and squawfish, dull green silver-marked fish of the Columbia River (1881). Interestingly, the word squaw was often applied to Indians for whom this Algonquian term was not native.

Other terms now found in good dictionaries are squawbush (dye or cranberry tree); squaw cabbage (used as potherbs by Indians); squaw carpet (used by squaws for making mats); squaw currant, with white flowers and a crimson berry; squaw-drops or squawroot; squaw or eider duck; squaw flower or purple trillium; squaw grass, a turkey beard of the mountains of the Pacific northwest also called pine lily; and, finally, squaw hitch, or knot to tie a pack on an animal. Should we presently rename all these words?

Speaking of language, with which I have carried on an eighty-year love

Vandalism	From the sacking of Rome, 445 A.D., by Genseric, king of the Vandals (who were members of the Germanic people that overran Gaul, Spain, and northern Africa in the 4th and 5th centuries).
Windfall	English nobility, required to reserve all timber for the Royal Navy, were not allowed to fell trees even on their own estates. *However*, they were free to use any trees *blown down by the wind*. A *windfall* thus brought good fortune!

affair, fence, defend, offend, offense, or offence all have the same root — all include the meaning of beating off. Robert Frost, intentionally or unintentionally, punned with these terms in his poem "Mending Wall," which you will allow me, I hope, to quote here as appropriate:

> Before I built a wall I'd ask to know
> What I was walling in and walling out,
> And to whom I was like to give offence.

Epilogue

I SUPPOSE EVERY book should have an epilogue. My editor insists on one, so what choice do I have? Besides it gives us an additional word, possibly now deemed fancy, with an originally simple, straightforward meaning, to add to our list. Formed from the Greek *epi* (meaning on, upon, to), prefixed to *logos* (meaning word), *epilogue* is quite simply something added to what was said or written before, and the verb *epilegein* means to "say in addition." If I substitute the Greek word *graphein* (to write) for *logos*, with the same prefix *epi-*, the result is *epigram*, a short poem, treating concisely, often satirically, of a single thought or event and ending with a witticism. If I add graph for epigraph, God forbid, it means writing permanently affixed to — among other solid surfaces — a tombstone. I have translated the following epigram from the French writer Voltaire, about Elie Fréron (Voltaire refers to him as "Jean Fréron"), 18th-century French critic, founder of the *Literary Year*, and enemy of Voltaire and his fellow philosophers:

> Not long ago, in the deep grass,
> a snake bit Fréron in the ass.
> Do not fret about Fréron's lot!
> The snake is who croaked on the spot!

Definitely, if you'll excuse the pun, mordant humor, from a French word signifying "biting."

I hope this book has served a more serious purpose than merely satisfying your curiosity about how some of our words and strange expressions originated. Its aim, more ambitious, was to show you *language in action*. Why? Because I truly believe that the mystery of language is beyond the grasp of human intelligence. We can, however, observe it, watching close up the miraculously ingenious way it communicates meaning, and thereby acquire a feel for its nature and spirit. We may never fully capture its capricious, lifelike character, which can be the case with anyone or anything you love and respect, but we can still achieve productive results. The womb of all meaning, especially linguistic meaning, resides in our thought processes, and the latter display kaleidoscopic and diapasonal features. Every perception, be it stimulated by sight, hearing, taste, smell, or touch, relying on countless associations and connotations gleaned from life experience, *rings a bell*, generating and evoking a myriad of familiar images, memories, related facts, and emotions. Look where the three letters *epi* took us in the first paragraph! Straight to the heart of the meaning of *epilogue*!

Our words are more than symbols, but they still never reflect or express the entire reality of what they refer to and represent. They allow us to deal with reality *vicariously*, an interesting word from the Latin *vice* meaning "in place of." The earlier adoption from this Latin *vice* was *vis* or *vi*, as in viscount and vicar. Thus, words are often no more than mnemonic devices helping us recall some aspect of what is represented, and we must infer and complement the rest of the meaning from the context or from our previous knowledge. In some languages, such as Hebrew, the situation is even worse. In writing, only consonants are used, and the reader must supply the vowels, a process requiring a continuous interpretative effort. In many cases, if we do not know the etymology of a word, as in *epigram*, we must commit the meaning of the word to memory. Knowing the "image behind the word" (one of the purposes of this book is to show you there usually *is* one), obviously helps greatly in providing us with a reason, a *why*, for the word's semantic evolution.

When Alfred Korzybski gently reminded us that "The word is not the thing; the map is not the territory," he had another semantic aspect of language in mind: its use and possible misuse. Simply put, he warned us that "talking about it" is not the same as "dealing with it itself." Lest we forget, theory is no substitute for life! And words are more than symbols in that they have a life of their own. The semantic possibilities they suggest increase exponentially, often almost beyond our control. Consider *capricious*, which I have used in connection with language! If you know that it comes from the Latin *caper*, meaning he-goat, your thought processses will start jumping and cavorting about like one and, "*before you can say Jack Robinson*" (now where did that come from?), will even remind you that the island of Capri was so named because of the goats that graze on it.

The best-known quotation in all philosophy may be Descartes' "*Cogito ergo sum* — I think, therefore I am." With language, the reverse works just as well. Perhaps Descartes "*put the cart before the horse*" and should have proposed instead, "I am, therefore I think." In this regard, never forget how much the written alphabet and writing affected the role of language. Once written, language exerted its own powerful effect on perception, while with indigenous oral tongues the effect on perception rather sprang from the natural universe.

One thing is certain: thought preceded language and communication. Prehistoric humans saw, touched, smelled, heard, tasted — in short perceived — and realized they could somehow communicate their perception, first probably by sign language, then by emitting sounds. The same mental mechanism perceived reality, received meaning, and, within a specific social group or community, emitted mutually agreed-upon signs or sounds to express this meaning. Signs and sounds might vary with groups. Reaction to pain elicits an "*Au!*" in German, an "*Ouch!*" in English, and an "*Aie!*" in French. It is what happened afterward, especially the invention of the alphabet and writing, that complicated everything, maybe even "*threw a monkey wrench in the machinery*" of language. See! . . . That's what I mean. I could have used "*gum up the works, caused confusion*," but, somehow, this "*monkey wrench*" intruded on my mind.

We are not even sure when this expression was first used. The tool itself was known in 1858, and an item appearing in the Boston *Transcript* (sometime in the winter of 1932-1933) credits the invention, in 1856, to a man named Monk, employed by Bemis & Call of Springfield, Massachusetts. It was called "*Monk's wrench*" and somehow, no doubt as a joke, evolved into *monkey wrench*. The American origin is more likely, since the English refer to the tool as a "spanner wrench." The date 1856 agrees with the first appearance of the term in the *Oxford English Dictionary*. What is really important for us here is how the human brain operates. One of the most basic human impulses in the cognition process is *to compare*. When positively inclined, we look for similarities; when negatively inclined, we search for differences, and cognition may even rely on a process of elimination to come up with a solution. Throughout everyday life we compare and find similarities. We look at the world around us, gaze at clouds, notice shapes of people, even evaluate certain sounds, and, willy-nilly, our mind plays tricks with our imagination, evoking new ideas or expanding on the ones suggested.

Strange-sounding words might inspire new ones through folk etymology (as in the Spanish *juzgado*, which ended up as *hoosegow*, or Cabez de Vaca's *cayo hueso*, which ended up as Key West) and customary terms suggest new meanings when needed. Consider also *heel*, for instance. From the Indo-European *kenk*, changing *k* to *h* and dropping the nasal sound, we have Old English *hēla*, the back of the foot. Necessity and similarity produced the meaning of "a bluntly rounded object," or "the end of a golf club near the shaft." Its low position may have suggested a "despicable person." Then it became a verb, when asking a dog to follow close behind. Countless other meanings followed, in cascades: *down at the heels*, *ward heeler* (minor politician), *under the heel of* (oppressed), *take to one's heels* or *show a clean pair of heels*, *cool one's heels*, *head over heels* (from the idea of falling, although illogical, because logic requires "heels over head"). From cockfights we have *heeled* (at first, razor-sharp spurs strapped to the legs of a fighting cock; then, in slang, armed with a weapon), and finally *well-heeled* or affluent, probably because of a bulging wad of banknotes in one's pocket.

How did it all happen? Newly equipped with the foregoing linguistic facts, form your own theories! If, as Nobel Prize winner Sir Francis Crick of DNA double-helix fame claims in *Astonishing Hypothesis*, consciousness is an evolved capability like binaural hearing and binocular color vision, perhaps language too evolved over millennia in the same manner.

You have herein a good start to ponder the puzzle. If you find a solution, or have any questions, feel free to contact me through the publisher or via e-mail at maxojr@earthlink.net.

Enjoy the miracle of language!

❧ Selected Reading ❧

Almond, Jordan. *Dictionary of Word Origins: A History of the Words, Expressions, and Cliches We Use.* New York: Kensington Publishing Corp., 1995.
Ciardi, John. *A Browser's Dictionary.* New York: HarperCollins, 1980.
_____. *A Second Browser's Dictionary.* New York: Akadine Press, 1983.
_____. *A Third Browser's Dictionary.* New York: Akadine Press, 2001.
Ehrlich, Eugene, H. *The Harper Dictionary of Foreign Terms.* 3rd ed. New York: HarperCollins, 1990.
Funk, Charles Earle. *2107 Curious Word Origins, Sayings and Expressions.* New York: BBS Publishing Corp, 1993.
Funk, Wilfred. *Word Origins and Their Romantic Stories.* New York: Funk & Wagnall's, 1950.
Mallery, Garrick. *Sign Language among North American Indians.* Mineola, NY: Dover Publications, 2001. (Unabridged republication of pp. 263-552 of the *First Annual Report of the Bureau of Ethnology of the Smithsonian Institution, 1879-1880.* Washington, D.C., Smithsonian Institution, 1881.)

Rheingold, Howard. *They Have a Word for It: A Lighthearted Lexicon of Untranslatable Words and Phrases*. Louisville, KY: Sarabande Books, Inc., 2000. (Interesting, but flawed in some of the translations.)

Safire, William. *Let a Simile Be Your Umbrella*. New York: Crown Publishing Group, 2001.

Shaw, Harry. *Dictionary of Problem Words and Expressions*. New York: McGraw-Hill, 1975, Rev. 1987.

Shipley, Joseph T. *Dictionary of Word Origins*. Westport, CT: Greenwood Publishing Group, 1970; Lanham, MD: Rowman & Littlefield, 1989.

Skeat, Walter. *The Concise Dictionary of English Etymology*. Hertfordshire, UK: Wordsworth Reference, 1993, 2001.

Wallraff, Barbara. *Word Count: Wherein Verbal Virtue Is Rewarded, Crimes Are Punished, and Poetic Justice Is Done*. New York: Harcourt, 1999.

Webster's Third New International Dictionary. Springfield, MA: Merriam-Webster, Inc., 1976.

For readers who know French, the outstanding:

Martinet, André, ed. *Encyclopédie de la Pléiade Le Langage*. Belgium: Editions Gallimard, 1968.

For readers who know German, the scholarly:

Porzig, Walter. *Das Wunder der Sprache*. Bern, Switzerland: Francke Verlag, 1950, 1957.

Index
by Lori L. Daniel

— A —
acronym, 176-177
Addison, Joseph, 146
adjective clause, 178
Aesop, 115
 Fables, 169
Africa, 113, 184, 194
 French West Africa, 184
  Senegal, 184
 North Africa, 17, 120
  Carthage, 9
 South Africa, 10
African, 83, 184
African Negro, 27
Afrikaan, 167
"aggrégation," 132
Alaska, 34
Aleut, 76
Alexander I (Tsar), 6
Alexander's Ragtime Band, 184
Alexander the Great, 70
Alexandrine line, 71
alphabet, 40, 63, 198
Amadis of Gaul, 10
America, 98, 106, 108, 117, 135, 147
 Colonial, 106
Americas, 76
American, 2-3, 19, 34, 38, 54, 60, 67, 76, 78-79, 90, 125, 135, 142, 149, 167, 173, 198

American *(continued)*
 East, 194
 Pacific Northwest, 194
 South, 86, 155, 183-184
 Southwest, 74
 West, 86, 194
American Name Society, 129
Amor, 165
Ancient Mariner, 133
Anglo-French, 31, 70
Anglo-Saxon, xv-xvi, 3, 7, 11, 14, 17, 23, 33, 35, 38, 46-47, 50, 61, 63-64, 67, 70-71, 74, 87-89, 92-93, 100, 106-108, 116, 122-123, 141, 151, 167, 174, 178
animals, 123
An Outline of Intellectual Rubbish, 102
Antony and Cleopatra, 63
antonym, 181
aphesis, 98
Aphrodite, 165
Apollo, 39
Arab, 4, 14-15, 118
Arabian, 4, 69
Arabic, 15-16, 77, 118
Arctic, 89
Arcturus (star), 89
Ares, 165
Argentina, 71
Aristocles, 127
Aristotle, 22, 99, 117, 122

Aristotelian language structure, 19
Aristotelianism, 83
Arizona, 2, 59, 131, 138, 193
    Scottsdale A&P, 169
    Squaw Peak Mountain Piestewa Peak, 193
    Sun City, xvii, 32, 111, 150
    Tempe, 74
        Monti's *La Casa Vieja,* 74
        Rio Lago restaurant, 74
Arizona Republic (AZ), 137
Arizona State Transportation Board, 193
Arizona State University, 74
Arizona Senior World (AZ), xvii
Ars Poetica, xvi
article
    definite, 179
    indefinite, 179
artificial intelligence, 80
artificial language, 80, 94
Art of Poetry: "Saepe stilum vertas," 90
Aryan, 7, 14, 26, 67, 128, 174-175, 178, 186
Asia, 12, 70
    Central
        Bukhara, 14
        Uzbekistan, 14
    Phrygia, 12
Asian, 154, 177
Astonishing Hypothesis, 199
A Table Alphabeticall of Hard Unusual English Words, 190
Attab, Prince, 17
Audi, 56
Australia, 106
Austria, 93, 146
    Vienna, 7, 23, 93-94, 108
        Congress of, 6, 37
        Vienna Castle, 94
            Children's Animation Tent, 94
Austrian, xvii, 99
Autumn Tale, 54
Avesta, 88
Avignon, 13
AWOL, 67
Aztec, 2

— B —

Babel, Tower of, 76, 94
Babylonia, 25
Bacchic rite, 57
Bacon, Francis (Sir), 106, 135
Banting, F. G. (Dr.), 18
Barber Paradox, 112
Bard, 173
Baret, John, 63
Barnum's Circus, 121
Barton, B. S., 78
Bas-bleu Club, 60, 188

Basque, 2, 25-26, 75
Battle of
    Hastings, xv, 87
    the Bulge, 65
    the Wilderness in Virginia, 174
Baudelaire, Charles Pierre, 104
Beaumont, Francis, 135
Bede, Venerable, 151
Belgium
    Bastogne, 65
    Ypres, 137
Benedictine, 103, 160
Berlin, Irving, 184
Berlitz, Charles, 5-6, 44
Bethlehem, 173
Bible, 25, 31, 46, 115, 124
bilingual education, 144-145
binary logic, 80
Blake
    James W., 19
    William, 1
Blumenau, Evelyn, 93-94
Boer War, 10
Borrow, George, 18, 128
Boston Transcript, 78
Brazil
    Guanabara Bay, 72
    Rio de Janeiro, 71-72
Brewer, E. Cobham, 4
Britain, 23, 107
British, 3, 8, 54, 75, 84, 107, 128, 161, 177, 189
    Blue Book, 189
    Order of the Garter, 183
    Parliament, 189
    Privy Council, 189
    Royal Navy, 162, 194
    White Paper, 189
Bronx cheer, 9
Browning, Robert, 73
Bruno, Giordano, 83
Buddhist, 12
Bukhara
    see Asia, Central
Burma, 147
Burton, Robert, 184
Bush, George W. (President), 155, 168

— C —

Caesar
    Augustus, 75
    Julius, xiv, 10, 47, 145, 181
California, 10, 34, 129
    Los Angeles, 57
    Monterey Language School, 145
California Proposition 187 on Immigration and Illegal Aliens, 159

Camembert (cheese), 3
Canada, 7, 106
Cantonese, 149
Cassell (Publishers), 129
Casti, John L., 80
Castile, 189
Catalan, 28, 174
Catholic, 10, 115
  Church, 20, 115, 125
Caucasian, 25-26, 113
Caxton, William, 17
Celtic, 174
century
  1st, 161
  2nd, 161
  5th, 152, 166
  6th, 22, 107
  7th, 140
  11th, 4, 40, 69
  12th, 74, 162, 168
  13th, 1, 12, 117, 119-120, 155
  14th, 5, 116
  15th, 2, 11, 17, 70, 105, 117, 163
  16th, 106, 120, 126, 152
  17th, 30, 36, 73, 84, 117, 167
  18th, 167-196
  19th, 16, 55, 119, 135, 154, 184
  20th, 184
  21st, 94, 109
Charlemagne, 75
Charpentier, Henri, 34
Chase, Stuart, 20, 159
Chaucer, Geoffrey, 5, 52, 191
Cheever, George B., 194
Chenault, Claire (General), 147
  Flying Tigers, 147
Chesterfield, Lord, 190-191
Cheviot Hills, 12
Chile
  Valparaiso, 71
China, 13, 147-149
  Beijing, 13, 164
  Canton, 149
  Chuanchow, 14
  Hong Kong, 147, 149
  Kunming, 147
    Yunnan Normal University, 147-148
    Yunnan TV, 147
  Nankin, 12-13
  Shanghai, 13
  Tzu-Ting, 14
  Yunnan province, 149, 180
    Nakhi, 180
Ch'in dynasty, 148
Chinese, xiii, 3, 12-14, 16, 33, 50, 120, 148-150, 162, 164, 190
Christian, 5, 10, 97, 115, 189

Christianity, 9, 115
Christie, Agatha, 65
Chung Kwo (Chun Kwo), 148
CIA, xv
Ciardi, John, 4, 167, 169
Cicero, 146, 152
Civil War, 174
Clinton, Bill (President), 12
Clio, 183-184
Clovis I, 154
cognition, 164, 199
Coinage Act of 1792, 106
Coleridge, Samuel Taylor, 133
Collected Essays and Reviews, 90
collective unconscious, 129
Colorado, 4, 132
Columbia University, 145, 185
Columbus, Christopher, 76
common semantic denominator, 164
communication theory, 44
Communist, 20-21
comparative, 10
Condit, Gary (Congressman), 129-131
Conestoga wagon, 77
Connecticut
  New Haven, 189
contraction, 177-178
Cooper, James Fenimore, 75
Cordax, 151
Coriolanus, 63, 151
Cornish, 9
Corsican, 28
Cossack, 5
Cowdrey, Robert, 190
Craig, Jenny, 64
Cratylus, 58
Creole, 120, 156, 184
  Gullah, 184
Cresollius, Ludovicus, 151
Crèvecoeur, J. Hector St. John, 78
Crick, Francis (Sir), 199
Cromwell, Oliver, 146
Cronos, 69
Crusades, 1
  Eighth (1270), 51, 154
  Seventh (1248-1251), 51, 154
Cutler, Charles L., 75-76
Czechoslovakia, 106
  Joachimsthal, 106

— D —

Daily News-Sun (AZ), xvii
Dalgarno, George, 151
Danish, 68, 113
Daphne, 74
Davydov, A. S., 164
Decline and Fall of the Roman Empire, 10

A Treasure Trove of Word Origins 205

Demetrius, 152
Democrat, 21
Dennis, John, 117
De Quincey, Thomas, 52
Descartes, René, 198
dialectical materialism, 21
Dianthus, 189
dictionary, 131, 191
  Alvearie, or Triple Dictionarie, 63
  "big dictionary," 191
  Dictionary (Samuel Johnson), 63
  Dictionary of American Regional English, 169
  Dictionary of Modern English Usage, 170
  Dictionary of the English Language, 190
  Dictionary of Word Origins, 39
  Larousse, 131
  Latin and English Dictionary, 129
  neo-Babylon, 94
  New Standard Dictionary of the English Language, 85
  Oxford English Dictionary (OED), 72, 173-174, 190-191, 198
  Robert, 131
  "rolling dictionary," 93
  The American Heritage Dictionary, 172
  The Dictionary of Phrase and Fable, 4
  Webster's, 148
Dionysus (Bacchus), 57
dissyllable, 63
Dixieland, 184
DNA, 199
Domesday Book, 102
double entendre, 59, 111
doublet, 18, 37, 40, 61, 74, 96-98, 121
Douglass, William A., 2
Duncombe, Sanders (Sir), 30
Dutch, 8, 10, 15, 29, 42, 46, 50, 55, 87, 92, 119, 122, 163, 167
  Middle Dutch, 29, 118

— E —

East Island, 29, 151
Ebonics, 25
Ecclesiastical History of the English People, 151-152
echoic, 33
Edward I, 116
Edward III, 154
Edward VII, 34
Egypt
  Carnac, 27
  Damietta, 14
Egyptian, 18, 149, 165
Einstein, Albert, 156
El Dorado, 71
Elizabethan, 183
Emerson, Ralph Waldo, 85

Engels, Friedrich, 21
England, xvi-xvii, 2, 8, 34, 60, 87-88, 98, 105-107, 122, 135, 141, 154, 157, 166, 173, 176, 183, 188-191, 194
  Berkshire County, 174
    Crowthorne, 174
      Broadmoor Asylum, 174
  Cambridge University, xvii, 83-84, 163
    St. Johns College, 83
  Dover, 126
  Jersey, 12, 124
  Leicestershire, 12
    Melton Mobray, 12
  London, 13, 30, 38, 109, 126, 173-174
    Covent Garden, 109
    London Library, 191
    St. Mary of Bethlehem, 173
    Victorian Lambeth Marsh, 174
  Stonehenge, 27
  Westminster, 191
English, xiv-xvi, 2, 7-8, 10, 18-19, 23-24, 28, 31, 33-35, 37-38, 40-42, 48-49, 52, 54-57, 59-61, 63, 66-68, 74-75, 77-78, 80, 82, 84-88, 90, 92, 94, 100-101, 106, 108, 116, 118, 120-121, 123, 125-126, 128, 133, 135, 139-141, 143-149, 151, 154, 156-157, 162, 168, 170, 173-175, 177-178, 180-181, 184, 186, 188, 190-191, 194, 198
  British, 65
  Middle English, 37, 128, 141
  Old English, 3, 9-10, 12-13, 15, 31, 33, 46, 50, 55, 63, 67, 96, 101-102, 104, 107-108, 115, 123, 130, 135, 157, 179, 199
English Channel, 8, 126, 141
Epimenides, 22, 112
epistemological theory, 58
Eros, 165
Eskimo, 76
Estonian, 114
ETC, 20, 171
Etruscan, 39, 60
etymology, 6, 31, 39, 76, 102, 129, 134, 176-177, 179, 197
  folk, 1-4, 10, 15-16, 18, 92, 116, 125, 141-142, 148, 176, 199
  popular, 3
Eumelia, 151
euphemism, 161
euphemistic, 142
Europe, 17-18, 25, 78, 113, 119, 166
European, 6, 78, 107, 145
"Everything at Reilly's Must Be Done in Irish Style," 19
exotic tongues, 25

— F —

Faulty Diction, 145

Faust, 95
Fawkes, Guy, 191
Fawkes Day, Guy, 191
Fester, Richard, 26-27, 113-114
Feuerbach, Ludwig, 21
Fierro, Martin, 71
figuration, xiii, 192
Finnish, 114
Finno-Ugric, 26
five senses, xii, 40, 128, 138
Flanders, 12
    Cambrai, 12
Fletcher, John, 135
Florida, 2, 91, 98, 184
    Florida Keys, 1-2, 87, 141, 199
    Florida State University, 164
Four Plays in One: The Triumph of Honour, 135
Fowler, H. W., 170
France, 4, 8, 12, 27, 34, 51, 93, 107, 109, 123-124, 126-127, 132, 154, 161, 165, 188
    Aigues-Mortes, 51
    Alyscamps, 161
    Antwerp, 12
    Arles, 51, 161
    Aurillac, 27
    Bergerac, 27
    Brittany, 27
        Carnac, 27
    École Polytechnique (Polytechnic School), 132
    Figeac, 27
    Guincamp, 14
    Laon, 12
    Lille, 12
    Limousin, 30
    National School of Administration, 132
    Nérac, 27
    Nîmes, 12
    Padirac, 27
    Paris, xiv, 5-7, 32, 59, 93, 126, 131, 139, 144, 146, 188-189
        Charles de Gaulle Airport, 12
    Provence, 51, 114, 161
        Rhône Delta (Camargue), 51
    Tulle, 13
France, Marie de, 169
Franks, 107, 117
French, xiv-xvi, 1-2, 4-5, 7, 10, 12-18, 23, 25, 27-35, 37-39, 41-42, 45-50, 52, 54-55, 57, 60-63, 67, 69, 72-75, 77, 81, 85-89, 95-96, 98, 100-101, 103-110, 114-117, 119-128, 131-135, 137-145, 148, 152, 154-155, 157-158, 160-163, 165, 167, 169-170, 172, 175, 177, 180-181, 183-184, 187-188, 190, 192, 196-198
    Modern French, 18, 118

French (*continued*)
    Norman French, 87, 100, 123
    Old French, 12-13, 17-18, 31, 33, 38, 60, 62, 67, 73, 81, 89, 107, 121, 130, 169
    Western French, 6
French Academy, 6-7, 131
    "forty immortals," 131-132
French Norman invasion, 35
French Revolution (1794), 142
French-Tunisian crisis of 1958, 132
frequentative, 36, 48-49, 61, 82
Fréron, Elie, 196
Freud, Sigmund, xiii
Frost, Robert, 106, 195
Fugger, 126
Funk & Wagnalls Company, 85, 146

— **G** —

Gaelic, 28-29
Galician, 28
Gallic, 4
Garden of Gethsemane, 125
Garibaldi, Giuseppe, 190
Gates, Bill, 45
Gauguin, Paul, 51
Gaul, 4, 101, 107, 117, 194
General Semantics, 159, 163
Genseric, 9, 194
German, xiv-xvi, 3, 7-8, 10, 12-14, 16, 23-27, 29, 31-33, 35, 37, 41-42, 46, 50, 53, 55-58, 60-61, 64-65, 68-70, 78, 80, 85, 87-89, 92-94, 96, 100-103, 106-108, 113, 116, 118-119, 122-124, 127-128, 133-135, 137-138, 141, 144, 154, 157, 163, 165-167, 180, 187, 198
    Modern, 67, 99
    North, xiv
    Old High German, 8, 11, 37, 68, 99, 107, 157
    POW, 130
German-Yiddish, 33
Germanic, xv-xvi, 35, 50, 68, 89, 92-93, 96, 100, 108, 117, 122-124, 154, 157, 194
    Anglo-Saxon, 87
Germany, 8, 11-12, 16-17, 56, 93, 108, 122, 145, 165
    Augsburg, 126
    Autobahn, 81
    Berlin, 108
    Frankfurt, 107-108
        Frankfurt Palace Hotel, 11
    Hamburg, xiv, 108, 144
    Leipzig, 146
    Regensburg, 145
        Detachment R, 145
Gibbon, Edward, 10
Goethe, Johann Wolfgang von, 95
Goody, Jack, 83
Gore, Al (Vice President), 12

Gothic, 58, 90
grammar, 85, 90, 112, 120, 131, 142-143, 168-169, 171, 188
"Great Cham" (Samuel Johnson), 190
Greco-Roman mythology, 138
Greece, xv, 39, 84
  Athens, 2, 22, 60, 147
    Pantheon of Athens, 60
  Attica, 2, 60
  Corinth, 138
  Macedonia, 84
  Olympus, 165
Greek, xii, 2, 8-9, 12-14, 18-20, 22, 24, 32, 39, 46-47, 50-51, 55, 57-60, 64, 67-69, 73-74, 77, 81, 84, 89, 92-93, 96, 98, 102-103, 105, 109, 114-118, 120, 125, 127, 133-136, 140, 151, 158, 160-161, 163, 165, 168, 176, 179-181, 196
Gregorian calendar, 190
Grimm, Jakob, 68, 75, 108
Gwyn, Nell, 55
Gypsy, 18, 177

— H —

Hamlet, 173, 192
Harrigan, Ned, 19
Hart, Tony, 19
Harvard University, 133
Harvey, Paul, 1, 193
Hayakawa, S. I., 20, 159, 171
headwords, 191
Hebrew, 135, 187, 197
Hegel, Georg Wilhelm Friedrich, 21
Heisenberg, Werner, 43
Heisenberg uncertainty principle, 43
Hellenic, xv
Hellenize, 84
Henry VI, 61
Henry VIII, 166
Hermes, 165
Heywood, John, 63
Himalayas (the Hump), 78, 147
Hindi, 3, 16, 160
Hindu, 18, 103
  Old Hindu, 58
Hippocratic oath, 174
historical linguistics, 25
Hobbes, Thomas, 193
Holland, 8, 12
Holmes
  Oliver Wendell, 135
  Sherlock, 157
Holstein, 21
Homer, 113, 188
Homeric Gallery, 152
homonym, 95-96, 111
homo sapiens, 164

Honduras bark, 61
Hopper, Karl, xvii
Horace, xvi, 90
Horch, 56
Horus, 165
Humboldt
  Alexander von (Baron), 93
  Wilhelm von, 26, 113
Hundred Years War, 154
Hungarian, 114
Hungary, 93
  Budapest, 93
Hussein, Saddam, 7

— I —

ideogram writing, 149
Illinois
  Chicago, 108
Incas, 71
India, 12, 16, 18, 42, 57, 126, 177
  Srinigar, 16
Indian, 60, 76-80, 133, 153, 194
  Algonquian, 76-79, 193-194
  American, 15, 75, 78, 193-194
  Apache, 78
  Caddo, 79
  Cheyenne, 77
  Chippewa, 77, 193
  Delaware, 77, 193
  Eastern Abenaki, 79
  Hopi, 79, 193
  Iroquoian, 77
  Massachusett, 193-194
  Narragansett, 77, 193
  Natick, 193
  Native American, 75-76
  Navajo, 79
  North American, 76, 153
  Ojibwa, 77
  Pima, 2
  Plains, 76
  Salish, 78
  Shawnee, 78
  Sioux, 77
Indo-European, 26, 101, 108, 113, 199
Inquisition, 56, 83
Iran, 155
Iraq, 12, 86, 155, 193
  Baghdad, 15, 17
  Mosul, 12
Ireland, 18, 74-75, 141
  Dublin, 75, 85, 191
Irish, 19, 174
  Old Irish, 28, 101
IRS (Internal Revenue Service), 124
Irving, Washington, 75, 105
Islam, 116

Islamic, 7, 23
Island of Reil, 18
Israelis, 159
"Is that Mr. Reilly?," 19
Italian, 4, 12-15, 28, 34, 37-38, 42, 61-62, 74, 83, 94, 104, 111, 114, 118, 125, 151, 155, 162-163, 165, 168, 190
Italy, 47, 82
   Capri, 29, 198
   Milan, 141
   Naples, 30
   Rome, xvi, 9, 35, 39, 70, 75, 89-90, 130, 147, 182, 194
      Palatine Hill, 75
   Venice, 60, 188
Ives, Burl, 128

— J —

Jacobin, 190
James, William, 90
Jansen, Cornelius, 137
Jansenist, 137
Japan, 44-45
   Hiroshima, 44
   Nagasaki, 44
Japanese, 44, 146
   Imperial government, 44
Japhetic, 26, 113
jargon, 119-120
Jeffers, Bill, 193
Jehovah, 25
Jeopardy, 69
Jesuit, 62, 137, 151
Jew, 115, 133, 189
Jewish, 161
Jimmy the Greek, 91
Johnson
   Samuel, 63-64, 190-191
   Wendell, 20
Jonson, Ben, 106
Jordan, Michael, 34
Journal of the West, 75, 150
Julius Caesar, 136
Jung, Carl Gustav, xiii, 129

— K —

Kansas, 136
Karakasidou, Anastasia (Dr.), 84
Kennedy, Jr., John F., 46, 108
Khitan dynasty, 148
King Henry V, 157
King Henry V, 129
King James Bible, 6
King John, 73, 154
Knight of La Mancha, 10
Korean Conflict, 145
Korzybski, Alfred, 19-22, 159, 163, 197

Kosovo, 67
   affair, 35, 37
Kreuz, Walter, 93-94
Krushchev, Nikita, 44-45
Kuno, Susumu, 133
Kurdish, 12
Kurzweil, Ray, 109

— L —

La Fontaine, 115
language, xvii, 59-60, 180-185, 187, 191, 197
   ancient roots, 88-90
   and chemistry, 142-144
   and mathematics, 43, 111
   and migration, 113-114
   archetype of human language, xiii, 26-27, 114
   borrowing, 40-42
   boundaries, 100-102
   colloquial, 64
   complexities, 191-193
   consistently inconsistent, 54-55
   differing views, 126-127
   entropy, 44-46
   exotic, 25
   fossilized poetry, 1
   games, 93
   hostility in, 8, 65
   humor, 23-24, 59-61
   learning foreign, 144-145
   loom of, 24, 185
   migration, 113
   misinterpretation, 44
   mistranslation, 44
   misuse, 19
   mystery, 25
   nonsensical, 69, 141
   origin, 25, 60, 150
   policies, 132
   primeval (*Ursprache*), 25-28
   principle of, 146, 155
      abstracting, 21-22
      degree, 22
      "non-allness," 20, 22
      perpetual flux, 20
      structural differential, 21
      uniqueness, 20
   radio and TV, 155-156
   role of, 198
   Romance, 28, 37, 87, 114, 174
   rules, 99-100, 111-112
   to communicate meaning, 40
   sacred, 120
   shaping, 58
   sign, 150-153, 198
   slang, 119-120, 125, 158
   subjectivism, 52-54
   thought and, 163-165

language (*continued*)
    usage, 21-23, 31-32, 44, 64, 99, 117, 121, 145-146, 155, 164, 168-172, 174, 178, 184
    Western, 149
    xenophobic, 8, 10-11
Las Ergas de Esplandián (*The Heroic Feats of Esplandián*), 10
Language in Thought and Action, 20, 159
Latin, xii-xiv, xvi, 1, 4-6, 10-17, 23-25, 28-32, 34-39, 41-42, 45-50, 52, 55-64, 66-69, 71, 73-75, 81-82, 87, 89-90, 93, 95-101, 103, 106, 108, 114-115, 119-121, 123-126, 130-131, 133-137, 139-140, 143-146, 148, 151, 154, 157-160, 163, 165-166, 168, 172, 175-179, 181-184, 186-187, 189, 192, 197-198
    Late Latin, 18
    Lower Latin, 36, 38, 57, 70, 81, 100, 141, 189
    Pig, 93
    Pre-Latin, 89
    Vulgar Latin, 55, 69
Latin American, 76
Latinist, 135
Lavoisier, Antoine Laurent, 142
Lawlor, Charles E., 19
League of Nations, 99
Leaves of Grass, 135
Lederer, Richard (Dr.), 187
Let a Simile Be Your Umbrella, 188
Letters from the Frontiers, 75
Levett, William, 79
Liar Paradox (Epimenides), 22, 112
Lincoln, Abraham (President), 125
linguistic, 164
    ability, 138
    aspects, 88
    collectibles, 187
    contamination, 51-52
    data, 80
    fossil, xii
    handicraft, 93
    historical, 113
    idiosyncrasy, 99
    meaning, 197
    paleontology, 26, 113
    phenomena, 54
    research, 53
    root, 175
    slang, 119-120
    unified field theory, xvi
linguistics, xii, xiv-xvi, 25-26, 40, 43, 51, 53-54, 56, 58-59, 62, 79-80, 97-101, 105, 110, 112-114, 119-120, 129-130, 138, 142, 146, 153, 164, 175-176, 185-187, 193, 197, 199
Literary Year, 196
Lithuanian, 113, 134
Lives of the Saints, 160
Livy, 151

loan translation, 41, 135
loan-word, 41, 75-79, 194
Local Examinations Syndicate (Greece), 84
"Lone Ranger," 78
Lorelei, 168
Louis IX (Saint Louis), 51, 154
Louisiana, 155
    New Orleans, 156, 184

— M —

Maccabees, 161
Machan, Tibor, 131-132
Macrobius, 152
Mafia, 3
Magellan, Ferdinand, 72
Magellan Straits, 72
Malay, 14
Mallery, Garrick, 150
Mandarin, 149
Maori, 29, 151
Marks, Edward B., 19
Marr, Nikolai, 26, 113
Marx, Karl, 21
Massachusetts, 194
    Springfield, 198
        Bemis & Call, 198
    Worcester, 156
        Podunk, 156
Mayan, 71
Mazda, Ahura, 88
McAuliffe, Anthony C. (General), 65
McCall, George A., 75
Medieval, 116, 166
Mediterranean, 51, 154
Melanchthon, Philipp, 24
memory
    associative, 81, 99, 128, 197
    connotative, 81, 99, 128, 157, 197
    the art of, 83
Mencken, H. L., 19
"Mending Wall," 195
Merrett, George, 174
Mesopotamian, 149
Messner, Reinhold, 78
metaphor, xi-xii, xiv, xvi-xvii, 15, 30, 33, 40-41, 43, 45, 53, 59, 77, 88, 94, 106, 114, 126-127, 134, 138, 141, 162, 186
    spatial, 181
Mexican, 74
Mexico, 76
    Acapulco, 59
Middle Ages, 4, 24
Middle Eastern crisis, 159
Middle West, 19
Military Intelligence Service, xv
Milton, John, 128, 140
Minor, William Chester (Dr.), 174

MIT, 80
Mitterand, Francois, 132
Moeso-Gothic, 174
Moirae, 11
Moldavian, 28
Molière (Jean-Baptiste Poquelin), 120
Mongol, 190
Montana, 9
Monte VI, 72
Moors, 15, 17, 189
moral virtues, 155
Moreau, Basil Antoine-Marie (Father), 6, 189
Mortes, Aigues, 154
Morton, George, 194
Mozart, Wolfgang Amadeus, 24
Mt. Parnassus, 74
Much Ado about Nothing, 63
Murray, James (Dr.), 173-174

— N —

Na-Dene, 25
Napoleon I, 5-6, 34, 37
Napoleonic reforms (1805-1815), 132
Nazi, 115, 118
    Party, 131
Negro, 184
neologism, 170-171
Nepal, 78
Nero, 75, 152
Netherlands, 8
    Friesland, 12
    Scheveningen, 118
Nevada
    Las Vegas, 91
    Reno, 2
New Age, 28
New England, 174
New England's Prospect, 194
New Jersey, 189
    Newark, 12
New Mexico
    Atalaya Mountain, 118
    Santa Fe, 118
New Theory of Language, 26, 113
Newtonian, 126
New World, 76
New York, xiv, 7, 33, 55, 101
    Gloversville, 38
    Manhattan, 9
        Broadway, 55
        Bronx, 9
    New York City, 29, 113, 126, 134, 139
        Ground Zero, 139
        Wall Street, 192
        World Trade Center, 134
New York Times, 173, 182
New Zealand, 106

Nixon, Richard (President), 172
Noah, 25-26
Nobel Prize, 199
Norman, 87, 123, 133, 141
    conquest, xv
Norman French, 122
Normandy, 12
    Creton, 12
Norse, 57, 157
    Old Norse, 33, 42, 50, 55, 70, 127
North America, 76
North Korea, 155
Norwegian, 32, 59
Nostradamus, 4

— O —

O Brave New Words!, 75-76
Odin, 57
Offa (King of Mercia), 107
101st Airborne Division, 65
Ono, Kent A., 159
onomatopoeic, 4, 17, 33, 53, 70, 76
Operation Infinite Justice, 137
O'Reilly, Bill, 182
Oriental, 120
Othello, 64
Oxford University, 190

— P —

paleolinguist, xii, 26-27, 113
Palestine, 12, 124, 159
    Gaza strip, 12, 124
palindromes, 187
Pallas Athene, 152-153
Pamphilus, 168-169
Pamphilus, seu de Amore, 168
Pan, 8, 39, 105
Panzerkraftwagenaufselbstfahrlafetten, 29
Parcae (the Fates), 11-12
Parsee, 88
Pascal, Blaise, 137
Pei, Mario A., 185
Peninsular & Oriental (P&O) Line, 177
    packet boat, 177
Pennsylvania, 10, 77
    Philadelphia, 77
People's Republic of China (PRC), 149
perception, xiii, 43, 128, 138, 159
Pericles, Prince of Tyre, 129
Persia, 148
Persian, 16, 116
Personae, 39
phallic symbol, 176
Philbin, Regis, 114
Philistine, 140
Philological Society, 191
philosophy, xvii, 56, 159, 163, 181

phonetic symbol, 94
Phrygia, 70, 138
Phrygian oracle, 70
Pictet, Adolphe, 26, 113
pictogram, 149
pictograph, xiii, 33
Piéchaud, Louis, 6
Piers Plowman, 116, 128
Pinker, Steven A., 80
Plante, Georgette de La (Madame), 16
Plato, 58, 127, 151, 160
Plutarch, 73
Poetics, 131
Poland, 7, 23, 74
Polish, 19
Polo, Marco, 14
Pompeius, 182
Pontius, 182
Pope, Alexander, 139
"Popeye," 162
Portuguese, 28, 61, 72, 114
Poseidon, 69
poststructuralism, 159
Pound, Ezra, 39
prefix, 14, 16, 30, 35, 42, 48-49, 82-83, 95, 97, 100, 116, 133, 136, 139, 141, 157-159, 161, 175, 186, 192, 196
preposition, 143, 146, 158
Presbyterian, 189
primeval vocabulary (language), 26, 113-114
Primeval Words of Mankind: An Archeology of Language, 26
Prince of Wales, 34
prohibition, 183
pronoun, 178, 187
Protestant, 24
Protestantism, 24
Provençal, 28, 154-155, 174
Prudential Insurance Company, 4
psychiatry, 23, 187
psychology, 65, 82, 90, 187
Pulitzer Prize, 188
pun, 125, 133-135, 141, 167, 195, 197
Punica, 9
Pyrenees, 75
   Roncesvalles, 75
Pythagorean, 56
Python, 74

— Q —

Quaker, 62
quantum
   physics, 54, 126
   theory, 126
Queen Victoria, 34
Quintilian, 151-152
Quixote, Don, 10

— R —

Rabelais, François, 152
Reagan, Ronald (President), 155
redundancy, 30-31
reduplication, 32-33
relative pronouns, 178
Republican, 20
Republic of Macedonia, 84
restrictive clause, 178-179
Reynard the Fox, 17
Rhaeto-Romance, 28
rhetoric, 85, 131, 137, 151, 158-160
Rhodes, 147
Rice, Thomas D., 193
Richelieu, Cardinal, 131
Richepin, Jean, 7
Rio Salado (Salt River) Sun Cities Lifelong Learning Center (AZ), 59
River
   Camargue, 154
   Columbia, 194
   Elbe, 28, 113
   Labe, 28
   Main, 107
   Mississippi, 79
   Oder, 113
   Oise, 28
   Penneus, 74
   Picketwire, 4, 132
   Rhine, 113, 168
   Rhône, 154, 161
   Río de las Ánimas Perdidas (River of Lost Souls), 4, 132
   Rivière du Purgatoire (Purgatory River), 4, 132
   Rubicon, 476
   Saône, 28
   Seine, 28
   Thames, 47
   Tiber, 182
   Tweed, 14
   Vistula, 113
Rockefeller, John D., 34
Roman, 9, 11-12, 28, 47, 50-52, 71, 75, 82, 90, 107, 109, 114, 117, 119, 122, 124, 130, 136, 141, 148, 151-152, 160-161, 165
   Catholicism, 24, 178
   Empire, 9, 115
Romance language
   see language, Romance
Romance of the Rose, 155
Romani, 18
Romanian, 28
Romany, 177
Romeo and Juliet, 17, 63
Ronsard, Pierre de, 109
Rooney, Pat, 19

Roscius, Quintus, 152
Rossetti, Christina Georgina, 135
Ruhlen, Merritt, 25-26, 28, 113-114
Rumania
   Bucharest, 146
Rumanian, 94, 114
Russell, Bertrand, xvii, 102
Russia, 5, 45
   Moscow, 59, 147
   Red Square, 190
Russian, xv-xvi, 6, 8, 13, 26, 36, 41, 44-45, 49, 70, 92, 101, 107-108, 112-113, 122, 138, 145, 147-148, 155, 164, 180, 189-190

— S —

Safire, William, 133, 170, 188
Samoyedic, 26
Samson Agonistes, 140
Sanskrit, 3, 11-12, 14-15, 18, 31, 50, 57, 60, 67-69, 78, 88, 93, 102-103, 107-108, 121, 128, 160-161, 182, 186
Santa Claus, 106
Saracens, 75
Sardinian, 28
Sasquatch, 78
Scandinavian, 70, 122, 141, 162, 175
Science and Sanity: An Introduction to Non-Aristotelian Systems and General Semantics, 19-20
Science Fiction, xv
Scot, 14, 50
Scotch, 37
Scotland, 116, 167, 191
Scotsman, 173
Scottish, 28-29, 97, 100, 103, 115-116, 179
Sea of Galilee, 125
Sea Islands, 184
Segar, E. C., 162
semantic, xiii-xiv, xvi, 19, 21-22, 29, 40, 52, 58-60, 65, 79, 81, 87, 92, 99, 101-102, 107, 110, 112-113, 117, 138, 143, 164, 167, 171, 181-182, 188, 192, 197-198
Senior World (AZ), 188
Serbian, 94
Shakespeare, William, 17, 39, 61, 63, 71, 73, 85, 89, 104, 128, 136, 140, 151, 154, 157, 173, 190-191
Shangri-La, 32
Shifting Borders, 159
Shipley, Joseph T., 10, 39, 51, 108, 182
Siberia, 26
Siberian Finno-Ugric, 114
Sicinnis, 151
Sidney, Philip (Sir), 191
signature phrases, 121-122
signifier, 101
Sign Language Among American Indians, 150

Silesia, 13
Sinatra's Rat Pack, 142
Sinologist, 150
Sinology, 148
Sino-Tibetan, 25
Sisyphean, 138
Sisyphus, 138
slang
   see language
Slav, 8
Slavic, xvi, 44, 84, 92
Sloop, John M., 159
Slovakia, 93
Smith
   John, 77
   Nadine L., 188
Smollett, Tobias, 190
Sobieski, Jan III (King), 7, 23
Socrates, 159
Sons of Terra (Earth) and Titan, 66
South America, 71
South Carolina, 184
Soviet, 130, 145, 147, 190
   defector interrogation, xv
   Regime, 92
Spain, 9, 15, 17, 71, 189, 194
   Cordova, 9
   Granada, 17
Spaniard, 189
Spanish, xv, 1-2, 4, 10, 13-16, 28-29, 31, 37-38, 57, 60-62, 67, 73, 79, 81, 84, 103, 106, 114, 118, 120, 123, 128, 132, 138, 141-144, 146, 148, 154-155, 163, 180, 189, 199
   Modern, 10
Speech through Finger Gestures, 152
Spenser, Edmund, 128, 155
Spic and Span, 167
Stalin, Joseph, 26
St. Edward the Confessor, 154
St. Martin's Day, 78
St. Nicholas, 32, 106
St. Peter, 124-125
structuralism, 159
substantive, 63
Suez Canal, 177
suffix, 14, 30, 48, 82-83, 88, 92, 98, 103, 169, 180, 187
superlative, 10, 86
Swinburne, Algernon Charles, 135
Swiss, 26, 113, 129, 146
Switzerland, 178
synchronicities, 129
synonym, 24, 31-32, 41, 70, 73, 87, 163, 192
syntax, 112, 120, 164, 171, 188
syphilis, 8, 61
Syria
   Damascus, 12

Syro-Arabic, 174

— T —
Tahitian, 29, 151
Talleyrand, Charles Maurice de, 37
Tantalus, 66, 138
Tarik, 4, 169
Tarik's Mountain, 4, 169
Tartarus, 56, 138
Tatar, 148, 190
Tennessee, 183
Teutonic, 12, 33, 37, 50, 55, 64, 70, 101, 103, 136, 141, 166
Texas, 79
The Atlantic Monthly, 168, 171
"The Bane of Our Linguistic Insensitivity," 40
The Bermuda Triangle, 6
"The Best in the House is None Too Good for Reilly," 19
The Cambridge Quintet: A Work of Scientific Speculation, 80
The Canterbury Tales, 52
"The Cracked Bell," 104
The Creole Village, 105
The Faerie Queen, 128, 155
"The Far Side," 78
The Ideal Husband, 54
The Journal of the Pilgrim at Plymouth, 194
The London Evening Standard, 84
The Mystery of Atlantis, 6
The Origin of Language: Tracing the Evolution of the Mother Tongue, 28, 113
Theory of Molecular Excitons, 164
The Picayune (LA), 156
The Practice (TV show), 90
The Professor and the Madman, 173
The Provok'd Wife, 193
"The Road Not Taken," 106
The Romany Rye (*The Gypsy Gentleman*), 18
"The Sidewalks of New York," 19
The Song of Roland, 75
Thessaly, 74
The Stone Age Is at Our Door, 26
The Taming of the Shrew, 53
The Tempest, 63, 71, 140
The Tyranny of Words, 20
Thor, 57
Thoreau, Henry David, 91-92
thought sequence, 164
Thoughts, 137
Tiberius, 75
Tibet, 78
Tinker Toys, 11, 143
Titan, 138
Tongue of the Ice Age: The First Six Words of Humanity, 26
Torquemada, Tomás de, 56

Tractatus Logico-Philosophicus, 181
Transcript (Boston), 198
travel, 56, 108, 119
Trench, Richard Chenevix (Dr.), 191
Triscuit, 15
Turk, 7, 23
Turkic, 148
Turkish, 94, 118
  Medieval, 190
Turner, Lorenzo Dow, 184
Twain, Mark, 68, 75

— U —
Umayyad, 17
Umbrian, 68
unified field theory, 180
Union, 79
  Army, 174
United Nations, 148
United States, 11, 44, 86, 127, 142, 174-175, 183, 193
  Army, xv, 145, 162, 174
    Regular, 145
    Reserve, 145
    Russian Area and Language Training Program, 145
  federal government, 188
  Marine, 148
  Navy, 122, 125
University of
  Athens, 90
  Nevada (Reno), 2
  Paris, 131
  Sorbonne, 6
  Toronto, 18
Uralic, 26
Uruguay
  Montevideo, 72
Ushuaia, 72
USSR, 145, 155
Uzbekistan
  see Asia, Central

— V —
Vaca, Alvar Nuiñez Cabeza de, 1, 142, 199
Vanbrugh, John (Sir), 193
Vandals, 9, 194
Van Gogh, Vincent, 51
Venus, 165
verb, 143
  inceptive, 143
  inchoative, 143
Vergil, xiv, 145
Verner, Karl A., 68, 75, 108
Vienna hot dog, 108
Vienna Sausage, 108
Viennese, 93

Virginia, 78-79
Volkswagen, 108
Voltaire, 196
von Humboldt, Wilhelm, 58
Voss, Johann Heinrich, 152

— W —

Waelisc (Welsh), 9, 28, 88, 101
Wallraff, Barbara, 168, 171-172
Wall Street Journal, 109, 175
Walters, Barbara, 34
Washington, D.C., 170
  Pentagon, 134, 145
  Smithsonian Institution, 83, 150
Washington, D.C. *(continued)*
  White House, 91
Weapons of Mass Destruction, 86
West, Mae, 128
Western Civilization, 22
West Indies, 141
Whateley, Richard (Archbishop), 85
Whitman, Walt, 135
Wild Peter of Hanover, 57
William the Conqueror, 122
Winchester, Simon, 173
Windows (computer operating system), 65
Wits' Recreation, 63
Wittgenstein, Ludwig, xvii, 99, 101, 159, 163, 181
wolf-girls of India (Kamala and Amala), 57
Wood
  Anthony, 190
  William, 194
Woods, Tiger, 34
word
  coined, 137, 164, 170-171
  echoic, 124
  genealogy, xii
  images, 162-163

word *(continued)*
  makeup of, 42
  meaning, xii-xiii, xvi, 1, 13-14, 16-18, 29, 35, 37-38, 40-41, 44, 57-58, 60, 64, 80-81, 87, 92, 95, 99, 101, 103, 105-107, 111, 118-119, 122, 126-128, 133-135, 137-138, 143, 164, 166-167, 169, 171, 175, 186, 188, 197
  mnemonic devices, 197
  origin, 1-2, 6, 10, 29, 37-38, 45, 51-52, 56, 66-67, 117, 122-123, 142, 162, 165, 184, 189, 191, 193
  root, 13-14, 18, 24, 31, 33, 35, 37, 41, 48-49, 58-61, 67, 69, 88, 92, 94, 108, 115-116, 125, 128, 131, 133, 135, 186, 195
  sequence, 164
  sources, 86-88
Word Court, 171
Words and Rules: The Ingredients of Language, 80
World War I, xiv, 144
World War II, xv, 65, 108, 118, 122, 130, 147
Wyoming territory, 4
Wyoming
  Teton Mountains, 4, 160

— Y —

Yale University, 174, 178
Yank, 4
Yeats, William Butler, 39
Yeniseian, 25
Yiddish, 7, 187
York and Portland, 79
Ysopet (Aesop's Fables), 169
Yugoslavia, 147

— Z —

Zeus, 69-70, 165
Zoroastrian, 88

Word Origins Index
by Lori L. Daniel

— A —
absolute, 101
   truth, 101-102
   zero, 102
abscess, 42
abstruse, 21
accede, 42
accident, 62
ache, 62-64
acquiesce, 143
adjective, 48
adversely, 82
advert, 34
advertise, 34, 93
advocate, 98
aerie, 52
aeronaut, 52
affect, 81-82
affluent, 48
aggravate, 66, 179
aggression, 14, 121
agnostic, 179
agonoclite, 140
agony, 140
aid and abet, 30, 33
aisle, 17

allegory, 116-117
almighty dollar, 105
almighty gold, 105
alpaca, 15
ambrosia, 160-161
ambush, 162
amenable, 95
amenity, 96
amphigory, 117
animadversion, 36
ankle, 93
antecede, 42
antecedent, 42
antipode, 73
aplomb, 170
apologia, 114
apologue, 115
apology, 114
appetite, 58
apprehend, 181
area, 52
argot, 120
Aromunian, 28
arrest, 186
artery, 89
artificer, 82

ashram, 161
askance, 130
asparagus, 3
assault, 192
assiduous, 184
assist, 186
aster, 49, 136
asterisk, 49, 136
astrology, 50, 136-137
astronomy, 50, 136
atheist, 179
atom, 20
   bomb, 44
attest, 31
attic, 2
aureole, 52
averse, 35
avert, 35
avoid, 18

— B —
bail, 38
bailiwick, 38, 189
baldachin, 15
baldaquin, 15
bandage, 114

bastinado, 154
bawl, 104
bedizen, 142
bedlam, 173
beleaguer, 163
bell, 104
belly, 89
benefactor, 83
besiege, 163
bestiary, 169
beyond the pale, 74-75
biannual, 54, 69
bind, 88, 99
biscuit, 14, 23
bistro, 5-7, 189
blue blood, 189
Blue Book, 189
Blue Laws, 189
blue repeater, 189
bluestocking, 60, 188
body, 88, 92
book, 47
boom (ship's), 100-101
boot, to, 7, 178
bosom, 128
bound, 31, 33
bowel, 89
bribe, 12
broach, 42, 52, 168
broadcloth, 11
brocade, 15
broccoli, 42, 168
brochure, 168
broker, 42, 168
buck, 46
buckram, 14
buckwheat, 46
bulldozer, 60, 167-168
bureau, 98
Burushaski, 25
butcher, 47
buxom, 128-129

— C —

cabriolet, 29
cacophony, 9
cake, 42, 55
calamity, 134-135
calico, 12, 42
California, 10
Calicut cloth, 12, 42
cambric linen, 12

camouflage, 16
cap, 133
caper, 29, 33
capital, 133
capriccio, 29
caprice, 29
capricious, 29, 198
Cathay (*Kitai*), 148
Cascara amarga, 61
Cascara sagrada, 61
case, 62
 in case, 62
casemate, 62
cash, 62
cashmere, 12
cask, 62
casket, 61
casque, 61
casual, 62
casualties, 62
casuistry, 62
catapult, 117
catastrophe, 117
category, 117
caterpillar, 15
catholic, 115
caustic, 115
cauterize, 115
cease and desist, 30-31
cede, 42
cemetery, 161
cent, 32, 106
centipede, 15
cerebrum, 18
chad, 97
chair, 87, 124
chaise lounge, 3
chambray cotton, 12
chance, 62
chaplet, 133
chapter, 133
chenille, 15
chest, 61
cheviot, 12
chew, 89
chickadee, 77
Chink, 3, 148
chintz, 12, 15
chiromancy, 73
chiropody, 73
chute, 62
circumstance, xvi, 41, 186

city, 38
clavicle, 89
cloth, 12
cock-and-bull story, 167
codes, 47
codices, 47
coin, 156
cold, 68
collation, 160
comparison, 86
compassion, 45, 135
complexion, 24
complicate, 24
comprehend, 181
condiment, 130
congregation, 121
congress, 14, 121
consider, 49, 136
considerate, 136
consternation, 50
constitute, 186
contest, 31
contort, 56
convent, 109
converge, 36
conversation, 35
converse, 36
conversion, 35
cook, 123
Cordovan leather, 9, 17
corduroy, 16
cotton, 15
crane, 46
cranny, 32
Creole, 120
crepe, 15
 Georgette, 16
Crêpes Suzette, 34
Cretan, 22-23, 111-112
cretonne, 12
crinoline, 16
croissant, 7, 23
crossroads, 13
crucial, 106
crux of the matter, 106
Cupid, 165

— D —

dagger, 88
dale, 27, 106
damascene, 12
damask, 12

dandelion, 42, 68
dead, 124
debate, 61
debonair, 52
deceased, 42, 124
deer, 123
defeat, 14
degrade, 14, 121
degree, 14, 121
dejected, 48
delerium, xiii, 96
dell, 27
Della Calza society, 60, 188
delusion, 11
demean, 95-96
demeanor, 95
demise, 31
democracy, 98
denim, 12, 124
dentist, 68
depart, 124
depend, xvi, 41, 96
dereliction, 183
derivative, 35
desire, 49
desist, 31, 186
despair, 92
desperation, 92
destitute, 186
detest, 31
devil, 135
devise, 175
devoid, 18
dialect, 120
dichotomy, 19, 22
die is cast, 47
digress, 14, 121
diligent, 97
dime, 32, 106
dimity, 14
disaster, 49
discuss, 61
disparate, 87
distort, 56
diverge, 36
diverse, 175
divert, 175
divide, 18, 175
Dom, 103
domain, 96, 103
dome, 103
domestic, 103

dominant, 103
domino, 103
Don, 103
doom, 102
doomdom, 103
doomsday, 102-103
dose, 38-39, 60
Double Dutch, 9
dough, 116
dramatis personae, 39
drill, 14
Druid, 101
duffel bag, 12
dumbfound, 50
dungeon, 103
duodenum, 32, 89
duplicate, 24
duplicity, 24
Dutch anchor, 9
Dutch auction, 9
Dutch bargain, 9
Dutchman's breeches, 9
Dutch comfort, 9
Dutch concert, 9
Dutch courage, 9
Dutch defense, 9
Dutch feast, 9
Dutch gold, 9
Dutch luck, 9
Dutch nightingale, 9
Dutch praise, 9
Dutch reckoning, 9
Dutch treat, 9
Dutch uncle, 9, 66
Dutch wife, 9
dwell, 11
dyslectic, 98
dyslexia, 98

— E —

easel, 46
east, 68
eat, 64, 69, 124
éclair, 55, 69
Edison Mazda
 light bulb, 88
 "Frost Top" lamp, 88
effect, 81
egregious, 122
egress, 14, 121
elbow, 89
election, 97

elegant, 97
eligible, 97
elucidate, 178
elucubrate, 101
empathy, xv
employ, 24
encaustic, 115
enemy, 163
English leave, 8
enthusiast, 161
entrée, 123
epigraph, 196
epigram, 196-197
epilogue, 196-197
epistemology, 180
erudite, 73
escheat, 62
eschewed, 188
eulogy, 161
eunuch, 161
evil, 21, 154
"Evil Empire," 155
exit, 14, 121, 186
expedient, 74
expedite, 73
expeditionary force, 73
explicit, 24
extolled, 145
extort, 56

— F —

fabric, 14, 124
fact, 14
faction, 82
factitious, 82
factor, 82
factotum, 82
faculty, 82
fallow, 75
farding, 72
farewell, 108
fat, 87
Fates, the
 see Parcae
father, 68, 75, 108
feat, 14
feather, 68
fertile, 14, 48
fiction, 82
fictitious, 82
filet mignon, 125
finger, 11, 89

fish, 108
flak, 69
flake, 122
fleur-de-lis, 4
flock, 122
flotsam, 48
foot, 73-74
foreboding, 102
forlorn hope, 92
frankfurter, 107-108
frankincense, 107
free, 107-108
French illness, 66
French leave, 8, 66
French postcard, 8
French walk, 8
fret, 64
frieze, 12
frogs (the French), 4
fuddy-duddy, 179
fulminate, 131

— G —
gabardine, 16
game, 157-158
gams, 158
Gaulism, 132
gauze, 12, 124
Geber, 4, 69
general consensus, 30, 156
gesture, 150, 152-153, 165
    digital, 151
    finger, 151
    law of, 151
gibberish, 4, 69
Gibraltar, 4, 169, 118
giddy, 161
gingham, 14
Gordian knot, 70
Gordius, 70
gossip, 37-38
gourmet cuisine, 123
gout, 73
grade, 14
gradual, 14
graduated, 14
grenade, 163, 169
grenadier, 163
gross, 87
guest, 68
gyros, 117

— H —
Hand in Cap, 7, 178
handicap, 7, 178
harass, 66-67
Harpocrates, 165
hate, 35
haute, 123
    couture, 123
    école, 123
head, 15
heathen, 10
heel, 199
heeled, 199
Hell, 116
helmet, 61, 116
hero, 67
hieroglyph, 120
highfalutin, 4
history, 60
histrionical, 60
hocus-pocus filiocus, 10
hodgepodge, 116-117
hogan, 79
hoist the blue peter, 189
holocaust, 114-115
hoosegow, 2, 142, 199
hope, 91-92
hostile, xvi-xvii, 163, 182
house, 11, 103
hovel, 11
hubris, 46
hue and cry, 30, 33
humors, four
    black bile, 23-24
    blood (sanguine), 23
    phlegm, 23
    yellow bile (choler), 23
hurt, 134
hydrogen, 142

— I —
iacta, 47
impaled, 75
impeccable, 134
impede, 73
implicate, 24
implicit, 24
imply, 24
inceptive, 143
inchoate, 143
incipient, 143
idea, 127

indent, 68
Indian summer, 78-79
in Dutch, 9
infatuation, 45
insist, 186
insulin, 18
insult, 192
intelligence, 97
intercede, 42
interloper, 33
interlude, 38
interpretation, 95
interval, 38
intervention, 109
intestate, 31
intestine, 89
intrepid, 139
inundate, 139
invention, 109
Irish dividend, 9
irregardless, 30
island, 17-18
isle, 17
isolationist, 18
issue, 121

— J —
jaw, 89
jazz, 184
jeep, 162
jeopardy, 70
jersey, 12, 124
jetsam, 48
jettison, 48
jetty, 48
jouk, 183
juke, 183-184
jukebox, 183-184
jump, 192-193
jugular, 90
just, 192

— K —
Kachina Cult, 79
Key Largo, 1
Key West, 1-2, 141-142, 199
khaki, 16
kin, 68
king's evil, 154
king's touch, 154
kiva, 79
knave, 3

knight, 3
knit, 70
knot, 70
knout, 70
kowtow, 3, 50

— L —
Ladino, 28
lady, 2-3, 116
ladybird, 3
ladybug, 3
Langerhans, islands of, 18
lawn, 12
leaps and bounds, 33
legal, 97
legation, 97
legend, 97
legible, 97
legion, 97
legume, 98
liege, 99-100
life of Reilly (Riley), 18-19
ligament, 100
ligature, 100
limousine, 30
lisle, 12
lobster, 33
loft, 60
lofty, 60
log, 70
logistics, 163
lord, 2-3
loyal, 97
ludicrous, 158
lungs, 90

— M —
macabre, 161
maharajah, 18
maharanee, 18
malfeasance, 183
maroon, 141
mask, 39
mastodon, 69
maven, 187
Mazada automobile, 88
meager, 87
mean, 95-96
medicine, 80
melancholy, 24
melton, 12
merry-go-round, 161

metalanguage, 122
metamorphosis, xii
metaphor, xii
metaphysics, 122
metathesis, 122
meteor, 51
meter, 30
metes and bounds, 30-31
mile, 71
mill, 106
mind, 96
Minnelieder, 96
mohair, 16
moire, 16
Monk, 124, 198
    Monk's wrench, 198
monkey, 47
    board, 198
    boat, 198
    bridge, 198
    cap, 198
    foresail, 198
    gaff, 198
    rope, 198
    suit, 198
    wrench, 198
moose, 77
Moroccan leather, 17
mortal danger, 127
muslin, 12

— N —
nag, 92
nail, 92
nainsook, 16
nankeen, 12
nausea, 52
near, 10
necrology, 161
necromancy, 73, 161
necropolis, 161
nectar, 160-161
nefarious, 158
neighbor, 10, 50
neth, 10
nethermost, 10
nick, 32
nickel, 32, 106
nigh, 10
nook and cranny, 30, 32
north, 68

— O —
obese, 64
objective, 48, 53
obligate, 100
oblige, 100
obviate, 172
obvious, 24, 172
occident, 62
odious, 35
odontologist, 68
odontology, 68
odor, 123
Old Bailey, 38, 189
old fogey, 115, 179
omen, 102
on occasion, 62
on the carpet, 102

— P —
pagan, 9-10, 115, 161
palace, 75
pale, 75
paleface, 75
paleolinguist, 8
pallid, 75
pallor, 75
palmistry, 73
paloverde (*leguminosae*), 74
Pamphilet, 169
pamphlet, 168
panic, 8, 105
pantomime, 151-152
paper, 47
parachute, 62
paradise, 116
parallel, 116
Parcae (the Fates), 11
    Atropos, 12
    Clotho, 12
    Lachesis, 12
pardon my French, 8, 66
parrot, 124
parse, 133
parsley, 133
part and parcel, 30, 32
pass, 81
passage, 81
passion, 5
paste, 55
pastor, 121
pastoral, 121

pastry, 55
pedagogue, 74
peddler, 74
pederasty, 74
pedestrian, 73
pediatrics, 73
pedigree, 2, 73, 105
pedion, 74
pedodontics, 74
pedometer, 73
pedophilia, 74
pence, 107
peninsula, 18
penny, 107
percussion, 62
pernicious, 159
perplexed, 41
person, 39
perspiration, 124
pervert, 35, 175
pet, 125
peter out, 125
petite, 125
petition, 58
petrel, 124-125
petroglyph, 133
pettifogger, 126
petty, 125
pew, 73
philologist, 58, 68, 113
picayune, 155
pidgin, 120
pile, 16
pillage, 15
pilot, 74
pink, 189-190
pink eye, 189
pique, 1, 132
play, 157
pliable, 24
pliant, 24
plier, 24
plush, 16, 177
podagra, 73
podiatry, 73
podium, 73
podunker, 156
pole, 74
pongee, 16
pontiff, 182
pontificate, 182
poplin, 13

port, 108
portent, 102
portentous, 102
posh, 16, 176-177
posology, 39
pound, 106
prelude, 158
prestidigitator, 11
prestige, 11
profit, 83
progress, 14, 41
prolusion, 158
protagonist, 140
protest, 31, 183
provide, 175
provident, 175
Punic faith (*Punica fides*), 9
pylorus, 89

— Q —
quash, 61
quintessence, 56
quintuplets, 56

— R —
rajah, 18
rampant, 175
rat, 141-142
rate, 141
ratification, 141
recede, 42
recondite, 130
red herring, 190
red tape, 98
reluctant, 67
rendezvous, 187
replica, 25
reply, 25
reprehend, 181
resilience, 86
resist, 186
respect, xii
restaurant, 61
restore, 61
result, 42, 192
retaliation, 135
reticent, 67
retort, 56
reveal, 16
revenue, 124

revert, 35
rhetoric, 158
rigmarole (rigamarole), 116
rile, 18, 87
roanoke, 77-78
roil, 18, 87
rye, 18

— S —
sabir, 120
salary, 187
sannup, 79
satin, 14
savage, 10
sawbuck/sawhorse, 46, 87
sawing, 46
scapegoat, 46
scatological, 81
scholasticism, 83
scrofula, 154
secede, 42
secret, 130
sedan, 30
sedan chair, 30
sedation, 30
sedentary, 30
seek, 59
seersucker, 16
select, 97
sequence, 192
serge, 13
servant, 3
shilling, 106
shock, 45
sidereal, 136
sight, 88
silk, 13
silly, 133
similar, 25
simple, 25
simplicity, 24-25
simulate, 25
sin, 134
sinister, 89
sir, 49
sire, 49
slander, 135
slang, 119
slave, 8, 60, 100, 107, 119, 141, 168
sleazy, 13
sleight of tongue, 159

A Treasure Trove of Word Origins 221

smell, 123
solipsism, 58
somersault, 192
sophist, 159
south, 68
span, 166-168
spannend, 166
sparrow, 124
spic-and-span, 167
spike, 168
spoon, 167
squaw, 77, 193-194
star, 49-50, 136-137
"stealing my thunder," 117
stella, 50, 136
stellionate, 50
stereotype, 50
stern, 50, 136
sternum, 50
steward, 3
stiff, 50
stitch, 168
stogie, 77
stomach, 92
stomatology, 92
stool, 87, 124
store, 61
story, 60
strategy, 162-163
subject, 48
subjective, 48
sub rosa, 165
succeed, 42
surgeon, 73
sweat, 123
sweetheart, 55
sylvan, 10
symposium, 160

— T —

tabby, 17
tactics, 163
taffeta, 16
tale, 23, 151
tally, 32
tamp, 29
tantalize, 66, 138
tap, 29
Tarifa (Gibraltar), 118
tariff, 118
tart, 55

task, 30
tattoo, 28, 151
tautologies, 32
tax, 30
taxi, 29-30
temper, 24, 29
temperature, 24
tempest, 24
temple, 88-89
tennis, 89
terror, 139
terrorism, 140, 159
terse, 139
testicle, 6, 31, 183
testify, 6, 31
testimony, 6
thin, 87
thoroughfare, 108
thug, 3, 160
thunder, 57
Thursday, 57
thyroid, 93, 77
Tibbie, 17
tit for tat, 8, 77
token, 12
tomahawk, 79
tonsils, 93
tooth, 68
torch, 56
torment, 57, 119
tornado, 13, 57
torque, 56
torso, 57
tortoise, 56
torture, 56-57
tragedy, 46
traitor, 111
trajectory, 49
transgress, 14, 81, 121
travail, 119
treasure trove, 2, 13, 76
trespass, 81
tripalium, 119
trivia, 1, 13
true, 101, 118
true blue, 189
truth, 101, 159
tulle, 13
turtle, 56, 113
tweed, 14
twill, 14
two, 68

— U —

uvula, 93

— V —

vacuum, 18
valedictorian, 12, 81-82
valley, 27
vandalism, 9, 194
vanish, 143
velours, 16
velvet, 16
venison, 123
vent, 108
verge, 36, 176
  within the verge, 36
versatile, 36
version, 35
versus, 35
vertebrae, 93
vertex, 36
vertical, 36
vertigo, 35
vicariously, 197
view, 88
villain, 38
viola da gamba, 158
virgin, 36
vituperative, xvi, 182
void, 18
voile, 16
vortex, 36
vote, 98
vow, 98

— W —

walnut, 9
wampum, 77
wapiti, 78
war, 37
wealth, 45
Wehrmacht, 37
well-heeled, 199
welsh, 9
werewolf, 67
west, 68
wigwam, 79
will and testament, 30-31
wind, 108
windfall, 162, 194
window, 162

Wisconsin Dells, 27
within the pale, 74-75
wrist, 93

— Y —
yacht, 118
Yeti, 78

— Z —
Zwieback, 15